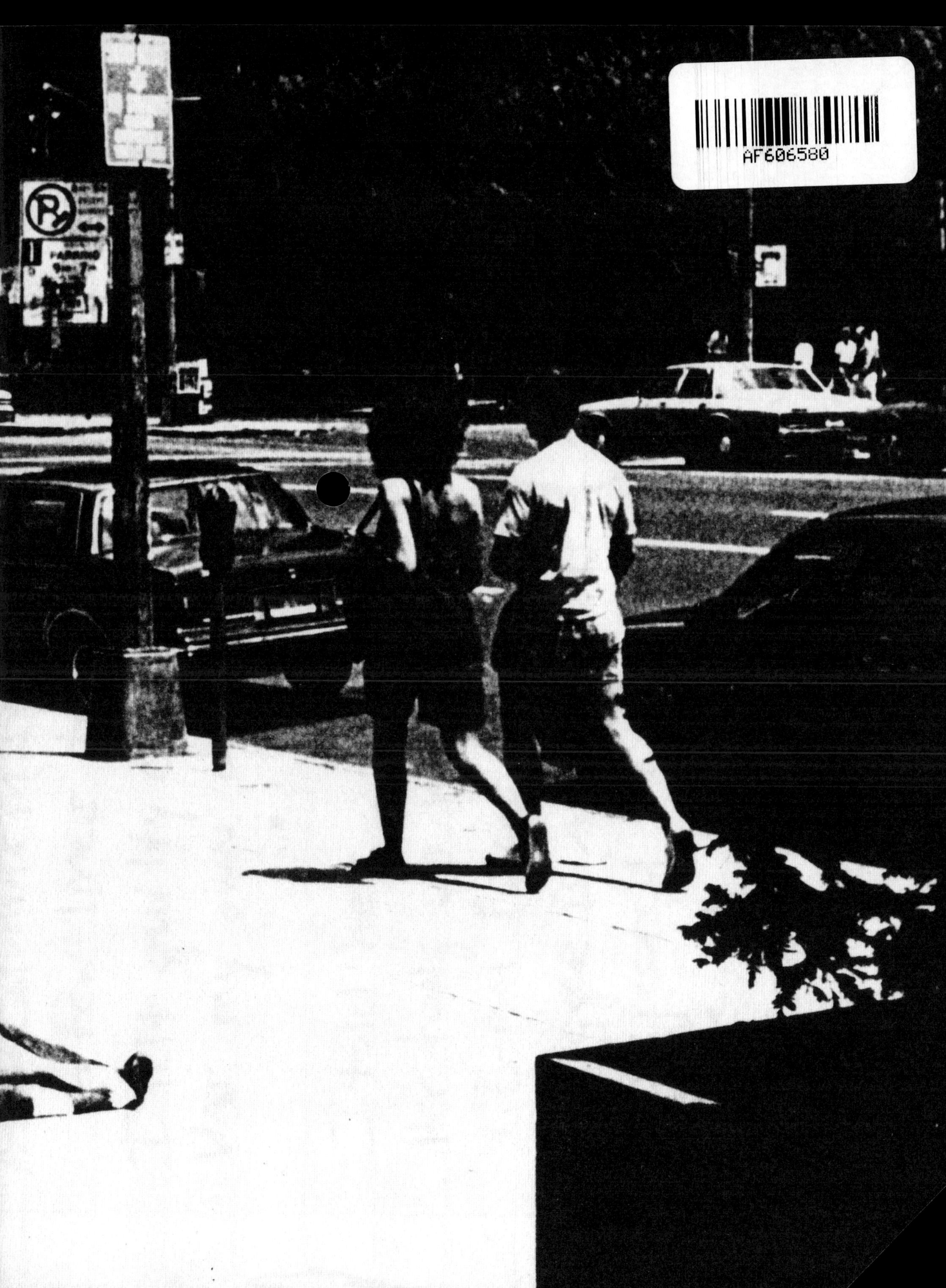

There's no such thing as clarity of vision
There's no such thing as clarity of vision
There's no such thing as clarity of vision
There's no such thing as clarity of vision
There's no such thing as clarity of vision
There's no such thing as clarity of vision
There's no such thing as clarity of vision
There's no such thing as clarity of vision
There's no such thing as clarity of vision
There's no such thing as clarity of vision
There's no such thing as clarity of vision
There's no such thing as clarity of vision
There's no such thing as clarity of vision
There's no such thing as clarity of vision
There's no such thing as clarity of vision
There's no such thing as clarity of vision
There's no such thing as clarity of vision
There's no such thing as clarity of vision
There's no such thing as clarity of vision
There's no such thing as clarity of vision
There's no such thing as clarity of vision
There's no such thing as clarity of vision
There's no such thing as clarity of vision
There's no such thing as clarity of vision
There's no such thing as clarity of vision
There's no such thing as clarity of vision
There's no such thing as clarity of vision
There's no such thing as cl[illegible]

26

Cashing my check over the bodies in Palestine
See 'em laid out on the Bowery,
The Port Authority Bus Station Terminal
Deep in New York City
People say there's supposed to be beauty
In ugliness
Pass the Haagen Daz, Vomit
Do it a thousand times, Don't let me spoil it
I got my own anorexia, it's kinda racy
I get down on belly and crawl
til I'm reality

Other folks said
The cartoon figures I used in the murals
And postcards looked more like whites
Than afrodites
As if blacks are the only hand bitten

There's no escaping the truth, you are
The work was not supposed to be a masterpiece
You want perfection buy a Smith & Wesson
Drink a slurpee, here's a lesson

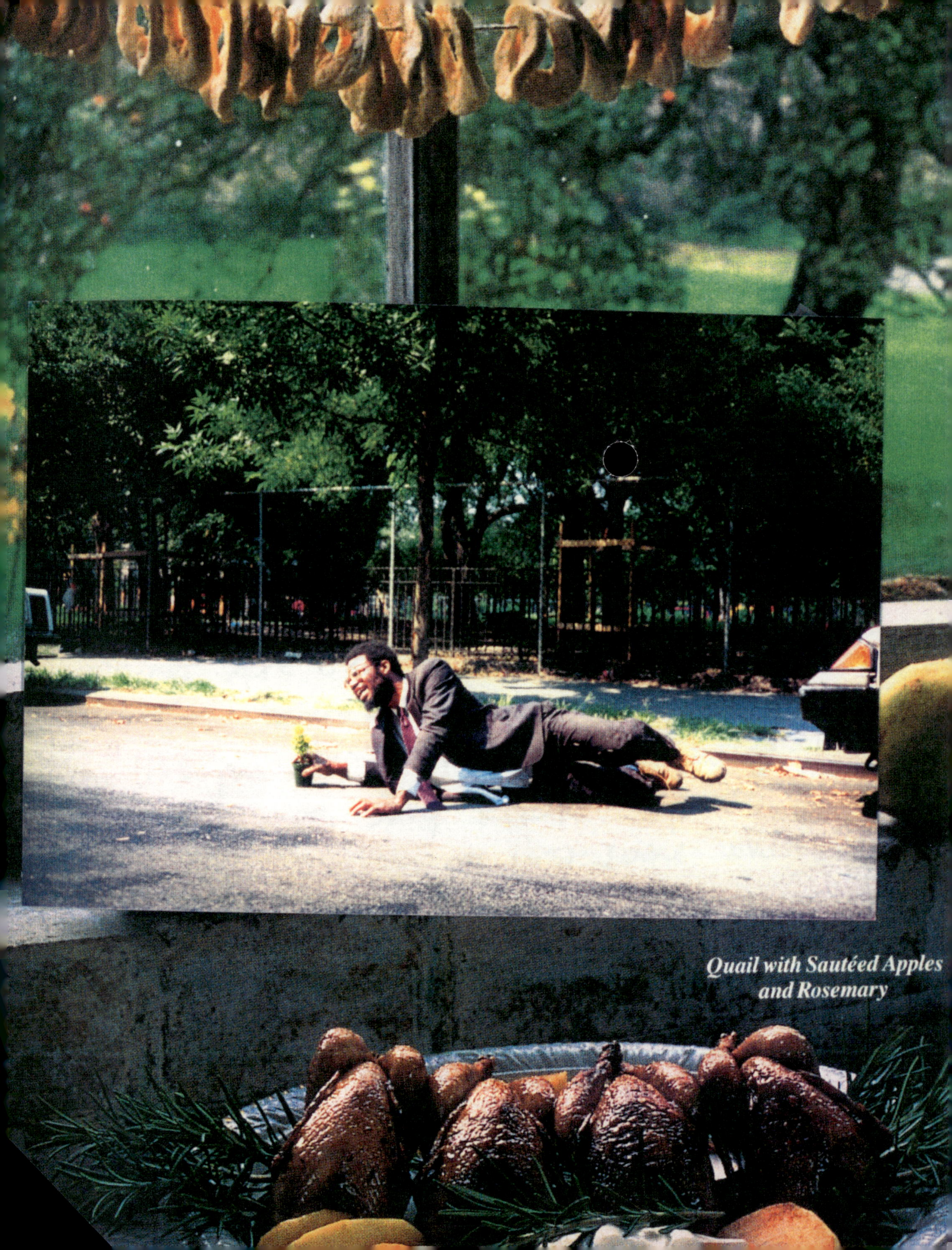

Quail with Sautéed Apples and Rosemary

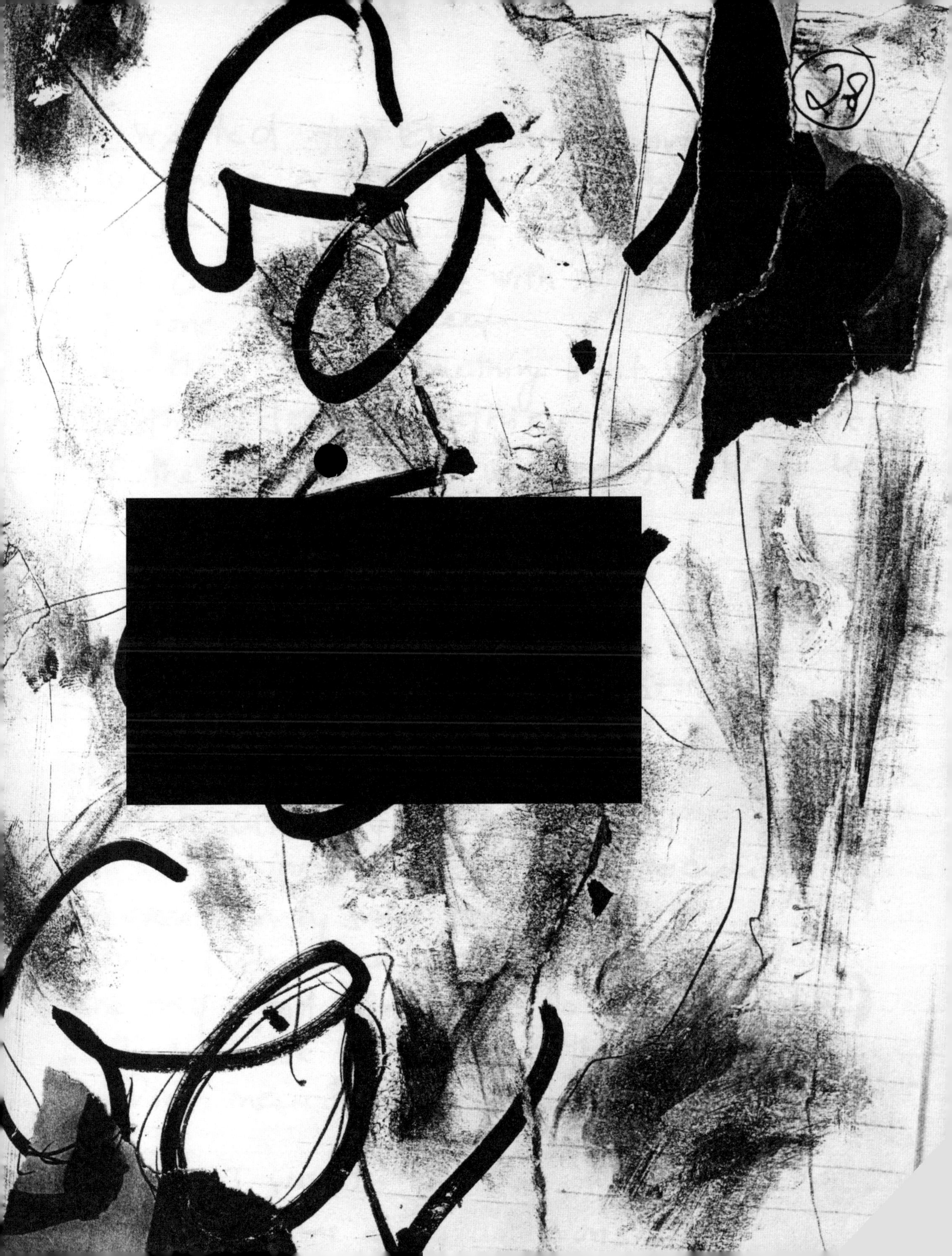

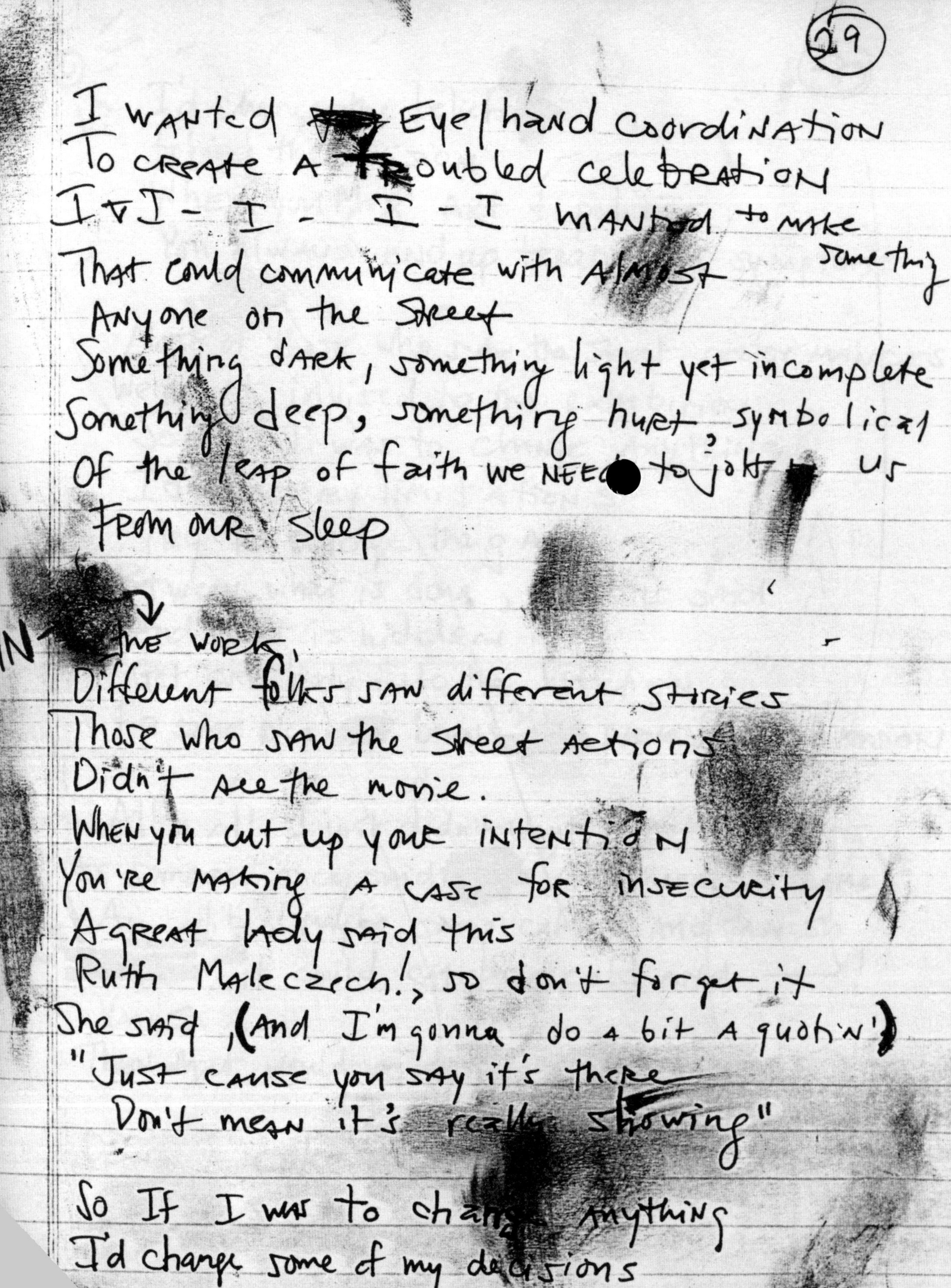

I wanted Eye/hand coordination
To create a troubled celebration
I-I - I - I - I wanted to make something
That could communicate with almost
Anyone on the street
Something dark, something light yet incomplete
Something deep, something hurt, symbolical
Of the leap of faith we need to jolt us
From our sleep

In the work,
Different folks saw different stories
Those who saw the street actions
Didn't see the movie.
When you cut up your intention
You're making a case for insecurity
A great lady said this
Ruth Maleczech!, so don't forget it
She said, (And I'm gonna do a bit a quotin')
"Just cause you say it's there
Don't mean it's really showing"

So If I was to change anything
I'd change some of my decisions

I'm lostin' . .

cause

The real question
Lies in the juxtaposition
Of destitution and plenitude
That's so un-nerving
And the sense, that is could be me tomorrow
So it's ultimately self-serving

portions of life
Are not evenly divided
If things were clearer, cleaner
Brighter, neater
More like the Ritz
If there were only rich or poor
Blacks or Moors or just white people
Biting the heads off Q-tips
I wouldn't be down for the gutter
Defending, pretending to suffer
For something supposedly totally other
I'm the darker, darker, darker brother
Working smother under cover
In a good job during bad times

I'd change the beliefs
behind the vision
When you mix art & politics
You always end up treating the symptoms

Most of those who saw the street performances
Weren't invited to the exhibition.
So - if I was to change anything
I'd accept my limitations
Try to bridge the gap
Between what is done, what is said
And what is hidden
Get everybody into the kitchen
For some rice 'n beans 'n pork fried subversion

All'n all I just didn't want to ruin my image
As someone once said "Art needs a frame"
An alibi, maybe coffee and danish
, it could catch cold and ——!
Vanish . . .
Then what would we do?

Drink a coke 'n get famished.

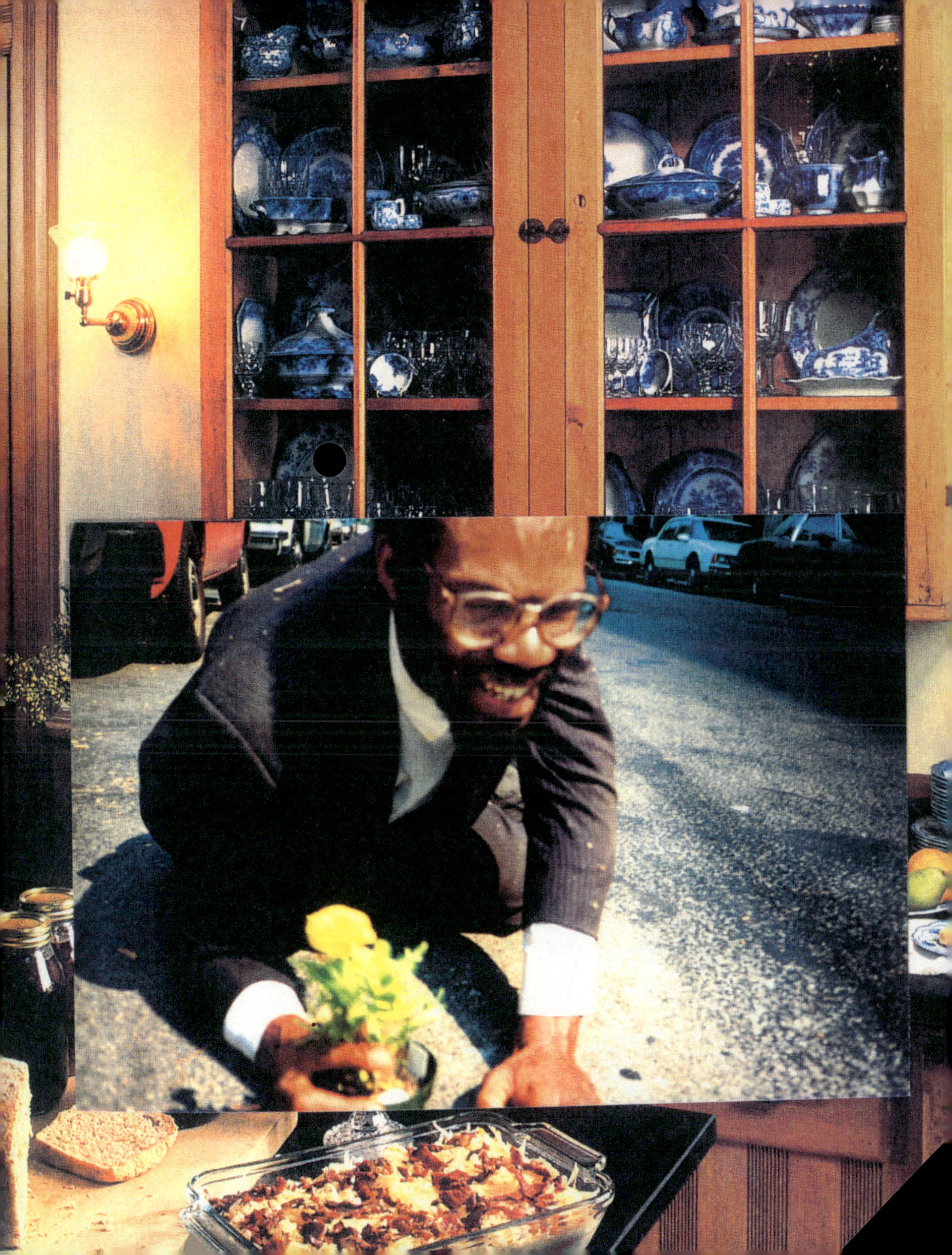

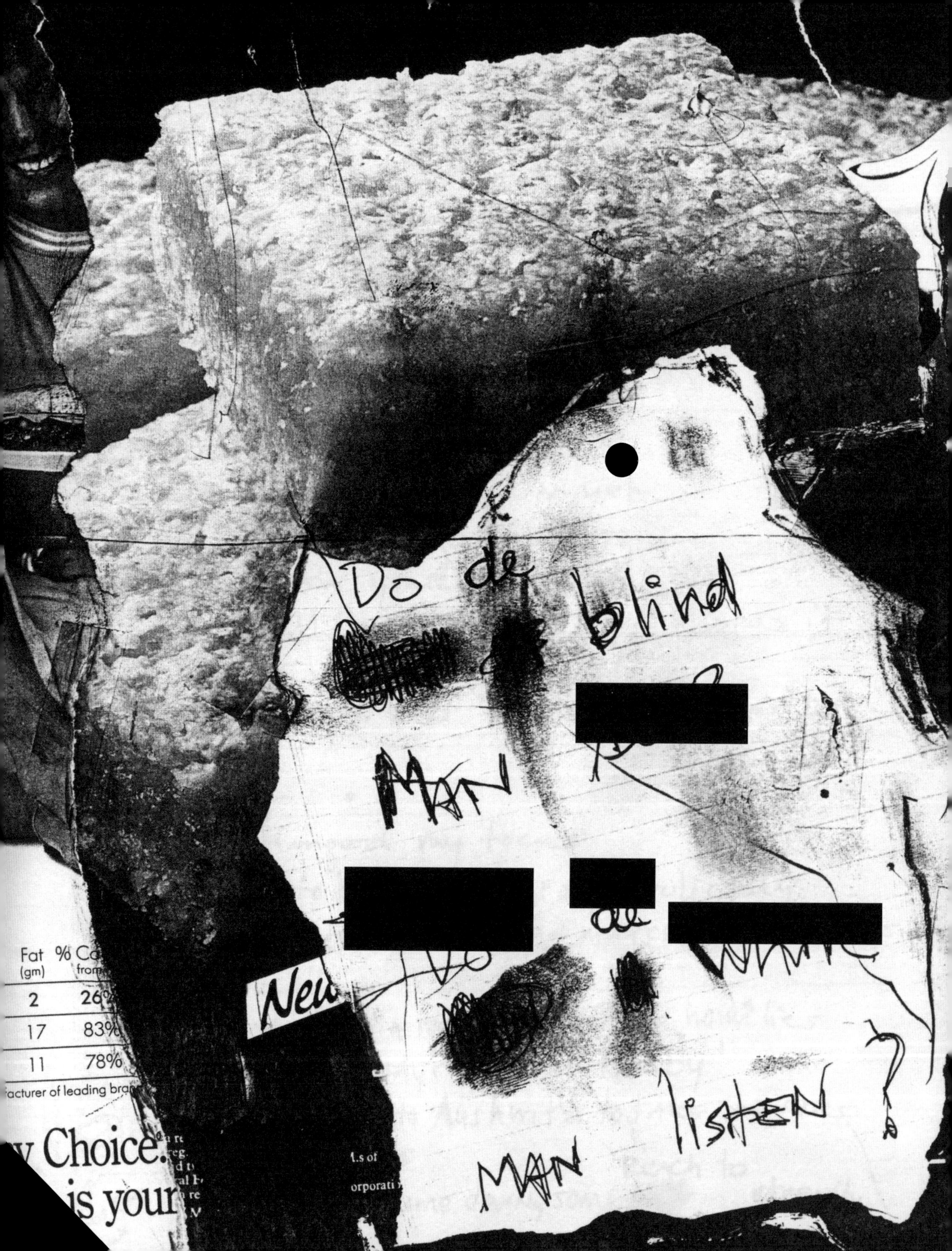

Do de blind
MAN
de
MAN lisHEN ?
New
Fat (gm) % Co from
2 26%
17 83%
11 78%
facturer of leading bra
y Choice.
is your

The work was slipshod and shameful.
Shame is the whip the cut and the apple,
How can you muzzle the now chain and the coffle?
What's wrong is to deny. Get awful and joyful.
The work was too large and small a mouthful

As for disrespect — well —
I down for wack, black is stacked
I'm deep for me, I'm down wit' street but I
Must diverge when it comes to hiding
Something up my sleeve
Cause I wanted to see something,
Yea, I-I-I-I- wanted to make something

GO!

Edited by Stuart Comer with Danielle A. Jackson

THE MUSEUM OF MODERN ART NEW YORK

member: POPE.L

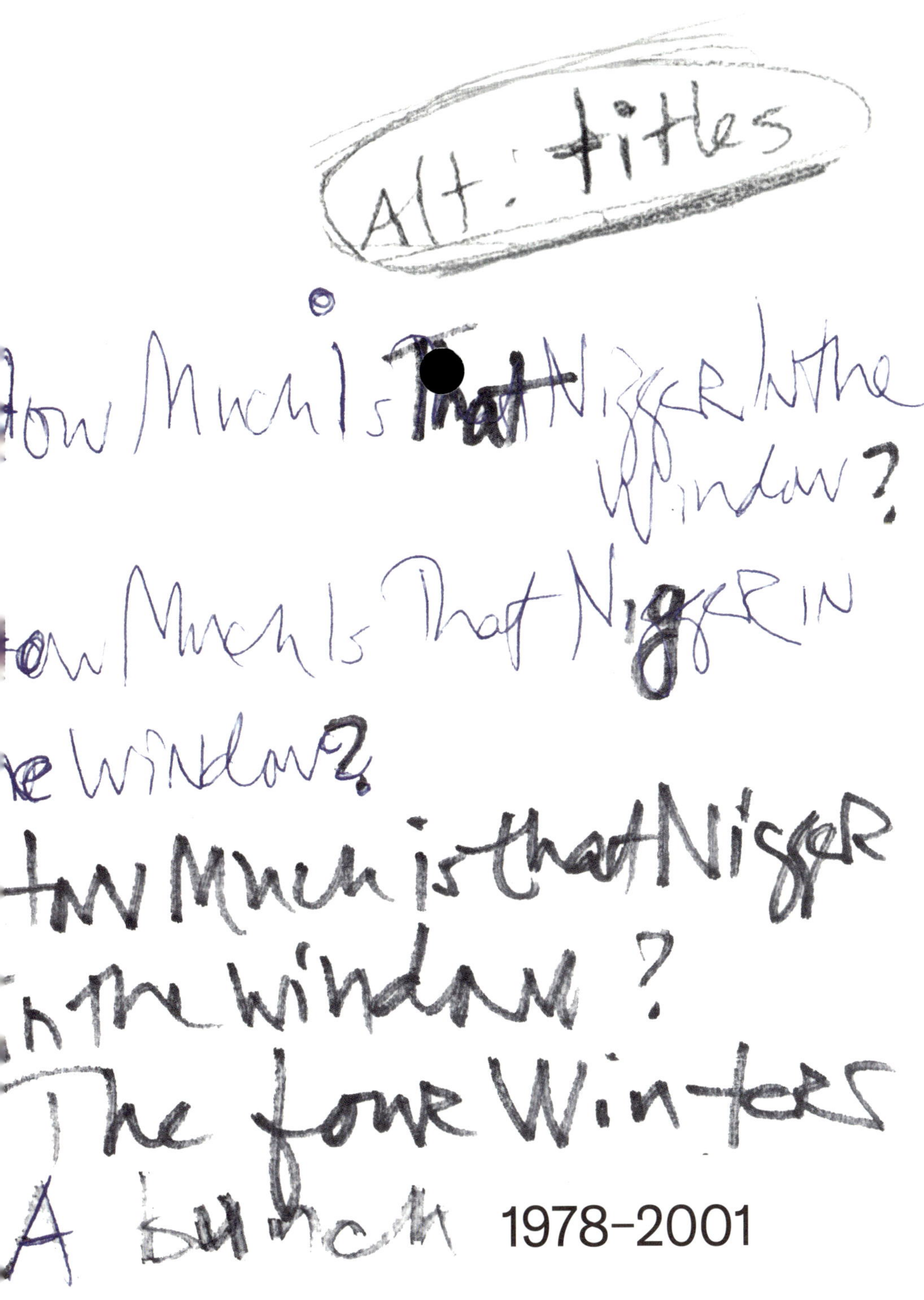

1978–2001

Hyundai Card

Hyundai Card is proud to sponsor *member: Pope.L, 1978–2001* at The Museum of Modern Art, New York, which surveys the singular early performance work of one of contemporary art's most influential figures. The exhibition presents a series of landmark performances, offering a rare opportunity to explore their role at the heart of Pope.L's unique multidisciplinary approach, spanning painting, drawing, street action, installation, sculpture, theater, and video.

Fully committing itself to creative disciplines, Hyundai Card seeks not only to identify important movements in culture, society, and technology but also to stimulate meaningful and inspiring experiences in everyday life. Whether Hyundai Card is hosting tomorrow's cultural pioneers at its stages and art spaces; building libraries of design, travel, music, and cooking for the members; or designing credit cards and digital services that are as beautiful as they are functional, our most inventive endeavors all draw from the creative well that the arts provide.

Pope.L has always been ahead of his time, and his longstanding practice of reinventing and recontextualizing the immaterial art of performance dovetails with Hyundai Card's drive to respond to our ever-changing times through creativity and innovation.

Hyundai Card hopes this exhibition will offer viewers a chance to rethink the relationship between the arts and society, as well as between the artist and the Museum's visitors. With gratitude to Pope.L and the exhibition's curators, Hyundai Card is delighted to be able to sponsor a major show of this powerful artist's work.

Cover: *Times Square Crawl a.k.a. Meditation Square Piece.* Times Square, New York, 1978. Inkjet print, 10 × 15" (25.4 × 38.1 cm). The Museum of Modern Art, New York

All works in the collection of The Museum of Modern Art are acquired in part through the generosity of Jill and Peter Kraus, Anne and Joel S. Ehrenkranz, The Contemporary Arts Council of the Museum of Modern Art, The Jill and Peter Kraus Media and Performance Art Acquisition Fund, and Jill and Peter Kraus in honor of Michael Lynne, unless otherwise noted.

FOREWORD

"Humans can make a difference with culture," the artist Pope.L told an interviewer in *Bomb* magazine in 1996. "It's a leap of faith to do any sort of cultural work. I choose to make troubled culture." Since the late 1970s, Pope.L (b. 1955, Newark, N.J.) has created poetic, symbolic, and at times troubling or even threatening images that reflect unpleasant truths about American society. His practice moves seamlessly across multiple mediums—painting, drawing, theater, video, sculpture, performance, and installation—targeting the relationship between whiteness and blackness and the insidious effect these racial categories have had on the most fundamental social, economic, and political conditions of our country. A trickster and provocateur, Pope.L deploys language, endurance, and absurdity to implode rigid categories of difference, making the everyday contradictions of an inherently unjust terrain impossible to ignore.

Today, Pope.L stands out as an influential critical voice in contemporary art who has inspired a younger generation of artists, particularly those whose work engages performance and media (for example, EJ Hill and Martine Syms, both of whom share their admiration for Pope.L in essays appearing in these pages). His groundbreaking performances can be understood as outcroppings of the Fluxus movement or as guerrilla street actions or manifestations of the artist's theatrical training. His work is often discussed in relation to influences as diverse as his late mentor, Geoffrey Hendricks; David Hammons and Adrian Piper; and the experimental theater troupe Mabou Mines.

member: Pope.L, 1978–2001 is the first museum exhibition to investigate the watershed early performances that helped define the artist's interdisciplinary career. Focusing on thirteen works from the late 1970s to the beginning of the new millennium, *member* features videos, photographs, props, costumes, and live actions. This selection of the artist's early work foregrounds documentation from theater, gallery, and street performances, including *Egg Eating Contest* (1990–91), *Eracism* (1992–2002), *Eating the Wall Street Journal* (1991–2020), and various manifestations of Pope.L's iconic Crawl series—most notably *Times Square Crawl a.k.a. Meditation Square Piece* (1978), *How Much Is That Nigger in the Window a.k.a Tompkins Square Crawl* (1991), and *The Great White Way: 22 miles, 9 years, 1 street* (2001–9)—in which the artist dragged his own body across the urban landscape of Manhattan. As much as these works highlight key strategies in Pope.L's practice during the initial stages of his career, they also provide a snapshot of the profound economic and cultural shifts that transpired in New York City over the course of the 1980s and 1990s.

Pope.L's political acuity is amply evident in the works around which *member* is organized. In *Tompkins Square Crawl*, as part of a residency at the alternative space Franklin Furnace, the artist crawled around the perimeter of Tompkins Square Park in New York's East Village in response to the park's closure by Mayor David N. Dinkins after the 1988 riots by homeless and squatter groups who sheltered there. For his 1996 performance *Member a.k.a. Schlong Journey*, Pope.L took a rickety white prosthetic phallus on a stroll through Harlem, stirring controversy among federal officials during that year's National Endowment for the

Arts reauthorization hearings. For *The Great White Way*, Pope.L crawled the entire length of Broadway, a grueling journey that decried the alarming growth of New York's homeless population and the community's refusal to acknowledge the problem.

Building on the model offered by recent exhibitions such as *Judson Dance Theater: The Work Is Never Done* (2018) and *Tania Bruguera: Untitled (Havana, 2000)* (2018), *member* joins the history of ambitious performance exhibitions staged at The Museum of Modern Art that have considered the afterlife of actions and performances and how these might be brought to life anew. The project coincides with a major acquisition of Pope.L's early work, a constellation of documentary photographs, costumes, props, video, and live performances that are the focus of the exhibition. This new acquisition brings more than 130 performance objects and relics into the Museum's collection, where they will complement another extensive body of work by the artist, *The Black Factory Archive* (2004–). The 210 objects that constitute the latter project were collected during Pope.L's 2004–6 performance tour across the United States, during which he asked visitors to his mobile "Black Factory" at various locations across the country to share objects that they felt represented "blackness." Together these substantial holdings, reflective of the Museum's ongoing commitment to the artist, deepen our understanding of Pope.L's practice overall.

Since the founding of the Department of Media and Performance in 2009, the Museum has intensified its engagement with live art. Today the department, led by Stuart Comer, is in constant pursuit of new ways in which the Museum might extend its core commitments—exhibiting, collecting, preserving, and documenting art—to performance and other time-based work. The diverse collection of works included in this major acquisition and featured in *member* joins other recent landmark acquisitions by the Museum's Media and Performance department, such as Simone Forti's *Dance Constructions* (1960–61) and selections from the Trisha Brown archive (1961–2005). Together, these influential bodies of work help the Museum champion artists whose engagements with performance have radically expanded the possibilities for art.

member is part of *Pope.L: Instigation, Aspiration, Perspiration*, a trio of complementary exhibitions being presented this fall across New York City, organized independently by The Museum of Modern Art, the Whitney Museum of American Art, and Public Art Fund, respectively. In keeping with Pope.L's practice, this expansive presentation involves both public and private spaces, and it includes not only a celebration of the artist's early work but a monumental new installation and a mass Crawl from a playground in the West Village to Union Square Park.

We are indebted to Stuart Comer, The Lonti Ebers Chief Curator of Media and Performance, and Danielle A. Jackson, Curatorial Assistant in the Department of Media and Performance. Guided by a spirit of innovation and cross-disciplinarity, they have crafted a groundbreaking exhibition and performance program and the volume you now hold, encouraging new critical readings of Pope.L's vital early performances.

We are truly thankful to our lead sponsor, Hyundai Card, for their generous support. The exhibition is presented as part of The Hyundai Card Performance Series. Major support is provided by The Jill and Peter Kraus Endowed Fund for Contemporary Exhibitions and The Jon Stryker Endowment. Additional support is provided by The Friends of Education of

The Museum of Modern Art, Marilyn and Larry Fields, Nancy and David Frej, Barbara Karp Shuster, and Ann and Mel Schaffer.

Leadership contributions to the Annual Exhibition Fund, in support of the Museum's collection and collection exhibitions, are generously provided by the Kate W. Cassidy Foundation, Sue and Edgar Wachenheim III, Mimi and Peter Haas Fund, Jerry I. Speyer and Katherine G. Farley, Eva and Glenn Dubin, The Sandra and Tony Tamer Exhibition Fund, Alice and Tom Tisch, The David Rockefeller Council, Anne Dias, Kathy and Richard S. Fuld, Jr., Kenneth C. Griffin, Marie-Josée and Henry R. Kravis, Jo Carole and Ronald S. Lauder, Anna Marie and Robert F. Shapiro, The Keith Haring Foundation, and The Contemporary Arts Council of The Museum of Modern Art.

Major contributions to the Annual Exhibition Fund are provided by the Estate of Ralph L. Riehle, Emily Rauh Pulitzer, Brett and Daniel Sundheim, Karen and Gary Winnick, The Marella and Giovanni Agnelli Fund for Exhibitions, Clarissa Alcock and Edgar Bronfman, Jr., Agnes Gund, and Oya and Bülent Eczacıbaşı.

On behalf of the trustees and staff of The Museum of Modern Art, we would like to thank the lenders to the exhibition. We would also like to recognize our collaborators and partners on *Instigation, Aspiration, Perspiration*: the Whitney Museum of American Art and Public Art Fund. Finally, we extend our warmest thanks to Pope.L, whose courageous work has inspired us all. His dedication to this project and his generosity at every turn have been remarkable. We are immensely grateful.

Glenn D. Lowry
The David Rockefeller Director
The Museum of Modern Art

INTRODUCTION: A LACK IN THE WAKE

Stuart Comer

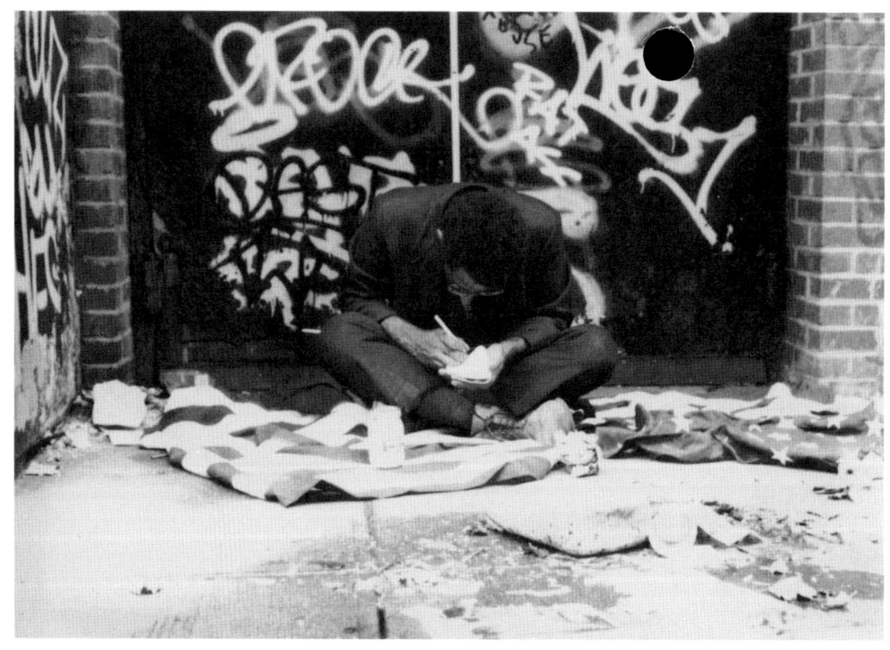

Writing/Sleeping/Living on the Flag, New York, ca. 1990–91

So—when I say
Holes are conduits or a 'means to'
Or a space or an intersection—
I mean holes are occasions—
Opportunities which can take
Many forms, materials, and durations
(imagine a hole that is only duration).

—Pope.L, *Hole Theory—Parts: Four & Five* (2002)

"Have-not-ness" is a hole at the heart of the body of work that forms this exhibition, a project defined as much by voids, ghosts, and the passage of bodies and time as it is by material objects and histories. To the degree that the multivalent work of Pope.L occupies a zone between actions and objects, between past and present, this hole becomes an occasion to problematize such binaries, structures of difference in aesthetic terms that find an echo in the heavily bifurcated social and racial relations Pope.L has endeavored to destabilize throughout his career. *member: Pope.L, 1978–2001* draws together a constellation of diverse materials constituting artworks that to varying degrees have attempted to inhabit this hole, this space of lack. Pope.L claims that it is a "lack worth having," a process of coming to terms with an absence of resolution that speaks to the "dynamic of pain, loss, joy, radicality, and possibility in the experience of being black."[1]

Pope.L's confession that "have-not-ness permeates everything I do" speaks to his own personal history emerging from a working-class family in which some members have lived in precarious conditions. Lack also defines a structural logic that frames the works in this exhibition, a series of performances and interventions focused on the condition of dispossession in a culture driven by aspiration, consumption, and violent social conflict.[2] Together these works offer a lexicon of actions and gestures that lay bare structures and behaviors that regulate difference in our society.

Pope.L defines lack as "an ongoing state of difference that evokes two conditions simultaneously: 1) failure and loss; 2) possibility and opportunity."[3] This schism is drawn out in actions such as his series of Crawls, in which the artist assumes the position of a homeless person, becoming horizontal in a vertical city, dragging his body across stretches of pavement in New York's East Village or Times Square clothed in a business suit, the armor of an aspirational society consumed with power. With each slog of his arms and legs, Pope.L slowly and steadily puts pressure on that metonym of privilege and authority, but he also claims membership in two camps simultaneously: the disenfranchised and those cloaked in the trappings of success.

The double entendre in the title *member* suggests the agency that Pope.L's form of role-playing offers in destabilizing the various positions of belonging he occupies across a range of institutions in our white, phallocentric society, beginning with his place in the family and extending to both his station among the marginalized underclass and his status in the art world as a successful, "legitimate" artist. A complex web of emotions, from shame and embarrassment to empathy and admiration, entangles Pope.L's connection to his family. Works like *The Aunt Jenny Chronicles* (1990–91) betray the frayed relationships produced by his father's absence and his mother's addiction. "Family is a potent but limited organizing concept," Pope.L notes. "Even so, a resemblance which suggests a beginning can be very compelling. Why? Because beginnings help us to locate where we are and who we are."[4]

Another mode of addressing such questions of place occurs in *Sweet Desire a.k.a. Burial Piece* (1996–97), but here the artist enacts a form of ending rather than a beginning. In contrast to the mobility of the Crawls, *Sweet Desire* required Pope.L to be buried from the neck down—in its first iteration, on the prestigious grounds of Skowhegan School of Painting and Sculpture in Maine—confined for several hours while he contemplated a bowl of vanilla ice cream placed in front of him, just out of reach. Having lowered himself to the pavement in the Crawls, he was now plunged even deeper, below grade. In the video documenting the performance, as Pope.L ponders the increasing formlessness of the melting white dessert from his makeshift grave, intertitles appear onscreen asking:

> what do black people want?
> who do they want it from?
> why do they want it?

Giving these questions physical and active form throughout his career, Pope.L has located himself on a broad range of faultlines in a dysfunctional society. Positioning the black body as an open question, he has intervened in the spaces of the city, the street, the stage, and the gallery to assess moments of collectivity and to test and exhaust the limitations of the structures that regulate them.

The thirteen performances that are the core of this exhibition were recently acquired by The Museum of Modern Art, a gesture that acknowledges the pivotal importance of Pope.L's early actions and reaffirms the Museum's commitment to bringing into its collection—despite the complexities of doing so—works that were once live and fugitive, whose negotiation between the living moment and the museum's space of memory provokes not resolution but a condition of multiple durations. These works are remade continually over time and play in the void between their initial iteration and the often troubled or degraded material traces that remain. Certain of the works in *member*, such as *Snow Crawl* (1991–2001) and *ATM Piece* (1997), exist primarily through documentation that Pope.L has edited and manipulated to short-circuit any linear reading of the work's evolution. Other projects, such as *Eating the Wall Street Journal* (begun in 1991), have existed in multiple versions over many years. Pope.L continues to restage, rethink, repeat, and restructure this work, sabotaging any notion of an original: "Originals should be tools not objectives," he stresses.[5] Coinciding with the presentation of this exhibition at MoMA, Public Art Fund has planned a mass crawl by Pope.L, a new iteration of the group Crawls he has presented since the early 1990s, opening up the central action of his early solo performances to a mixed community, treading the knife's edge between the power of collective action and utter precarity.

Pope.L's resistance to fixed states and rigid categories raises tough, compelling questions for a museum that seeks to corral the strategic slipperiness of his actions into its collection, a family of another kind. The artist has referred to performance's relationship to the museum as a canary in the coal mine, claiming that "institutionalized art performance reenactment is about emptying as much as it is about remembering. Memory is a smoke screen for a set of anxieties possessed by both the packrat and the king."[6] Pope.L's affinity for holes and voids suggests that he is comfortable with emptiness and its capacity to become a conduit or an intersection for multiple meanings and configurations. The works in this exhibition suggest the degree to which Pope.L has been willing to place his own body at the center of those intersections and to raise the stakes for what happens when various states of difference converge. He dives into the wake produced by the anxious history of blackness and its representations in this country, a space described by Christina Sharpe in her discussion of black life and the afterlives of slavery as "a region of disturbed flow." "We live in the knowledge that the wake has positioned us as no-citizen," she notes. "If we are lucky, the knowledge of this positioning avails us particular ways of re/seeing, re/inhabiting, and re/imagining the world."[7]

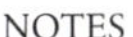

NOTES

1. The artist, quoted in Lisa Melandri, "Ritual, Archive, and Repetition: An Interview with William Pope.L," in *William Pope.L: Art after White People: Time, Trees, and Celluloid . . .* (Santa Monica, Calif.: Santa Monica Museum of Art, 2007), 21.
2. Martha Wilson, "William Pope.L," *Bomb* 55 (Spring 1996), 53.
3. The artist, quoted in Melandri, "Ritual, Archive, and Repetition: An Interview with William Pope.L," 21.
4. Pope.L, "On Versions," in *William Pope.L: snow, spraypaint, hair, sperm & baloney* (London: Kenny Schachter/ROVE, 2007), 35.
5. Ibid.
6. Pope.L, "Canary in the Coal Mine," in *Art Journal* 70, no. 3 (Fall 2011): 55.
7. Christina Sharpe, *In the Wake: On Blackness and Being* (Durham, N.C.: Duke University Press, 2016), 22.

MORE Alt titles

- Pointilism
- Empty Bottle
- From A hill below the Horizon
- Why I don't go to the Island anymore
- Afraid of the

A CONVERSATION WITH POPE.L
Stuart Comer and Danielle A. Jackson

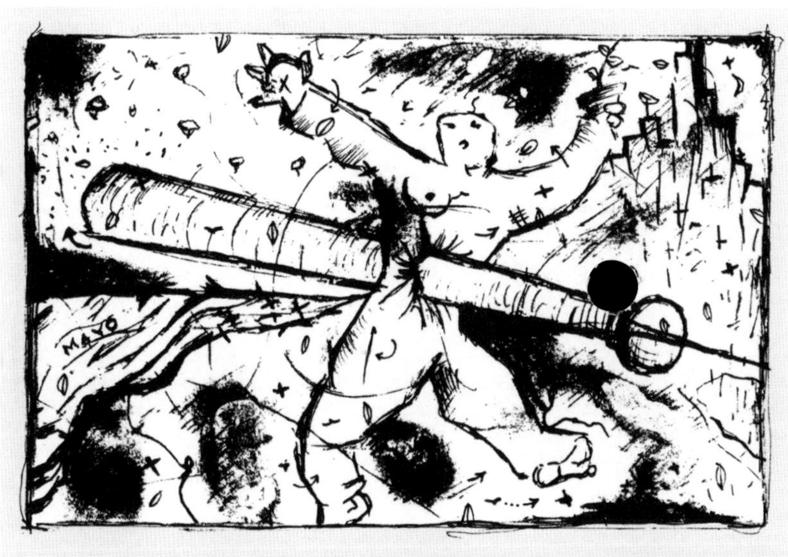

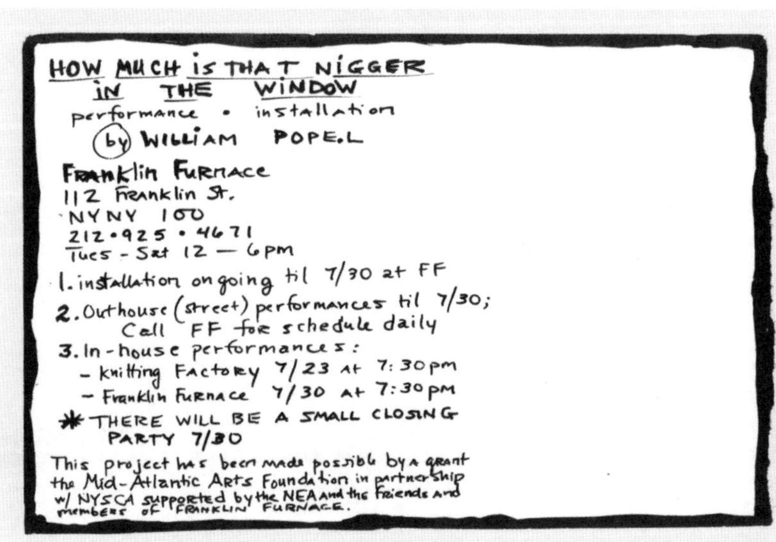

Postcard (recto and verso) for *How Much Is That Nigger in the Window*. Franklin Furnace, New York, 1991. Franklin Furnace Archive, Inc., New York

Stuart Comer: Where did your concern for the "mixed signal" originate?

Pope.L: I have always had neurological processing confusions between signifier and signified. I thought it was a mere problem. Later, as I got more involved with language, I saw the advantages in my deficit. Neurological gaffes could be spaces, opportunities, tools, even a manifesto for getting at consciousness.

SC: How would you link your language operations with the situations and actions to which you submit your body? It is generally assumed that your early work shifted from an emphasis on language in the theater works to a focus on tasks as you moved to the street. But I wonder if there might be deeper connections to consider.

P.L: The link between language and performance is duration; both exist only via the crucible of time and are continually remade in time.

Intuitively, I've always been drawn to images and actions that feel "sentient" without the support of words. However, I did not know how to get at that sort of condensation in an artwork; it took a while. Sometimes it seemed I could perform with an object and near get a sense of it—but the object or text or frame or my intention still had too much primacy... The unvoiced image stuff like the Crawls could only have happened after doing a shitload of language. I tired myself out and wrote myself into image. A situation plus action plus time equals some *x*. I made this physically palpable in terms of a choice of scape, a more porous social space than a gallery. On the other hand, writing comes off very proscenium to me. Meaning already framed by a context. But marking, painting with letters, tussling with their material character, making them out of graphite or potatoes or blood or this and that molecule unhinges the text in a way that machine writing cannot—scaping the world with the word...

SC: In many of your performances, you put your body under duress, and in your paintings, collages, and other works, you similarly distress words and images. When you take the word or image off the stage, or off the page, and create different arenas in which language is both enacted and deconstructed, what happens? How has your use of language been informed by your experience in theater? How have your street actions led to an "undoing" of language?

P.L: There's a space of language that is not accounted for by any substrate in art. This is what makes language unique as a hinge, as a tool. When you play in language, it's a recognition of your limits—this playing is always saying at least two things: what I CAN and CANNOT do. Playing betwixt, around, among, between the possibilities of what can be said. There is no above or beyond in language.

But how has my work in theater informed my work in language? Negatively. Not a bad thing. It's a craft thing. It's good not to be able to do anything I want. Theater asks questions of Art that to art folks' ears might sound dumb and whiny—unnerving. Theater asks Art: "Why don't you ask questions I can understand? Why you so fascinated with repetition? Why all this auteur shit? Where's the story, emotion, and payoff, bitch?!"

Regarding the street stuff: what it's led me to is shutting up a little more—undoing language with silence . . .

DANIELLE A. JACKSON: What initially propelled you to make proscenium work? How did you get involved with experimental theater groups such as Mabou Mines and Tesla Linkum Theater Collective?

P.L: My initial interest in proscenium work came from making artworks I called Communication Devices. These "CDs" came out of not knowing, pointless wandering, and illness. By the time I started thinking about CDs as performances, I'd more or less found a format that did not respect medium specificity. Performance seemed to be the next thing. And I found it a very odd thing. It had so many parts, it was a head-fuck—it contained objects plus!!! TIME, PEOPLE, COLLABORATION, ACTUAL SPACE IN THE WORLD . . . It offered a nice bundle of formats all in one format: language, choreography, lighting, sound, props and machines, scenography, the play of "the group" via a continually changing network of ideas . . . collaboration as a kind of virtual collage. So when I say "proscenium," I don't mean it in the strict sense of an arch or box within which a text is staged; I mean any demarcation deal between an audience and a performer or between performer and writer or a prop and a movement, etc., etc.

Yeah, so after grad school I was looking for an interesting Theater experience, not an Art experience. I wanted to learn some other kind of conventions. Slow some shit down in my art-head. Step into a different flow of knowledge. Joni Harmon, also a grad from Mason Gross, was working on a piece and told me about her boyfriend who was making "this really interesting stuff," Joni called it. The boyfriend turned out to be Jim Calder. Eventually Jim introduced me to Joe Daly, and we began to make a piece together for the next three or four years. We worked out of Mabou Mines' rehearsal space in the East Village, at First and Saint Marks. Every week or so we'd bring in parts of the piece and perform it for Ruth Maleczech or her partner, Lee Breuer. It was the perfect postgrad situation. I mean, Ruth and Lee were Mabou Mines! Like what IS THAT!?? Their example inspired us to create Tesla Linkum, our own collective, which though short-lived produced a ton of really interesting work, not always successful but really interesting.

DAJ: Last year, during a lecture at New York University, you spoke about theater, collaboration, and authorship. "Theater will fuck your shit up!" you declared. You also talked about how director, writer, actor, et al. engage in a kind of riff or cypher. Can you speak about those ideas in the performances with Calder or Daly, who became recurring collaborators for several years?

P.L: First off, I think a person's ignorance and curiosity can teach them a lot. I had a lot of both going into the world of theater. I learned a LOT from working with Calder and Daly. They were kind of my reluctant big brothers and assholes all at once. I also learned a lot from Tom Miller, Jessie Allen, Carl Schnedeker, Ledlie Bogerhoff, and Barbara Hiesiger. I was with the right people in the right place at the right time. It was up to me to make something of the opportunity. Without those folks I would not have had the wherewithal to do it. In the very beginning it was funny and upsetting. I did not understand the difference between Theater as something you see or read and Theater as something you make or do or live.

SC: Could you describe the process that took you from proscenium space to outdoor performance?

P.L: Hmm. I was already in outdoor or nontraditional spaces doing CDs. I just did not recognize that work as performance since at the time I had no frame of reference except a conceptual one. My goal with CDs was to explore communication conundrums and confusions within as many situations and formats as possible; medium followed challenge, not the other way around. SO—formalizing performing or performance was a logical next step. My first formal performance works were indoors, but simultaneously I was doing less obvious performance-y things outdoors.

SC: Your best-known outdoor works include the Crawls, which you did as early as 1978. Your first notion for them involved group crawls, but the initial performances were solo. What happened when you extended the process to a mass crawl, which first happened in 1992? How did the dispersal of the action across a community impact the work?

P.L: Community is a diversity. Group or mass crawls tended to be confusions and a letdown. A fruitful, giddy, what-the-fuck sort of confusion. Some people, usually male and young, thought it was a race. Others thought it was about me—usually the organizers—and mistook the group situation for the previous solo situation. Still, I thought they had to be done. It was important to move folks' thinking beyond the solo gesture à la Yves Klein's *Leap into the Void* or, in this country, Chris Burden's *Shoot*. I say this even though I believe that artists like Burden, Suzanne Lacy, Vito Acconci, Joseph Beuys, and more recently Santiago Sierra, Patty Chang, and Tania Bruguera have upped the ante on the performative gesture as a more expansive and layered thing.

DAJ: In 1978, you performed *Thunderbird Immolation a.k.a. Meditation Square Piece* in SoHo outside a building that housed art galleries, including those of Leo Castelli and Ileana Sonnabend. You sat on a square yellow cloth in a lotus pose surrounded by unlit matches, periodically pouring a mixture of Coke and Thunderbird on yourself. The event evoked the famous 1963 self-immolation of Buddhist monk Thich Quang Duc in Saigon to protest the repressive South Vietnamese regime. After his dignified yet grisly death, a few monks covered his charred body with a yellow robe.

I often see the yellow square—which also appears in the other two Meditation Square Pieces, *Times Square Crawl* and *Singing in the Rain* (both 1978)—as a symbol of resistance and protest. Did you see these gestures as a kind of activism? What role does symbolism play in these works and your work overall?

P.L: HMMM. I was thinking of SIMPLE and DIRECT ACTivities AS MARKERS OF CHANGE OR RESISTANCE. I WAS BLIND and INSISTENT about it A LITTLE BIT. SYMBOLISM? SYMBOLISM? HMMM. I prefer to think LANGUAGE and REFERENCE. COWARDLY? I am not comfortable with the popular usage of the word *symbolism*, a usage WHICH suggests, for many, a one-to-one strict protective meaning relation such that one thing must mean or equal ONE thing. I'm not comfortable with DAT.

I think of the yellow square, its use and reference, as more a means of marking or framing... It's interesting to note NOW that soon after this time I gave up framing so-friendly-like. Once I let that go, I learned, whether I liked it or not, how framing can limit reference rather than encourage it... so...

DAJ: What was your connection to Eastern spirituality?

P.L: I used to meditate. A lot. I gave it up eventually. A fa[illegible]e teacher asked me: "Maybe you're hiding from the world?"

DAJ: Can you describe *Singing in the Rain*, which took place at the Third Street Men's Shelter in New York?

P.L: It was a plan and an epiphany, both cause I enjoyed it and I wasn't expecting to... I set it up as a wandering like the *Cow Commercial* performance—so I'm stumbling around Lower Manhattan, just above Houston Street, stopping here there, doing impromptu, inept versions of the celebrated dance routine from the film *Singing in the Rain*. I wanted a change of pace, to get more vertical than crawling or sitting, something looser... Doing the piece was a challenge, to not rehearse, not overconceive—interesting to perform a routine, perform it incompletely and badly in public, stupidly as a shtick but repeat it as if what you're doing is cause your heart is guiding you. The work was supposed to suggest lightness and a relinquishing of cares while performed against and in environments that felt abandoned or on the edge of care. It seemed funny, callous, and poignant—all at once.

SO eventually I run into these guys sitting on a stoop near the men's shelter on Third Street, between Second and Third Avenues. My family used to live near there. You could see the day yard from our bathroom window. SO yep, I'm wandering and I see these guys and I do a version especially for them. They're sitting on the stoop like an accidental but enthusiastic audience, just sitting, clapping not in a hurry like the rest of the city; in a way, they were the proscenium...

DAJ: In your street interventions, the locations are always intentional—outside the galleries in *Thunderbird Immolation*, at the site of the 1988 Tompkins Square Park riot in *Tompkins Square Crawl* (1991). Why did you take *Member a.k.a. Schlong Journey* (1996) to Harlem, the mecca of black America, and in particular 125th Street?

> P.L: I knew 125th Street, especially near Seventh and Eighth Avenues. My grandmother lived on 136th between Seventh and Eighth for forty-plus years, so I knew that general area. It's the feel of 125th Street that I always remember. The feel was very singular: the gaggle, stop-and-go of people, clashing sounds, laughter, cars, music, always music, people yelling to each other for no apparent reason, just yelling, the smell of burning incense, always more than one color, bargain and fast-food stores with their doors open to the air, the hustle and bustle of the space, in the space, through the space. My sister worked for the Department of Corrections in the Adam Clayton Powell building across from the Studio Museum in Harlem. In siting *Member* on 125th, I wanted to make myself a spectacle and 125th Street my interlocuter. I knew black folks would appreciate the work in crucial ways. There would be someone who noticed, someone who ignored, someone who enjoyed the puzzle nature of it, someone who laughed—I wanted to be a site that galvanized in terms of ridicule, wonder, criticality, and enigma . . .

DAJ: *Snow Crawl* (1991–2001) was the first of the Crawls to occur outside New York City. Having taken place in Maine over several winters, it is simultaneously a performance, a video, and an installation. The mirrored tube through which the video is viewed kaleidoscopically fragments the image and renders your body nearly illegible. Can you speak about the process of making the work and how you developed the idea for the installation?

> P.L: I wanted to do something where the focus would be more on image, mood, and making via an apparatus rather than the performer's body—in this case, my body. The latter is more in keeping with the tradition of solo art performing, where it's a lot about the performer and their individual adventure. I wanted to make clearer my drive to divorce performance documentation from objectivity—SO when I used this sort of footage I was making a doppelgänger, fictional, narrative thingamajig. In the case of *Snow Crawl*, the fronting of context and mood over the performing body was an intended scheme.

SC: A number of your works have appeared in different versions. How do you view their evolution in time and for posterity?

> P.L: Hmm. Posterity. I'm a shell, it's a shell, and we are all together . . .

SC: New York City's Tompkins Square Park continues to have a strong association with the riot there in summer 1988, when its homeless and squatter population was forcibly evicted by police. That event coincided with the culture wars, which reached their peak the following summer during the Robert Mapplethorpe controversy, a vicious debate over government arts funding that hinged largely on homoerotic, idealized images of nude black men shot by a white photographer.

In 1991, you performed *Tompkins Square Crawl*, a work you had incubated at Franklin Furnace, a key participant in the alternative-space movement and no stranger to the culture wars. Your residency at Franklin Furnace, titled *How Much Is That Nigger in the*

Window, culminated in another performance, *I Get Paid to Rub Mayo on My Body* (also 1991), in which you smeared mayonnaise on your skin while wearing only underwear in the venue's storefront window. It was a shocking counterpoint to the image of black masculinity proposed by Mapplethorpe. Together, your two performances seemed to distill the cultural and political moment with uncanny insight, and they can be seen as DNA for many projects you produced later. They also suggest a remarkable moment in which three spaces you had been engaged in—the street, the gallery, and the theater—all intersected.

> P.L: Mistakenly or not, I always thought I had a more intimate, rubbery relationship to the black male body than just photographs. That may seem obvious, but I wonder ... Imagine a sort of person whose only relation to their own body was via photography—is that blackness? Is blackness a kind of femininity in that sense? Anywho, I feel the way I do not just cause I'm inside a black male body but because of the people before and around me who have had these bodies designed for them. Is this design a mode of theft, a denial, making bodies that zombie their own self-feeling? Black Zombie feeling is a way to feel you are in the world. It's a way to survive by discarding yourself like you're someone else's condom in your own pocket. There is a righteous stubbornness and poignancy in this denial that touches on the publicness, for example, in the spectacle that is in black male homelessness. I did not really care about Mapplethorpe's situation. Maybe I should have. I eventually cared a little more. I was too caught up with a lower horizon. The edge of a curbside when you pull yourself along an asphalt tributary...
>
> The residency at Franklin Furnace was a key moment. Franklin Furnace was always good to me. Meaning Martha Wilson was always good to me. She gave my work a home when no one else would, whether it was the early, wacky, smarty-pants theater work or the more art-performance work I was doing on the other side of the proscenium.

SC: To some degree, the alternative-space movement arose out of earlier provocations in the art world, such as those at the heart of Fluxus. Given your connections to the movement, how have scores and other of its strategies influenced you? What role did the Fluxus artist Geoffrey Hendricks, a mentor of yours, play in how you developed your performance practice and the rest of your work?

> P.L: Geoff wasn't the most talkative person. He led by example. He included me and other students—Vivian Vassar, Jonathan Leiter, Lydia Gray, François Morelli, John Patterson, Mark Semanchik, Darrell Wilson—in his public performance work as a gift, which was also a kind of training. From Geoff I got permission and encouragement. Not much detailed criticism, more a love for making and a generosity of spirit. Re: Fluxus: I've never gotten super-deep into their actual bric-a-brac—mail art, editions, boxes containing many small things, or publishing. It's more the way of Fluxus: inexpensive, indeterminate, open-ended, learned but stupid, fancy but poor, funny but sad, smart but down to earth.

SC: The violation of the body in your work has a number of historical precedents, particularly Viennese Actionism, and a number of your works evolved in parallel with those of artists like Mike Kelley and Paul McCarthy, who similarly turned to abjection and its peculiar relationship to consumerism. Did you ever feel your work was in dialogue with these projects? What's at stake when blackness is introduced into this equation?

> P.L: I was told that my work could be related to Kelley or McCarthy. I did not know their work. Once I looked at their stuff, I denied any connection! Ha! They were already packaging up their "mess" for galleries and museums, whereas I wasn't thinking about that.
>
> Even so, the more I looked at their work, the more of their work I encountered, I could see, separate from their gallery gaming, that some of their interests related to mine. But the Freud they were after was different than the Freud I dug. I saw Freud through Lacan or Wittgenstein and maybe certain contemporary trends in ethnology or anthropology. Working-class themes in Kelley definitely connected with me. In McCarthy, the use of food related, but I was less interested in food as paint than as a way of performing duration with objects or demo-ing a way of making without actually making. And when I use food, especially a lot of it, I always feel a little guilty—that's the underclass immigrant in me. I don't see this in McCarthy; he is free, he has no shame. Kelley and McCarthy bring race into their work via their use of European stereotypes of whiteness; it tends to feel a little bit quaintly morbid or perverse. When American black folk reference Africa, it feels more intimate to me, which could be another kind of perversity, I suppose, but maybe the two are more closely related than I thought...

SC: In January 2019, I saw *Choir of the Slain (part X)*, part of the performance installation *Black Power Naps* at Performance Space New York by niv Acosta and Fannie Sosa. Their program notes read, "Our culture has required that people of color present themselves as extraordinary performers, athletes, or entertainers in order to exist in the public realm. *Black Power Naps* refuses institutionalized exhaustion and demands the redistribution of idleness, down time, and quality sleep." This idea chimed with two consistent strategies in your work, exhaustion and "giving up verticality." Perhaps one key distinction is the fact that, in the Crawls, you situate the horizontal body on the sidewalk, a kind of provocation. Too, your work arguably does not provide for recovery; rather, it pushes the body to extremes with no reprieve.

You've written, "The supine body symbolizes indolence, passivity, sickness, and death... even though the horizontal body is central to lovemaking, birth, resting, and play."[1] Within current discussions about the violence done to black bodies, how might the reading of the earlier Crawl works shift? Do the questions change? Do the answers change?

> P.L: The answer is always basically the same: survival, because the history that created the problem is the same—how to unencumber oneself from an institutionalized past that has marked one before one is even in the world. The group crawls were a way to harness the power of a congregation of strangers, an ensemble of just-mets,

a polis of folks who empower themselves by performing an act that dirties them. Black power napping is witty and funny. Faggy and middle class in an odd way. Maybe perverse. The photo on the Performance Space New York site is wonderfully weird. They're asleep standing up. Typical herd behavior. Always on alert. They are dressed like they are out clubbing, very aggressive zombies, but I'm not sure which way the flesh is pointing.

SC: What role has autobiography played in your work? Performances like *The Aunt Jenny Chronicles* (1990–91) reference specific family members, and you have discussed the Crawls and your consideration of homelessness in terms of your family history. Where do you locate the self in your work, and what happens in performances where actions are distributed to others?

P.L: As if it were ever up to me. Not sure how to ponder this. I tend to be drawn to what is near. I AM NEARSIGHTED. The local speaks to me. That's why I'm drawn to domestic materials. Home is not only where the politics [illegible] it's where the substrate is. My family formed me. My country formed me. My time formed me. Agency? Agency? Who got the agency?

Distributing action to others? Experience has taught me distributing action to others can be a form of social justice; telling someone what to do is one of the most vulnerable, intimate acts a human can do. Telling people what to do is a transaction that makes the teller as much enmeshed as the one being told, maybe more.

DAJ: *member: Pope.L, 1978–2001* focuses on thirteen works that helped define your career. What is it about this selection that highlights your core concerns?

P.L: Welllllllll—I know that the curatorial head feels these thirteen works mean something key, for example that they highlight core concerns. I'm not sure I have core concerns. But let's say I do—let's say I do, then it's all projection, perambulation, and performance anywho which is HOW it should be. I mean, how could it be otherwise? The seam of the puzzle is the core of the puzzle and so on . . .

DAJ: You once said that the origins of *Eating the Wall Street Journal* (2000) stemmed from advertising for the paper suggesting that if you purchased a subscription, good things would happen. The ads led you to begin thinking of the *Journal* as a kind of modern fetish, imbued with mystical power: "Just having it near you, having it land on your doorstep, would multiply your wealth. So I took the logic to its absurd conclusion. Shouldn't ingesting it increase your wealth 10-fold?"[2] Can you speak about the absurdity of this act, its ritualistic implications, and the relationship between consumption and social mobility?

P.L: Capitalism is, at its root, a ritual based on superstition which is based on the myth and a training for empty consumption and endless evacuation in a loop of some perverse sort. We're always on the go, always vigilant, always on the potty

> about existence. To romance wealth is simultaneously an exorcism and a masturbation of contraries.Perhaps this is a key to the space between things . . . This is the point where I growl . . .

DAJ: In the first version of *Eating the Wall Street Journal*, from 1991, you sat on a flag. In the next version, in 2000, you sat on stacked copies of the paper and telephoned *Wall Street Journal* executives to invite them to lunch. In the third, later that year, you performed atop a kind of scaffolding. Why has the work evolved in the way it has?

> P.L: I'm not sure the work evolved . . . I think I forced anything that might have resembled an evolution. The street-flag version where I sat on the ground made sense. The city was dominant; OK, that seemed factual. Taking the work indoors, into a gallery, brought a scale shift. The sky suddenly lowered. The tower version required a shift in the sitter's status as peformer. The piece has always, since the very beginning, turn[illegible]n a power relation. The abused becomes the abuser.

DAJ: You've written extensively on holes and "hole theory." As you've put it, "Holes are conduits or a 'means to' or a space or intersection—opportunities that take many forms and materials, and duration."[3] Holes are also scattered throughout *member*, strategically placed as cuts in the walls, in the exhibition or institutional architecture. And there is a hole in this book. What's your thing with holes?

> P.L: Holes are machines. They are a tool. Complex and simple simultaneously. You can read them like a text—a secret, a code or a structure, a model, a mode of transport or transition from one state or condition or space to another. Frequently that other state or condition is not immediately apprehendable, because holes by their very nature only reveal a part of themselves. This withholding of legibility can make the aperture simultaneously more inviting yet more threatening . . .

DAJ: Let's talk about *The Black Factory*, a nomadic laboratory for dialogue and exchange that toured the United States in a delivery truck in 2004–6. The project included participants donating objects that were representative of "blackness." In a 2001 drawing for the piece, you describe it as a mechanism or machine: "The blk f. makes blackness / Refines it / Recycles blackness and makes it new." The piece also points to blackness's contradictions. How did *The Black Factory* begin, and how does it relate to some of your earlier proscenium work? I find that it complicates the idea of mobility by taking the proscenium on the road.

> P.L: I like that idea: taking the proscenium on the road! Very fucking idealistic!!! Back in the day, if you'd said that to me I would have turned up my nose, vomited even. Too-too-too fancy-pants! I wanted a floppy, goofy, stupid proscenium. Turned out, well-laid plans beshitted, the BF became truck-as-backdrop—too-too much. A wheeled theatrical pacifier! In time I forced the crews to operate sans truck. Even when the strategy did not work, it was more interesting than slavery to the backdrop—

DAJ: You often take on characters in your performances, in both the street interventions and the theatrical work. I'm thinking specifically of Mr. Poots, who appears in *Tompkins Square Crawl*, *Egg Eating Contest* (1990–91), and *Eracism* (1992–2002). In the press release for *How Much Is That Nigger in the Window* (1991), you call Mr. Poots a "hybrid nigger character... a cross between a black militant, a preacher, a street-crazy and a Buppie." How did Mr. Poots originate?

> P.L: Chicken or egg. Mr. Poots relates to my fiction writing around that time—which was mostly a bunch of pretty conventionally worded stories about this guy, Mr. Brown-Guy, who's in his head a lot and who drives around in an Eldorado Cadillac a lot. This is curious, cause in real life I don't drive. I did but I don't. I don't. For a few years, I wrote these stories very seriously and published a few things, but...

DAJ: When and why did you begin to publish your writing in the form of artist's books and zines?

> P.L: I first tried publishing in the '70s. It didn't work. Tried again in the '80s, small magazines and readings. The self-publishing deal came in the '90s. Drove home the idea that publishing was more layered and interesting than merely making publications. Publishing was simply being in the world in a heightened way—

DAJ: Earlier you noted that, for you, the link between language and performance is duration, and that writing is of the proscenium. With these ideas in mind, can you speak about your writing, specifically *Rap Street Journal* (1992) and other "street jottings," in relation to the performances that were part of *How Much Is That Nigger in the Window?*

> P.L: The jottings were a post + lintel deal to shore up concerns stirred up in the work, anxieties re: whether the stuff could honor, speak to something authentic re: poor folk, black folk, dispossessed folk, whatever patina or flavor. That is, could I make palpable these concerns with the tools I was using? I thought I could headlock the contradictions, the contraries. My ignorance was the authenticity was the contradictions.

DAJ: Why did you title that Franklin Furnace residency *How Much Is That Nigger in the Window?*

> P.L: The title had the right combo of play, hurt, and accuracy that every title should possess. To name is arrogant. Naming is a curse. You can't avoid it so so so you might as well do it with some guts—

DAJ: In the first version of *Sweet Desire a.k.a. Burial Piece* (1996–97), you were buried in the ground from the shoulders down for eight hours, and a bowl of vanilla ice cream was placed just beyond your reach, melting before it could be consumed. In the second version, the following year, you were dug out and rushed to the hospital after four hours. How do you approach durational work? Here, it's pushing the idea of "losing verticality" in the Crawls in a different way and to an extreme, without their mobility.

P.L: There's an unavoidable arrogance to durational work. Hard to deny when you're trying to put pressure on privilege. One's own, or . . . ? The verticality of the burial piece was a secret, kind of. . . A viewer had no access to what was below my shoulder blades—one had to imagine. Or look me in the face and judge. Funny; as painful as it was for me, some people really enjoyed it. Ahh, people.

NOTES

1. William Pope.L, "Crawling in Public," in *Intersection: Sidewalks and Public Space*, ed. Marci Nelligan and Nicole Mauro (Oakland, Calif.: ChainLinks, 2008), 77.

2. Quoted in Philip Connors, "The Man Who Ate the Wall Street Journal—A Performance Artist Has an Appetite for Spectacle; Next Up: A 22-Mile Crawl," *Wall Street Journal*, April 9, 2002, Eastern edition.

3. Pope.L, *Hole Theory* (2002), 8.

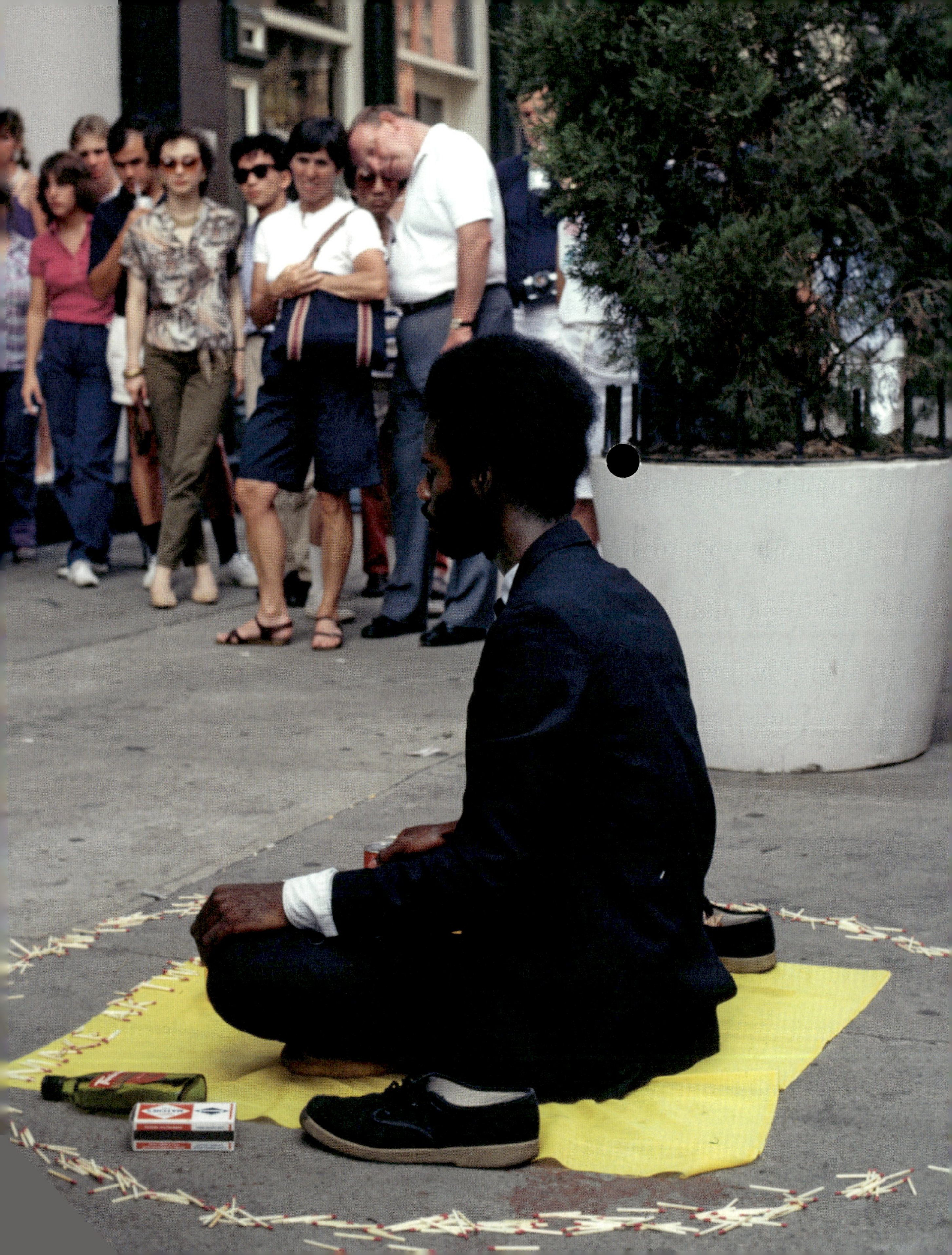

THUNDERBIRD IMMOLATION
A.K.A. MEDITATION SQUARE PIECE
1978

Performance History

Thunderbird Immolation a.k.a. Meditation Square Piece. West Broadway, New York, 1978.

WAITING FOR A LIGHT

ADRIENNE EDWARDS ON *THUNDERBIRD IMMOLATION A.K.A. MEDITATION SQUARE PIECE*

Throughout *Thunderbird Immolation* (1978), Pope.L meditates in a half-lotus or cross-legged pose on a sidewalk outside a building in the SoHo neighborhood of Lower Manhattan. The edifice housed art galleries, including those of Ileana Sonnabend and Leo Castelli, agents of some of the most influential Minimalist and Conceptualist artists. In his brown paper bag of tricks, a container that nods to the alcoholic beverages it often conceals while they are illegally enjoyed in public, were "two bottles of Thunderbird, a bottle of Wild Irish Rose, a can of Coca-Cola, a yellow plastic cup, and a box of wooden kitchen matches."[1] Pope.L placed a yellow cloth on the ground, sat on it, and removed his suit jacket, eyeglasses, and shoes, leaving him clad in a white dress shirt, black bow tie, and dark pants. He then encircled himself with the matches. During the performance, he did not speak, though he did occasionally fashion words out of the matchsticks. Rather than drink any of the beverages, he periodically combined the booze and pop and doused himself with the mixture. Eventually, a gallery employee asked him to leave; Pope.L responded by collecting his props and vacating the premises.

Thunderbird Immolation is part of a group of three introspective sidewalk works called Meditation Square Pieces. The performance is named in part for Ernest and Julio Gallo Winery's cheap fortified wine, created in the 1950s and targeted to black Americans in inner-city neighborhoods. As performance-art historian Kristine Stiles explains, the beverage "aimed to become the 'Campbell Soup of the wine industry.'"[2] Pope.L has made edible Americana recurring materials in his work—milk, Pop-Tarts, peanut butter, mayonnaise, baloney, and Cracked Wheat Biscuits feature in *Harriet Tubman Spinning the Universe* (1992); *Eating the Wall Street Journal*, Version 3 (2000); and *Claim (Whitney Version)* (2017). He shares this feral subversion of distinctly American mass-produced items and corporate food matter with Paul McCarthy, who symbolically uses ketchup, and Mike Kelley, with his proclivities for plushies.

Thunderbird Immolation directs us elsewhere, however, as it equally alludes to the act of self-immolation in Buddhist practice. Rather than actually performing such a self-annihilating event, Pope.L merely gestures to it. In reflecting on the work, the artist assessed:

> For the people on the street, perhaps for some, they were waiting for me to light myself up. Maybe, probably not since reconstituted wine isn't flammable. Maybe I was waiting for a light in them or a light inside myself. Drinking yourself to death and burning yourself to death are both modes of seeking. Seeking attention, seeking the ethereal, seeking absolution, seeking oblivion. No one ever says: he burned himself to oblivion. We do say: he drank himself into oblivion. Samadhi is not oblivion; it is a lively death that can be a kind of activism.[3]

Samadhi is the ultimate step in meditative concentration and enlightenment in Buddhism; it is also associated with self-immolation. In pursuit of samadhi, Pope.L designates *Thunderbird Immolation* an attempt to explore the unification of mind and right focus in which the object of attention is the self. Equanimity and concentration unite in a liberating practice of attaining wisdom and training one's awareness, one that for Pope.L is an act of resistance, rebellion, and self-care.

If Western culture values rationality, self-control, honor, and principle above all else, *Thunderbird Immolation* reveals its fault lines in relation to the overwhelming fungibility of black being/being black. The work performs such racialized effects through a circuit of affects teetering on the brink of social and real death. A fact of blackness is that it is always poised uncertainly under threat of annihilation by the self or by the state. In *Thunderbird Immolation*, Pope.L has been described by art historians as "threatening" to light himself ablaze;

they remark on the "visually volatile street situation" or his "making a scene," neglecting the metaphorical implications of his act.[4] Critics' perceptions of the work, or more precisely their anticipation of Pope.L's demise within it, says less about their interpretation and rather more about the racialized, gendered, and capitalist apertures that obstruct their view. One need only think of the importance of visualization in Tibetan Buddhist tantra, for example. The meditator's practice involves imagining oneself in relation to, and thus identifying with, the qualities of a deity. The deity is a vehicle and a symbol of what one already possesses yet must cultivate in a process of self-realization. In *Thunderbird Immolation*, which implicates "a light inside," Pope.L presents himself as the embodiment of a force for change, demonstrating a courage to challenge affliction (economic/sociohistoric, collective/individual). Accordingly, Pope.L's performance concerns the inextricable interrelations between sanctity and transgression, serenity and violence, abandon and restraint, particularly as it concerns matters betwixt the self and the state.

Arriving near the end of the 1970s, *Thunderbird Immolation* took its place in a concatenation of ritualistic performances involving fire over the decade. Take, for instance, Chris Burden's *Match Piece* (1972), an all-white work in every sense: white-butcher-paper-covered floors in a white cube at Pomona College, the artist dressed all in white while a white woman lay on the floor in the nude. (This stark whiteness recalls, among other whitenesses, that of Robert Ryman's monochromes, works that Pope.L has long seen as symbolic of individualistic creative freedom.) Burden lit matches covered in aluminum foil and fired the ligneous mini-missiles toward the woman with the help of a paper clip, occasionally hitting his target and leaving small burns, at times misfiring into the audience. In *Fire Roll* (1973), Burden saturated his pants in lighter fluid, lit them, and extinguished the flames by rolling his body over them. The following year, Marina Abramović performed *Rhythm 5*, in which she lay in the center of a blazing star construction on the floor; as the oxygen inside the pentagram waned, the artist lost consciousness and had to be rescued. Ritual is also a formal device and affective force in Ana Mendieta's Silueta Series, a group of performances for the camera made from 1973 to 1980. Centering the works around nature, landscape, and the body, Mendieta inscribed her contour into wood, earth, and fabric—and in some cases transformed it into an effigy with fire.

Instead of literally employing fire in his work, Pope.L summons an inner directive, a shine, as an exercise of diminishing the self by compassionately assimilating another's suffering as a means to acknowledging and relinquishing one's own. The recognition of desire as the preeminent cause of suffering is perhaps Buddhism's core tenet. The alcohol and sugary drinks of *Thunderbird Immolation* are powerful symbols of a soft violence always at hand, with their excessive consumption transposing the microaggressions and actual brutality of daily existence buffeted by racism and poverty. Such behavior serves as the tool of a slow self-destruction that renders life doubly precarious.

Thunderbird Immolation is an ethical artwork about witnessing desire as it teeters between abandon and restraint—witnessing an engaged and embodied desire for parity against the set-up that is inequality, an insistence to hold space for the self as well as for others. The possibility for redemption resides in that which eludes the visual, which Pope.L invokes when he summons the light. What is to be redeemed retains its position of withdrawal, concealment, restraint, and ambivalence as it must, holding the line as a necessary counterpoint to karmic and capitalist accumulations.

1. Kristine Stiles, "Thunderbird Immolation: Burning Racism," in *William Pope.L: The Friendliest Black Artist in America©*, ed. Mark H. C. Bessire (Cambridge, Mass.: MIT Press, 2002), 36. **2.** Ibid. **3.** Quoted in Sarah Jane Cervenak, "Before I Was Straightened Out," in *Wandering: Philosophical Performances of Racial and Sexual Freedom* (Durham, N.C.: Duke University Press, 2014), 155. **4.** Stiles, "Thunderbird Immolation," 36–37, and Cervenak, "Before I Was Straightened Out," 151.

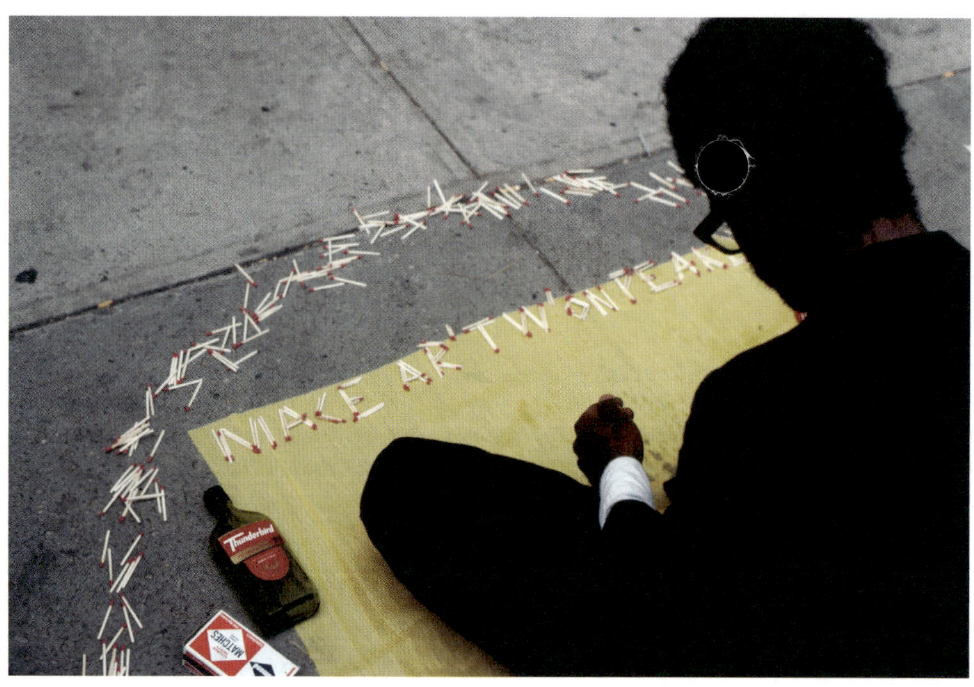

Page 38 and this spread: *Thunderbird Immolation a.k.a. Meditation Square Piece*. West Broadway, New York, 1978. Inkjet prints, 15 × 10" (38.1 × 25.4 cm) and 6 × 9" (15.2 × 22.9 cm). The Museum of Modern Art, New York

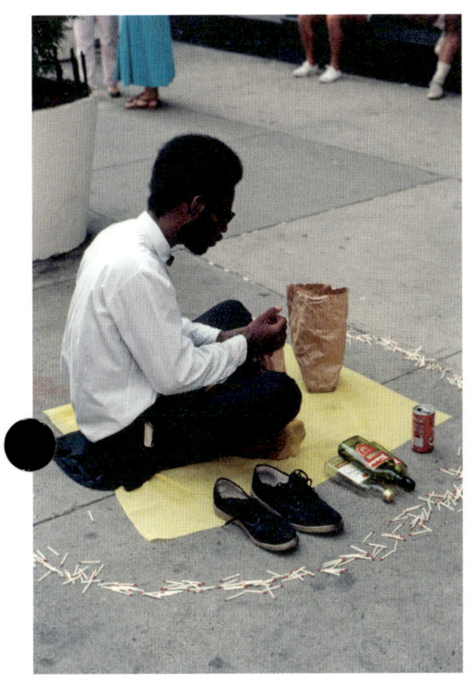

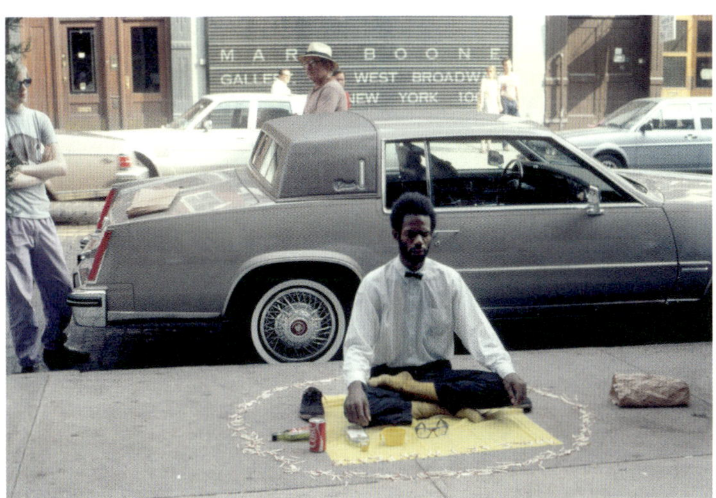
BOONE
WEST
YORK

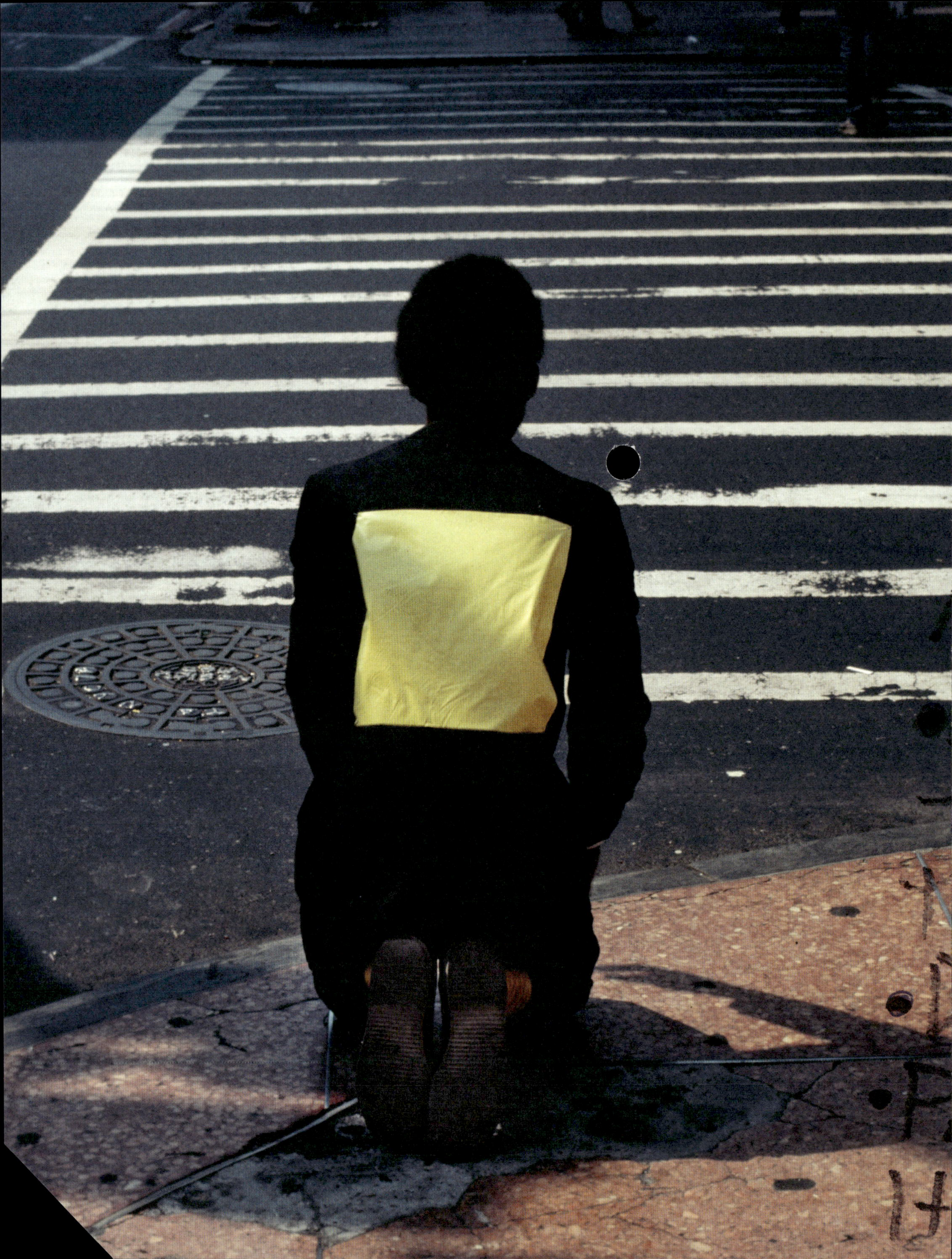

TIMES SQUARE CRAWL
A.K.A. MEDITATION SQUARE PIECE
1978

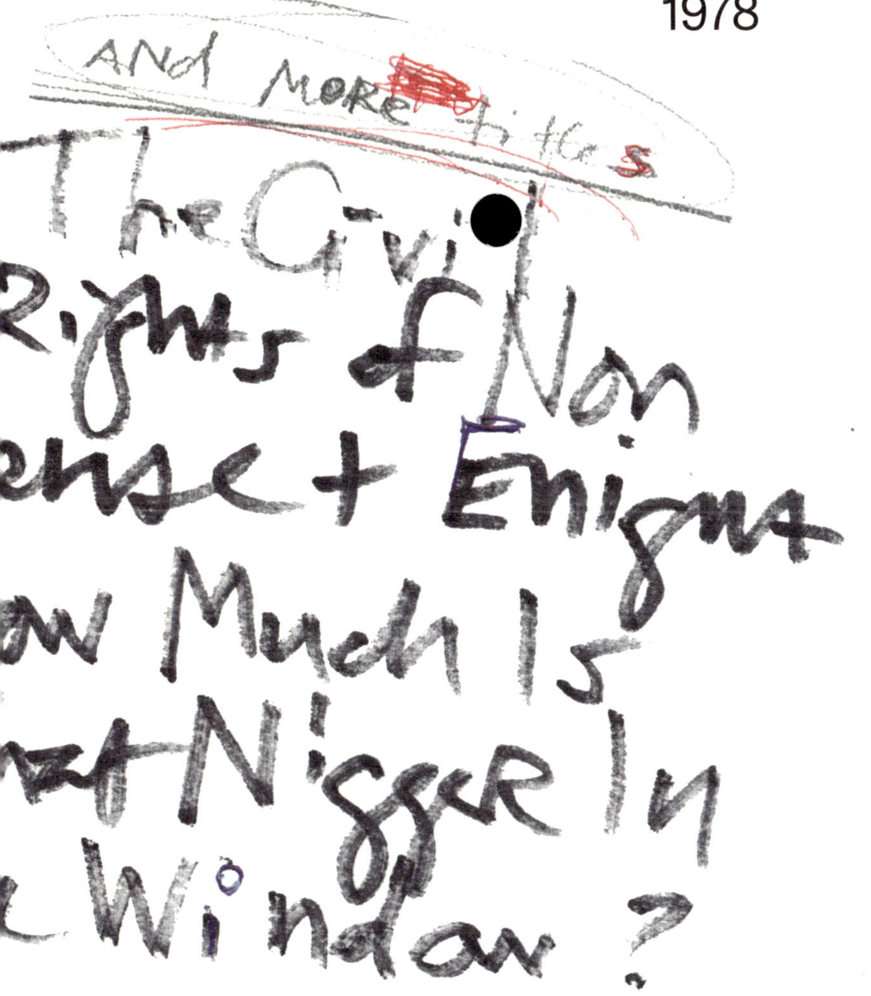

Performance History

Times Square Crawl a.k.a. Meditation Square Piece. Times Square, New York, 1978.

BEING HORIZONTAL

MARTINE SYMS ON *TIMES SQUARE CRAWL A.K.A. MEDITATION SQUARE PIECE*

Man, says that on December 3, 2018 Samone departed this life but no one knows the exact moment or hour she entered eternal life except God Almighty.

My cousin is found prone on the couch in her Inglewood apartment with the TV blaring and no face. My brother messages me, "Did you talk to mommy and daddy?" I'm on my way out. "Haven't heard from them."

Samone was discovered the previous day after not responding to phone calls for a week. Her body had started to decompose. The coroner's office had to get fingerprints to confirm it was her. "Crazy."

I call my mother from the car. She is spooked. "I hate thinking of her like that. Alone."

Back in my apartment I lean against the couch. I lift my eyes towards the 43-inch on the wall and pretend to watch television. I roll onto my side the way we do in yoga, tip forward and smush my face into the cushion. I stay there, applying more and more pressure.

My cousin and I looked alike. We were only three years apart, and I recognized myself in her face. I was afraid of dying like that. I thought about it constantly. I wondered which one of my neighbors would smell my rotting flesh first. Probably the nosy white lady I call Diane Keaton. I imagine her big, stupid dog barking and pulling her down the hallway like in an episode of *Lassie*.

I consider why I am alive and Samone is not. I think of all the choices that have kept me here. I hate being human. Ceaseless talking, eating, shitting, fucking, sleeping, masturbating, socializing, being pathetic and fleshy. I pitch myself off the sofa onto the floor. The aunties in my head yell at me to get my ass up off the ground.

Billy, put your money where your mouth is—put your ass on the line where the rest of us live.
—Pope.L, "Notes on *Crawling Piece a.k.a. How Much Is That Nigger in the Window?*" 1997

In the summer of 1978, Pope.L puts on a white shirt and a black suit and gets down on his knees in the middle of Times Square. He looks respectable. A bespectacled, studious youth. Hair picked out into a neat little fro, mustard yellow socks, a shiny wristwatch, a yellow square pinned to his back. The cloth is in part a reference to Buddhism, meditation, and martyrdom, marking his solidarity with Thich Quang Duc, the "Burning Monk." The color slips between a caution and a target. Pope.L advances his right elbow and left knee, then his left elbow and right knee. He is crawling. It is a bear crawl, to be specific. Great for moving through places where concealment is minimal and enemy violence or surveillance prevents you from getting up.

His bare hands touch the ground. The gravel is hard against his palms. His skin traces dirt and glass and shit and piss and vomit and dried malt liquor and probably a used condom or two. He bleeds on the concrete. The air is thick and his muscles ache. Pope.L makes his body at odds with the city. His head hangs. Slowly he raises it, picks the next position, and lowers it again. New York stretches up around him. Passersby try to ignore him, but their gaze meets his horizon line at street level. Aw shit—here come the cops. In the words of the artist himself, talking to Martha Wilson in *Bomb* in 1996: "Cops, you know, cops and black people—even if they're black cops."

Since that first Crawl, there have been about thirty others. Pope.L wanted to know what it felt like in the gutter, so he put himself there, in the space between heaven and hell. Why do people devalue the bottom? The Crawl is a hard thing to do. It's also hard to watch. The experience is as much a threat as it is an invitation. Sometimes people are supportive, offering water or their company; other times they curse, turn away, try to step on his head. They think if you're down there you must deserve it.

I don't require myself to want to.

It is because of Pope.L that I apply to a theater workshop. I haven't been sleeping and I'm not sure if it is blue light or drugs or caffeine or trauma. In the wee hours, I decide that recording is about death not memory like I always thought. "Today what can 'live' mean as a motor for production?" Pope.L asks, in an interview with Hamza Walker in the *Showing Up to Withhold* catalogue (2014). "Live-ness as a way of actively engaging viewers concerning their place as living, breathing, fleshy entities in a world full of screens." This quote becomes a mantra of sorts. I take a picture of it and look at it nightly the way one looks at party pics.

I write to my best friend about my broken spirit. I tell her I was weak, and then I was a [illegible], and now I'm a ghost. She calls me and reminds me not to kill myself. Before the ability to record, there was no concept of "live." There was no gap between the experience of an event and its representation. One of the first hit records was of a man and woman laughing alongside a melancholic horn solo. These popular tracks spawned copycats. Every label had their own version. In those days, the masters only lasted a few pressings. To meet demand, the artists were trapped chuckling into the mic all night and all day. Many of them went mad or committed suicide. Now they haunt YouTube alongside many others.

Pope.L's work suggests that I might learn something from the rub between duration and body. He proposes that the conflation of self and image could be useful and not only depressing. I do as much reading as I can, but eventually I need to put some skin in the game. I worry about solipsism. I am working on a piece about shame, and "acting" is the most embarrassing way I can spend the week.

The class begins with a reading of a transcription of James Brown's "Please, Please, Please." The teacher stops the student volunteer many times. She instructs him to read not only the word but also the punctuation. Period is a full stop; ellipses are a sustain. Her corrections are clear and precise. Over and over, he has to begin again from the top.

The teacher admonishes us for fidgeting and being clever. The little spasms—straightening a shirt, retying a ponytail—release the tension in the room. We crowd each other. The only time I'm this close to anyone is when I'm going to fuck them. It's difficult not to apply meaning to the position of our bodies. When my partner is directed to walk away from me, I feel loss. Quick, what's it about? Power, shame, vulnerability, exhaustion, and ecstasy. All I've been thinking about is power and powerlessness and how you go from one to the other. The teacher calls this "level."

In the *New York Times*, the playwright Tarell McCraney explains how taxing it is to move from poverty to the elite world of high culture. "When people say, 'I'm tired,' . . . it's not necessarily like, 'I've been working in a cotton field all day.' There's tired, like—you just don't know how much pre-thinking, post-thinking, anxiousness, anxiety, that one has to toggle in order to deal with the United States." I try not to say "I'm tired" the way I try not to say "I'm busy." The way I try not to say "I can't." The way I try not to say "L.A."

The workshop is intensely physical. We run around, and the teacher shouts, "This is an embodied practice!" I had been training: weightlifting, running, dance classes, voice lessons, Iyengar yoga, soccer. I started crawling several years ago after my aunt Gina and my cousin Dorrick died within months of one another. I do the bear crawl, too, a strengthening, stabilizing, and cardio exercise that involves nearly all your muscle groups. I like it because it feels impossible to drag my ass across the room. Sometime my trainer makes me do it ten times. I often collapse. Sometimes I cry. I fall onto the floor and hang around. I love it down there.

"The body is also a thinking organism," Pope.L says in that interview with Martha Wilson. "And black folk are bodies that think. We think all the time. Maybe that's our problem—we're too intellectual!" My body uses a different kind of cognition, bound to physical experience. No language. Only failure. There is no uplift. There is barely upright. There is only being horizontal.

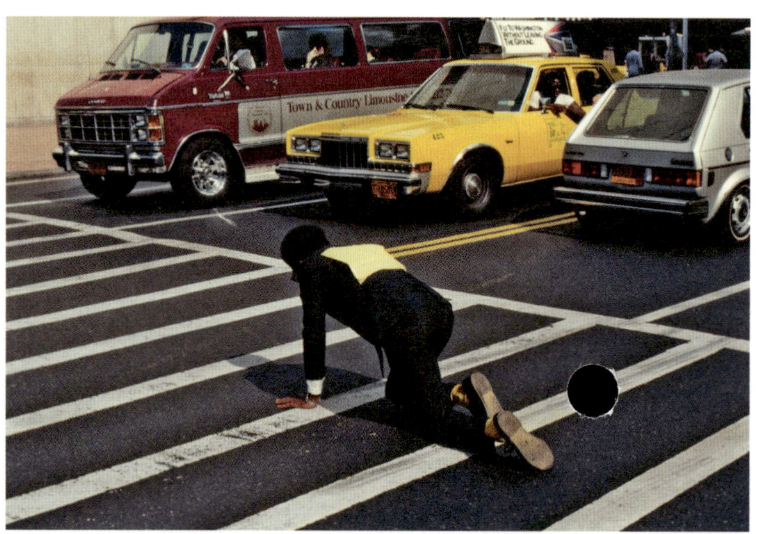

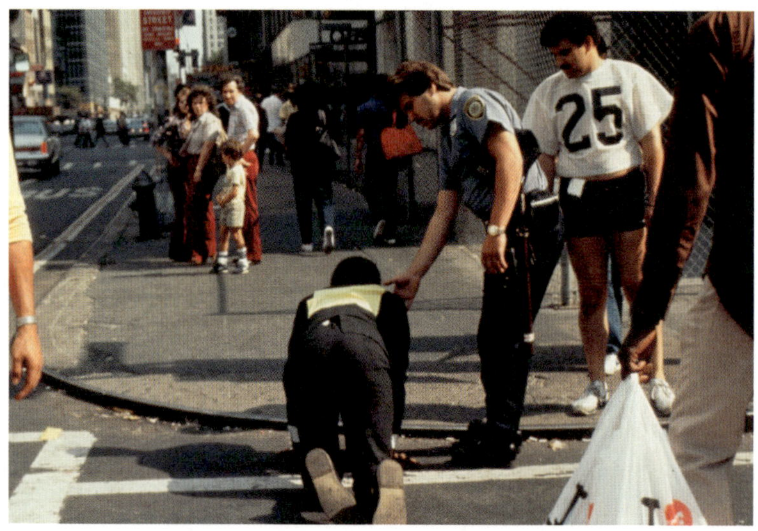

Page 44 and this spread: *Times Square Crawl a.k.a. Meditation Square Piece*. Times Square, New York, 1978. Inkjet prints, 10 × 15" (25.4 × 38.1 cm) each. The Museum of Modern Art, New York

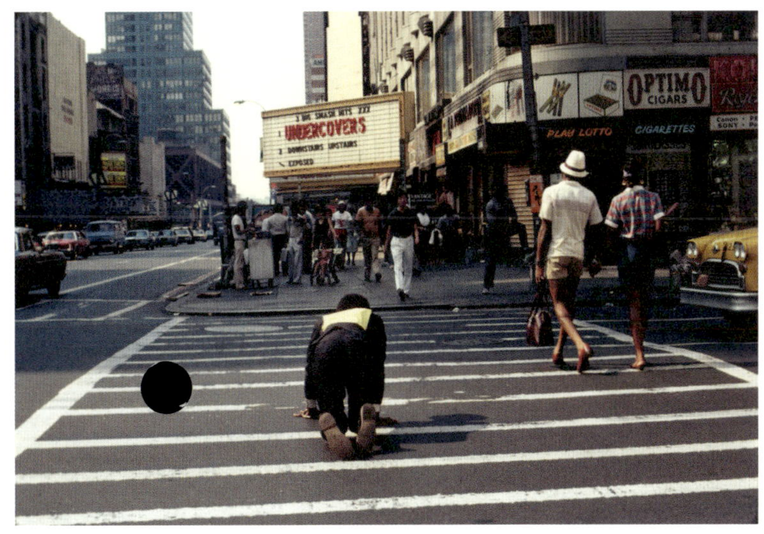
3 BIG SMASH HITS XXX
1 UNDERCOVERS
2 DOWNSTAIRS UPSTAIRS
EXPOSED
OPTIMO
CIGARS
PLAY LOTTO
CIGARETTES

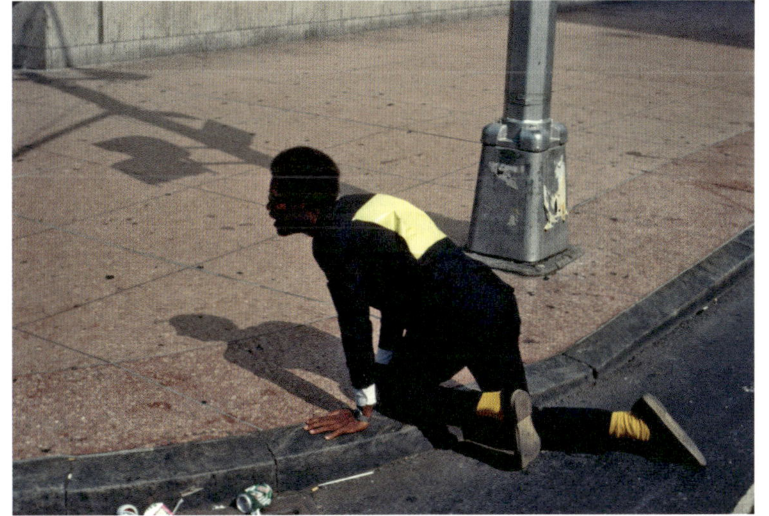

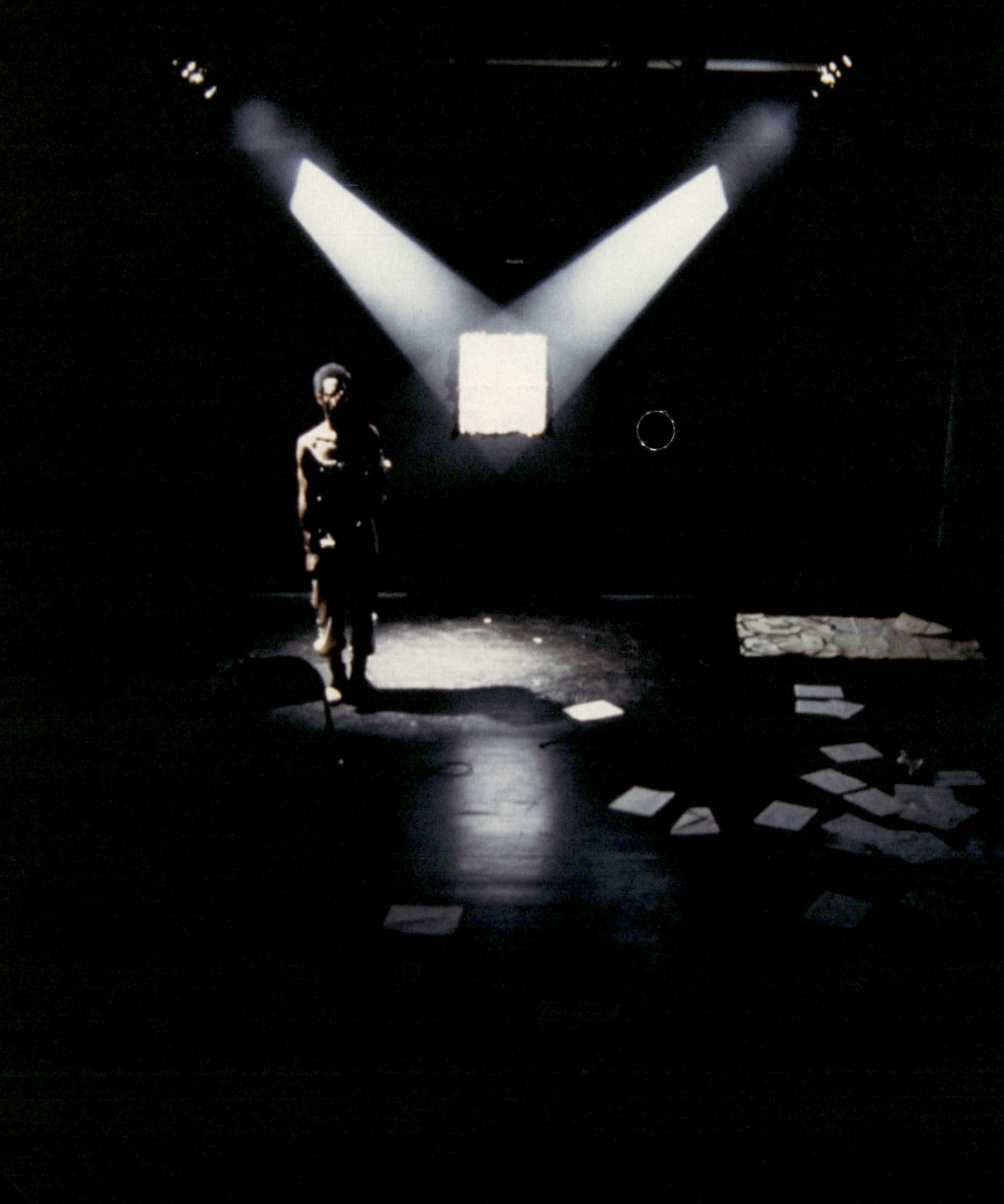

EGG EATING CONTEST
1990–91

Performance History

Egg Eating Contest, basement version. East Orange, N.J., May 30, 1990.

Egg Eating Contest, ensemble version. BACA Downtown, Brooklyn, N.Y., October 18–27, 1990.

Egg Eating Contest, solo version. Franklin and Marshall College, Lancaster, Penn., 1990.

Egg Eating Contest, ensemble version. Dixon Place, New York, 1990.

Egg Eating Contest, solo version. Cone Art Gallery, University of North Carolina, Greensboro, 1990.

Egg Eating Contest, ensemble version. Painted Bride Arts Center, Philadelphia, 1990.

Egg Eating Contest, solo version. Knitting Factory, New York, 1990.

Egg Eating Contest, solo version. Movement Research, New York, 1990.

Egg Eating Contest, solo version. Cleveland Performance Art Festival, March 1991.

FERTILITY RITE

MALIK GAINES ON *EGG EATING CONTEST*

In 1990–91, Pope.L toured the performance *Egg Eating Contest*. The work appeared at experimental performance venues in New York as well as at university and other arts spaces in North Carolina, Ohio, and Pennsylvania. The artist also produced a "basement version," made for video without an audience in East Orange, New Jersey, which remains as a trace, along with photographs of the more theatrical stagings that reveal a wider array of activities and objects in the piece.

In the basement version of *Egg Eating Contest* (1990), Pope.L enters a brick-walled, underground room dressed in a jumpsuit covered by a tattered trench coat and crosses the space making funny pivots. He approaches a large, cartoonish drawing of testicles displayed on a wall and produces a marker from his coat. In a clownish mode, he attempts to complete the image of the member that the balls suggest, struggling to reach the height required. The whole drawing comes falling down, covering the performer and revealing a smaller, complete cartoon cock on the wall behind it. This dick wears a bow tie and marks the edges of the performance and all that follows. Among other events that unfold, the artist produces a black egg from his mouth and parades it around, observing its form like it's a holy relic. He then launches into a monologue, using an agitated, stuttering voice and a children's storytelling manner to weave a convoluted tale of racial power relations. The story is an absurdist retelling of slavery's afterlife, focused on white power and black subjugation. "Once there was a patriarch who lived in a shoe; he had so many factions he didn't know what to do," the narration begins. The artist recounts scenes of dispossession and frustrated attempts to make up for what was lost. The telling is funny in a sad way, lifting peculiar details from an overwhelming history. He describes "that authentic black statuary" that was left behind in Africa, dispossessing black people of a cultural inheritance while imbuing European modernism with its frisson. Eventually, an apparently white man enters and connects a power cord to one attached to the artist's costume, completing the circuit. While the performance itself continues beyond this point, the video documentation of the basement version cuts off here, leaving the viewer hanging with this evocative image.

This performance, still relatively early in Pope.L's career, reveals an artist unafraid of theater. While his body of work overall offers a practice adept at exhibition and the manipulation of objects and materials, his roots in performance have oriented those drawings, paintings, and other static things toward activity. His works exist in time and operate in modes that are alternately critical, ironic, and sarcastic, but also vulnerable and sometimes abject, suggesting an artist subject to a dynamic world rather than as a maker of unchanging forms. Especially in *Egg Eating Contest,* production details depart from conventions of performance art that center on the body as material in unmarked space. Costume, character, narrative, and memorized text provide a basement-level theatricality that, while present in its own right, also points elsewhere. This theatricality is representational but not illusionistic. The looseness of this mode suggests the radical performances of Jack Smith and a kind of downtown avant-garde theater that offers presence unbound by minimalist priorities and unconcerned with the mandates of art institutions. *Egg Eating Contest* can serve as a hinge in a performance field that sometime after the 1990s got divided, placing experimental theatrical works on one side and performance art that can be aligned with a genealogy of sculpture on the other. While this separation suited art-world antitheatrical tendencies and high-modernist aspirations, it has been a little too convenient, as artists like Pope.L remind us.

Egg Eating Contest may be thought of as part of a solo monologue form that was a lively site of experimental performance in its day, associated perhaps most notoriously with the case of the NEA Four, performance artists whose 1990 theater grants from the National Endowment for the Arts were interrogated and vetoed by politicians objecting to themes of gender and sexuality. The fallout from this national controversy and subsequent court cases gutted the federal government's arts funding and had more than a little to do with a bifurcation that resulted within performance, separating identity-oriented theatrical performance from the more austere forms of performance art that thereafter ascended in art institutions. Pope.L, whose works appeared at New York performance spaces like Franklin Furnace and Dixon Place but have also populated the galleries of major museums such as The Museum of Modern Art, offers a remarkable way beyond [illegible] distinction.

Unlike the work of performance progenitor Smith or Pope.L's contemporaries Karen Finley, John Fleck, Holly Hughes, and Tim Miller—the four of the NEA case—Pope.L's performances, in particular *Egg Eating Contest*, thread gender and sexuality through race via a black critical position. "The problem with the white man is he's not very nice," asserts the artist at the start of his ranting soliloquy. A piece of press from 1990 describes the title of a proscenium version presented at BACA Downtown in Brooklyn as *Egg Eating Contest, or How Much Is That Nigger in the Window*, putting a finer point on it. Elsewhere in that *Village Voice* review, its author, Joe Wood, describes the performance as concerned with "the sick American fascination with our *things*."[1] In the performance, reproductive imagery is rendered both dominant and ridiculous. These tropes include the egg, a bra Pope.L wore beneath his jumpsuit, and the penis drawing on the wall. To call the cartoonish cock symbolic is an understatement, but the goofiness of its exposure plays games with the representational order that normatively protects phallic power. The hidden bra, however, suggests a preoccupation with gender that exceeds a gaze that might fix it, as well as the distortions black genders undergo within white-supremacist regimes. According to Wood, in the version at BACA Downtown, the white male participant urged the artist to show his own penis, which he did.[2] This play of exposure and revelation extends the historicizing narrative of the effects of slavery into a present where symbolic and literal elements lose their differentiation. "Humiliation for a good cause is ritual," Pope.L once wrote in a short essay on theater's social potential.[3] In ritual we may find the place where theater and performance art connect, and Pope.L offers that site as an apt location for reenacting the humiliating realities of race.

1. Joe Wood, "Color-Blinded," *Village Voice* 35, no. 45 (November 6, 1990), 116. **2.** Ibid. **3.** Pope.L, "Beyond the Proscenium," *Theater* 31, no. 3 (Fall 2001): 92–93.

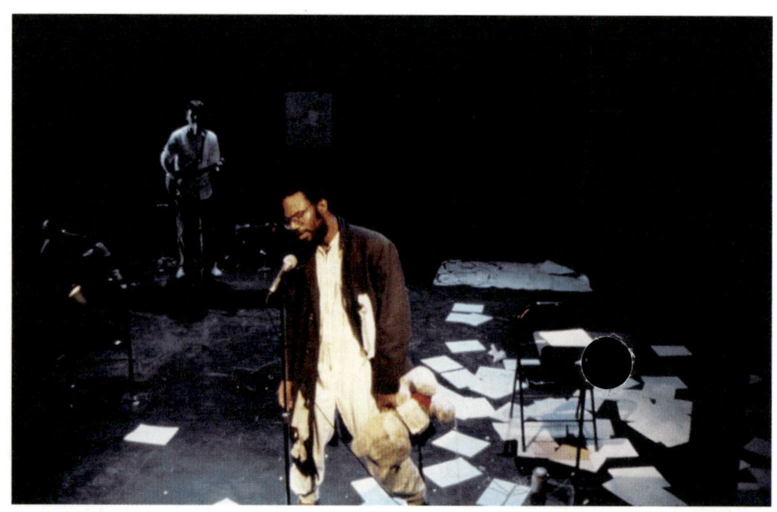

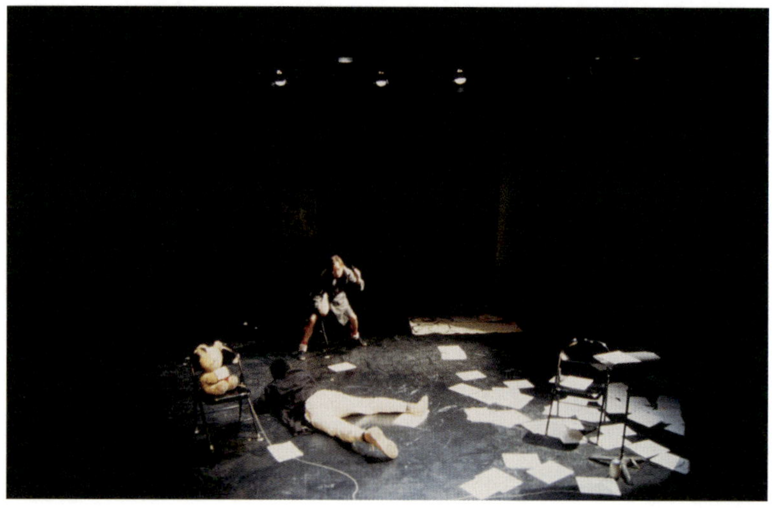

Page 50 and this page: *Egg Eating Contest*, ensemble version. BACA Downtown, Brooklyn, N.Y., 1990.
Inkjet prints, 10 × 15" (25.4 × 38.1 cm) each. The Museum of Modern Art, New York

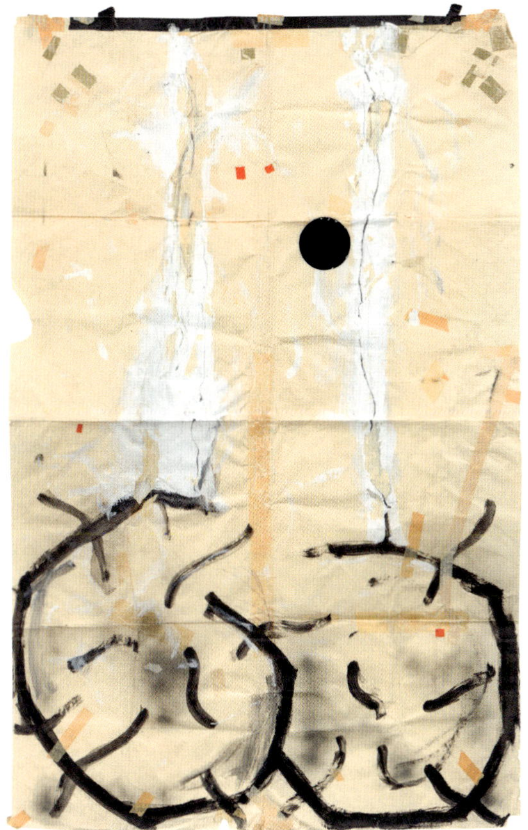

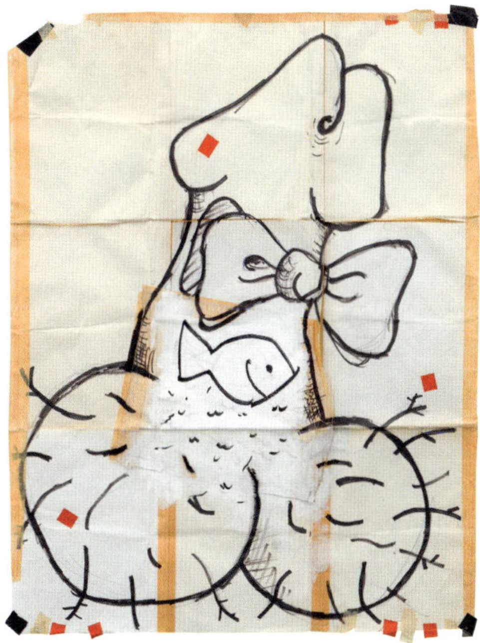

Drawings from *Egg Eating Contest,* basement version. East Orange, N.J., 1990. Synthetic polymer paint, ink, and tape on paper. Left: 65½ × 42" (166.4 × 106.7 cm). Right: 33½ × 26" (85.1 × 66 cm)

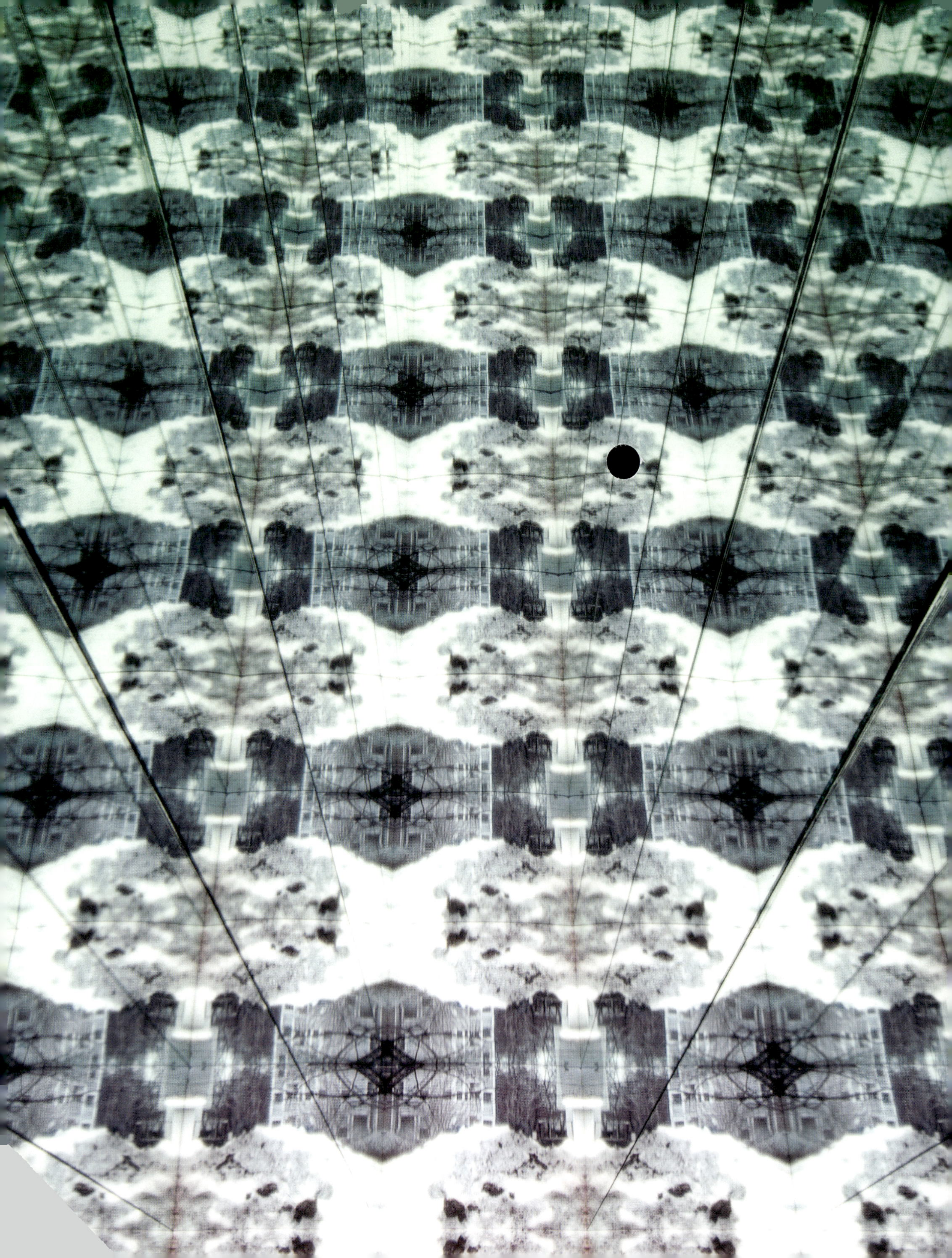

SNOW CRAWL
1991–2001

Performance History

Snow Crawl. Lewiston, Maine, 1991–2001.

FLOCK

DANIELLE A. JACKSON ON *SNOW CRAWL*

Between the sidewalks of the Earth and satellites of space is the body. Symbolically caught between heaven and hell, the body is an arena of conflict, contraries, and oppositions: lovely/filthy, noble/common, vertical/horizontal, epidermis/cavity, made in the image of God/forsaken by God.
—Pope.L, "Crawling in Public," 2008[1]

Amid the clamorous caws of unseen birds, the camera zooms in and out of focus on a white, wintery plain. The wind blows aggressively against a red triple-decker apartment building, causing vibrations that resemble a deafening thunderclap. Other homes and thin trees appear in shots intercut with this one, in various framings and at odd angles. The gale functions like a painter's hand on the red house, luring the snow onto it and dappling its vermillion surface with white. It whisks the snow off the home's roof into the ether, evoking a mist.

As the sharp winds chitter, our (super)hero, Pope.L, enters the frame, wearing a threadbare Superman costume with soggy kneepads, shabby mittens, and black boots. First the camera homes in on his torso as he crawls on his belly in the wet snow, willingly forsaking verticality. Then the frame goes aerial to give us a disorienting, upside-down overhead view of Pope.L's crawling that makes it look more like flailing. For about seven minutes, interrupted with shots of the red house's exterior, its presumed interior, and cryptic imagery, the video *Snow Crawl* (1991–2001) tracks the artist's progress across the white ground as he heads into a wooded area, ultimately to top and tumble over a dirty ice mound—this Superman's Fortress of Solitude, surrounded by ranch-style homes. I imagine Pope.L *feels* his body and his soaked attire adhering to it, gushing when compressed, exposing his flesh to the earth as though he were wearing nothing at all. Occasionally, visual effects turn the screen a brilliant white; at other moments, an eerie green. Church bells sound in the background, each frame ratcheting up the slowness of Pope.L's progress. A white cat's eyes and fur appear unexpectedly in close-up. Then the video's climax takes us back indoors: Superman walks slowly down a creaky wooden staircase, cuddling the stark white cat like a newborn. As he stands in the doorway, its fur becomes brighter and brighter, transforming into a radiant beacon of light that can only evoke the Gospel of John's "Believe in the light while there is still time" as well as the blindingly vivid light that those nearing death describe.

The cat's name is never provided during *Snow Crawl*. But a perusal of Pope.L's archive identifies the animal as—or at least with—a cat named Mr. Milk, whom the artist said he valiantly rescued from a treacherous snowstorm one bone-chilling night in 1987; supposedly, the cat remained silent for six years.[2] The imagery of rescue in *Snow Crawl* makes it clear that Pope.L is Mr. Milk's savior, his Jehovah Rapha. The work is rife with biblical undertones: the number six, of Mr. Milk's meowless years, is the duration stipulated in the Old Testament that slaves are to be held before being freed.[3] Gaining salvation is not something that Pope.L's black body affords him, however, at least not in a traditional sense. His crawl is ongoing, in *Snow Crawl* spanning ten years. Our (anti) hero can take on the guise of a deitylike figure, rescue Mr. Milk, release him from his voiceless prison, and adorn him in the armor of light, but he cannot himself be freed, because freedom, as defined by the American project, is a birthright of whiteness.

In his work, Pope.L is a kind of prophetic agitator, poetically performing social struggle to wrestle with troublesome feelings in a way that is unbearably tactile. In *Rap Street Journal*, writings assembled in 1991–92, the artist humorously proclaims, "The portions of life / Are not evenly divided / If things were clearer, cleaner / Brighter, neater / More like the Ritz / . . . / I wouldn't be down for the gutter."[4] This passage refers specifically to *How Much Is That Nigger in the Window a.k.a. Tompkins Square Crawl* (1991), a horizontal trip around the eponymous New York City park, which posed the question,

"What can a black guy with a teaching job at a private school in New England say about black disenfranchisement?"[5] Its protagonist, Mr. Poots, was described by Pope.L as "a cross between a black militant, a preacher, a street-crazy and a Buppie." But that work's themes, including its pastorly affiliations, resonate with the numerous other crawls the artist has performed over the years. Collectively, the crawls can be read as a flock, a set of epics that emerge from a deeply troubled society. In contrast to Pope.L's dozens of other crawls—including *Times Square Crawl a.k.a. Meditation Square Piece* (1978) and *The Great White Way: 22 miles, 9 years, 1 street* (2001–9), which also uses the Superman costume—*Snow Crawl* focuses on image making and narration via an apparatus rather than the performer's body and improvisation. *Snow Crawl*, while compiled partially from documentation of a performative action, turns the body into a kind of unreliable narrator, amplifying the work's distortioning properties. The live event and the resulting video are cousins, produced via a multiplication of the real.

Snow Crawl was shot and edited over several winters while Pope.L taught theater and rhetoric at Bates College, located in Lewiston, Maine. Far from the bustling metropolis, Lewiston was, as Pope.L described, "a very depressed, white working class town."[6] The overall arc of the Crawl works thus moves from the most urban of landscapes to the woodsy, where whiteness is all-encompassing, inescapable and everywhere evident: Mr. Milk's fur, the town's population, the white-out video effects, and the weather. Is Maine Pope.L's Fortress of Solitude, or is this sea of whiteness merely a reminder of his have-notness? But perhaps a respite is not the point. Maybe our hero wants to be in the belly of the beast to renew a troublesome spirit, or as a way of making the world's injustices and contradictions more difficult to deny.

Snow Crawl has another dimension: it is viewed through a long, mirrored tube that takes the form of a chimney, like the one on the red house in the video. Viewers are required to ascend a platform and peer down a hole to experience it.[7] The result is a kaleidoscopic view that disrupts and multiplies the video and its methodical crawl. The mirrored mechanism mechanically rearranges Pope.L's Superman image, the route of the action, and his body, transforming it all into a complex pattern. Here the mirror acts as a kind of mist—a billow of fragmentation and dispersion that harkens back to the work's beginning. The movements and allegorical details in the video itself are all but lost to the eye, but their residue remains.

Cycling through iconography, Pope.L draws on a variety of references: biblical scripture; symbols of class and privilege; the familial; the black church where folks speak in tongues, preach dynamically from pulpits, and roll down aisles, depending on one's denomination. Is the salvation that our street prophet Pope.L preaches—if it's attainable at all—encountered from the earth, that space between heaven and hell? Does it require a humbling experience with the filthy, getting down in the cold muck of the snow or the gutter?

1. William Pope.L, "Crawling in Public," in *Intersection: Sidewalks and Public Space*, ed. Marci Nelligan and Nicole Mauro (Oakland, Calif.: ChainLinks, 2008), 76. **2.** See "William Pope.L: Times, Life, and Work Version #10b," in *William Pope.L: The Friendliest Black Artist in America©*, ed. Mark H. C. Bessire (Cambridge, Mass.: MIT Press, 2002), 223. **3.** The six-year duration is specific to slavery and labor laws in Exodus, Leviticus, and Deuteronomy. See Raymond Westbrook, "Cultural and History Notes: Slavery and Labor Laws in the Ancient Near East," in *New International Version Archaeological Study Bible: An Illustrated Walk through Biblical History and Culture* (Grand Rapids, Mich.: Zondervan), 117. **4.** *William Pope.L's "How Much Is That Nigger in the Window": Rap Street Journal* (New York and Lewiston, Maine: self-published, 1992), 25. **5.** This quote and the next from the press release for *How Much Is That Nigger in the Window*, June 15, 1991. Event Records, Franklin Furnace Archive, Inc. **6.** Martha Wilson, "William Pope.L," *Bomb* 55 (Spring 1996), 54. **7.** Pope.L has written extensively on "hole theory," including the self-published *Hole Theory* (2002). In *Snow Crawl*'s presentation in *member* at The Museum of Modern Art, the visitor encounters the work by walking through a hole in the wall, then through another that leads onto a staircase ascending to the viewing platform. A third hole, in the ceiling, provides the clearance by which one looks down the chimney.

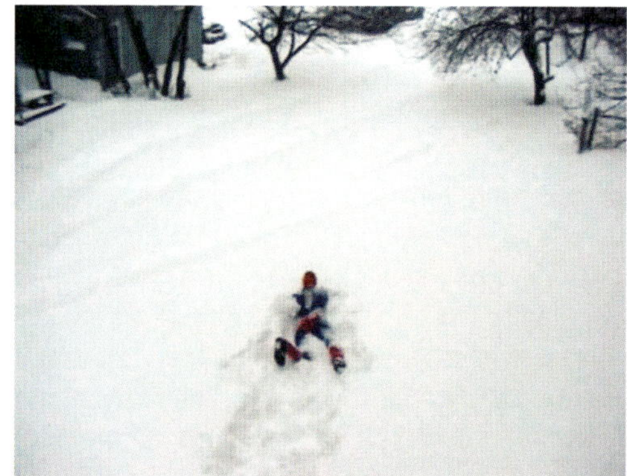

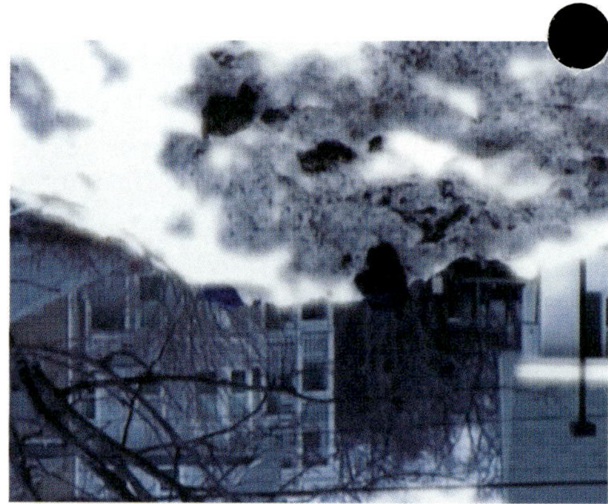

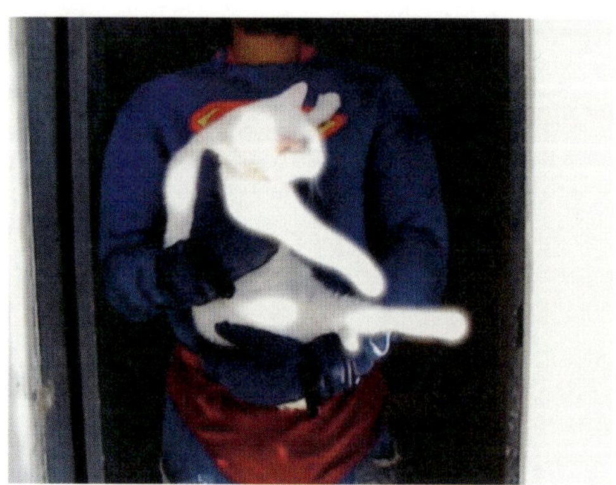

Page 56: *Snow Crawl* (detail). 1991–2001/2015. Video: color, sound, 7:41 minutes, and wood, mirror, TV, and DVD, 114 × 206 × 110½" (289.5 × 523.2 × 280.7 cm). The Museum of Modern Art, New York. Installation view: *William Pope.L: Trinket*, The Geffen Contemporary at the Museum of Contemporary Art, Los Angeles, March 20–June 28, 2015
This page: *Snow Crawl*. 1991–2001. Video: color, sound; 7:41 minutes. The Museum of Modern Art, New York

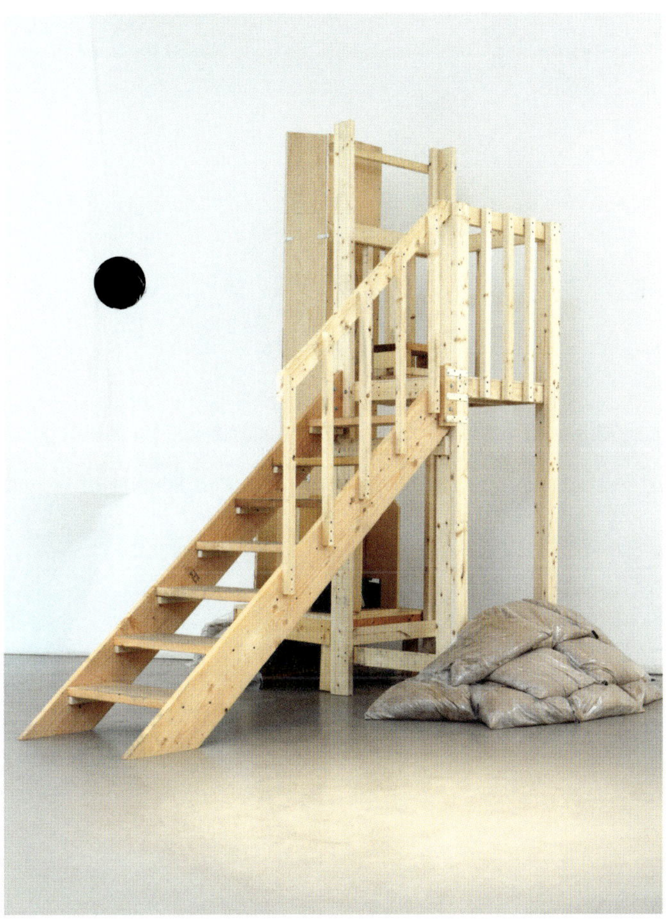

Snow Crawl. 1991–2001/2010. Video: color, sound, 7:41 minutes, and wood, mirror, television, DVD player, and sandbags, 117 × 30 × 30" (292 × 76.2 × 76.2 cm). The Museum of Modern Art, New York. Installation view: *Landscape + Object + Animal*, Mitchell-Innes & Nash, New York, May 20–June 28, 2010

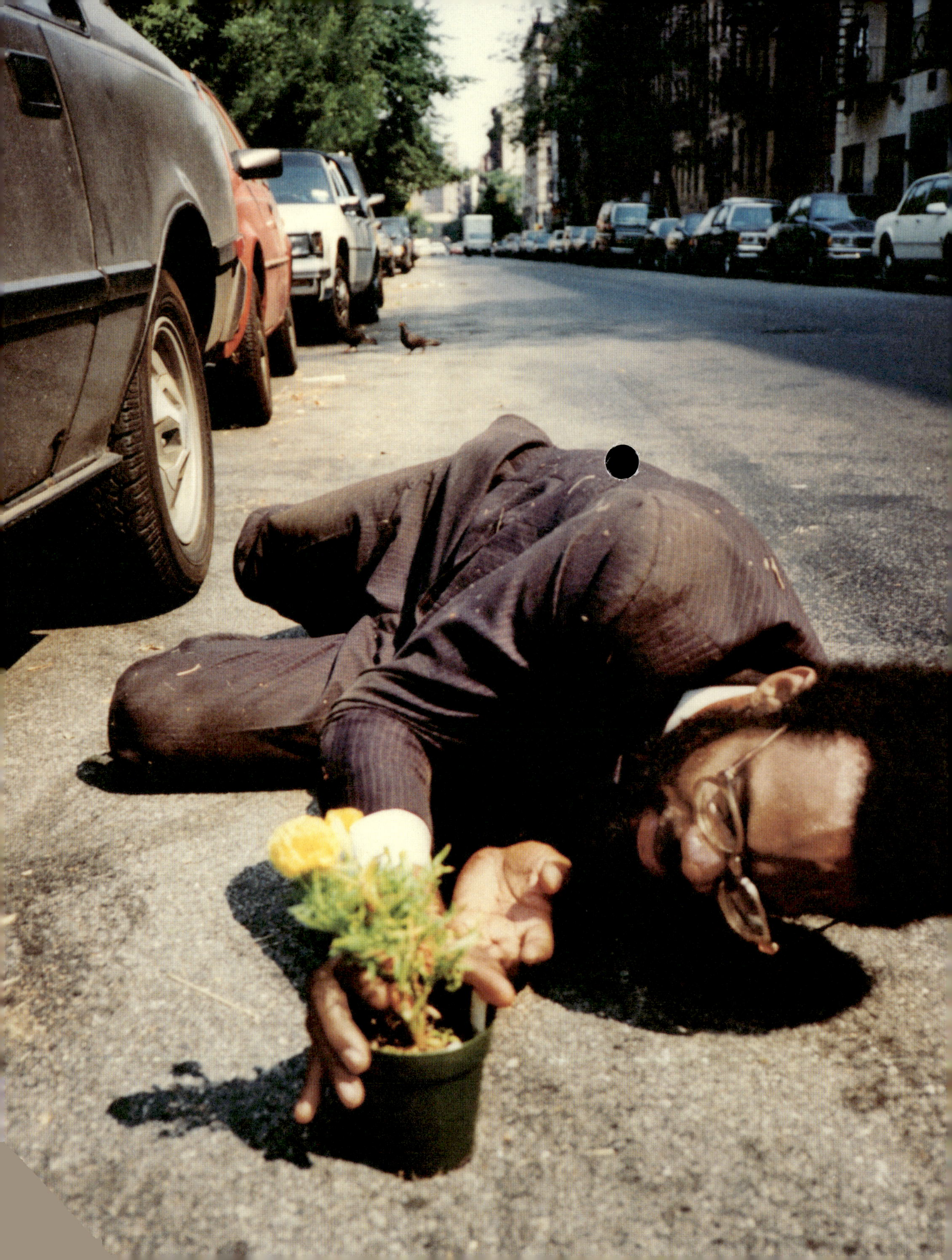

HOW MUCH IS THAT NIGGER IN THE WINDOW A.K.A. TOMPKINS SQUARE CRAWL 1991

Performance History

How Much Is That Nigger in the Window a.k.a. Tompkins Square Crawl. Tompkins Square Park, New York, July 1991.

A BUSINESS SUIT AND A FLOWERPOT

MARTHA WILSON ON *HOW MUCH IS THAT NIGGER IN THE WINDOW A.K.A. TOMPKINS SQUARE CRAWL*

Franklin Furnace, a not-for-profit arts organization I established in 1976 in my storefront living loft in the Tribeca neighborhood of New York, began as a part of the alternative-space movement of the 1970s and '80s. The proliferation of shoestring venues was an attempt to undermine the capitalist system represented by commercial galleries and major museums by showing cheap art such as artists' books, "unsalable" works of temporary installation, and even less salable performance art. What the galleries and museums did in response was establish spaces to show these ephemeral practices alongside painting and sculpture. I think the alternative-space movement can be proud that it fostered the development of postmodernism in its many forms, forever changing art theory and practice.

The first time I ever laid eyes on Pope.L, then William Pope.L, was January 8, 1988, when he was performing at Franklin Furnace in *Bombs*—an evening, per the subtitle, of "three ordnances" created by a group of writers, actors, musicians, directors, dancers, and technicians. I saw *Bombs* because, as Franklin Furnace's director, it was my policy to see every performance event selected by its peer panel reviewers, and as a performance artist myself, I wanted to keep up with evolutions in the field. *Bombs* was part of the group's ongoing experimentation in collaborative work, which used as many forms as possible for the stage. The members' backgrounds and training included classical dance, rock and roll, television, film acting, mime, and puppetry; yet they all shared a common interest in the American musical as a form. My impression of *Bombs* was that it was creatively chaotic, with cultural and intellectual references flying everywhere.

The second time I saw Pope.L in action was January 13, 1989, when he and Jim Calder presented *George Is in the Lake*. The basement performance space of Franklin Furnace was covered with a giant sheet of plastic, representing an icy Delaware River. A boat carrying General George Washington, played by Pope.L, has capsized, landing him in the drink. The work investigated American origin myths, with an ensemble similar to the one behind *Bombs*. Pope.L's notes on the piece, which I found in Franklin Furnace's archives, give a sense of his playful but pointed sensibility and his querying, inverting impulses: "The play asks and tries to answer the question: What would have happened if George hadn't crossed the Delaware? And again, what would ensue if George were Sue? Or once again, if history tells the truth, what do fairy tales? Or lastly, but not finally but maybe, if a man is a woman and a woman is a man, then what is a fish?"[1]

By this point in our relationship, Pope.L had become aware that Franklin Furnace went quiet in the summer months as we prepared the program for the coming season. He asked if he could do a residency during the summer of 1991, using Franklin Furnace as a home base from which to plan and execute one of his Crawl works, prepare an installation, and end his residency with a performance, which became his first (and ultimately, only) solo performance at Franklin Furnace. Pope.L provocatively titled the exhibition *How Much Is That Nigger in the Window*. Throughout this multilayered body of work, Pope.L would perform as Mr. Poots, a character he described in the press release as a cross between a black militant, a preacher-figure, a homeless person, and a buppie (a "black upwardly mobile professional," the African American version of the era's yuppie).[2]

In *Tompkins Square Crawl*—the best-known of the residency performances—Pope.L as Mr. Poots crawls around the perimeter of Tompkins Square Park wearing a business suit and holding a flowerpot. At the time, the park was shut down and enclosed by a fence. Tompkins Square had been a gathering place for the homeless and drug users amid the disorder of New York's East Village in the 1980s. Nearby, squatters were taking over buildings. Fighting with the police was a regular occurrence, including rioting, famously in 1989 and again in 1991. That year, the city closed the park for renovations that were a guise for evicting those living there.

Tompkins Square Crawl itself was jarring, incongruous—a black man in a suit crawling in the gutter. During the performance, an upset bystander, also black, crossed the street and started shouting at Pope.L: "Get up, get up!" he said. "Stand upright! You're degrading the image of black people!" To Pope.L, this was a sign that the piece was working. *Tompkins Square Crawl* takes him out of the upright posture representing power and places him in the position of the destitute, forcing his audience to directly engage with a disenfranchised black body that mirrors those others that have been rendered invisible.

How Much Is That Nigger in the Window included several other parts developed in the course of the residency—an artist's book titled *William Pope.L's "How Much Is That Nigger in the Window": Rap Street Journal*; performances titled *Suck Harder*, *Writing/Sleeping/Living on the Flag*, and *Selling Mayonnaise for 100 Dollars a Dollop*; and the first version of the performance *Eating the Wall Street Journal*, which took place on the sidewalk on an American flag. The residency culminated with the first iteration of *I Get Paid to Rub Mayo on My Body*, performed in the Furnace's storefront window on Franklin Street, the artist's back to the passersby outside. Meanwhile, a crowd inside watched as a nearly naked Pope.L, wearing little more than Jockey shorts, smeared mayonnaise on his skin in an attempt to become "white." Poised behind a video monitor that displayed footage from *Tompkins Square Crawl*, he performed silently, sitting in a white fold-out chair on a platform draped in an American flag. When applied, the mayonnaise oxidized and became transparent, constantly revealing his black skin underneath. For twenty or thirty minutes he continued, gathering a blob of mayonnaise with his hand from a nearby jar and smearing it on himself. The condiment appeared to dissolve almost as quickly as it was applied. In the scorching summer heat, the smell quickly became terrible. Pope.L's body became shinier and shinier, the few white marks that remained appearing on his skin like scars.

When *I Get Paid to Rub Mayo on My Body* concluded, Pope.L walked off the platform, leaving the chair, jars of mayonnaise, monitor, and flag in the window. The worn and dirty suit from *Tompkins Square Crawl* hung on the wall nearby, the boots leaning below it, all on a wall/floor painting showing a homeless person being penetrated by a skyscraper. The once-beautiful flower from the trip around the park sat in the center of the gallery, completely deteriorated; presumably it wasn't watered for the six weeks of the residency.

The denouement of *I Get Paid to Rub Mayo on My Body* made Franklin Furnace into a kind of stage in much the same way that Pope.L's public works like *Tompkins Square Crawl* turned the city into one. It also strongly underscored the cultural context of the time—the "culture wars" attack on government funding of the arts that had begun to heat up and, more generally, the assault by the right wing on poor, black, queer, and all othered bodies that had been ongoing throughout the 1980s.

A few years later in an interview, Pope.L and I discussed the crux of *I Get Paid to Rub Mayo on My Body*: "Mayonnaise was a very useful and fresh way for me to get out of [a] dead end: whiteness constructs blackness. . . . The idea that there's a pure good blackness or a pure bad whiteness is untenable for me. I use contradiction to critique and simultaneously celebrate."[3] He also touched on *Tompkins Square Crawl* and its relation to privilege:

> In New York, in most cities, if you can remain vertical and moving you deal with the world; this is urban power. But people who are forced to give up their verticality are prey to all kinds of dangers. But, let us imagine a person who has a job, possesses the means to remain vertical, but chooses to momentarily give up that verticality? To undergo that threat to his/her bodily/spiritual categories—that person would learn something. I did.[4]

1. Pope.L, "A Few Notes on George," ca. 1989. Event Records, Franklin Furnace Archive, Inc., New York. **2.** Press release for *How Much Is That Nigger in the Window*, June 15, 1991. Event Records, Franklin Furnace Archive, Inc. **3.** Martha Wilson, "William Pope.L," *Bomb* 55 (Spring 1996), 51. **4.** Ibid.

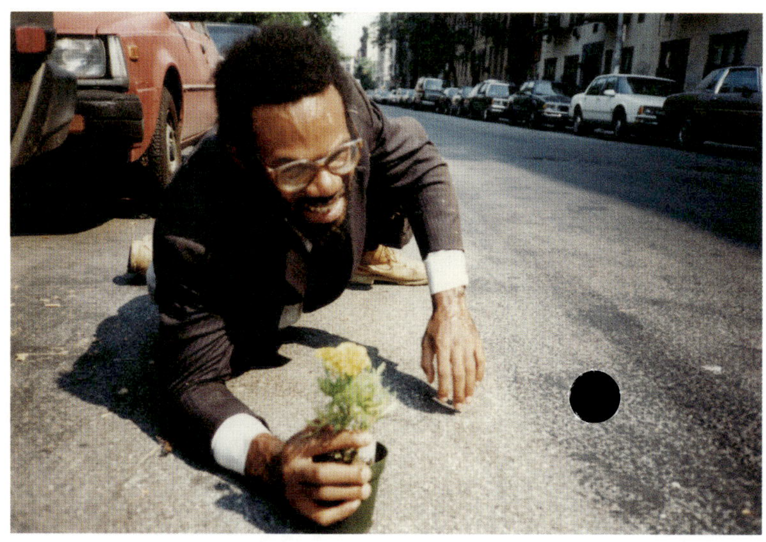

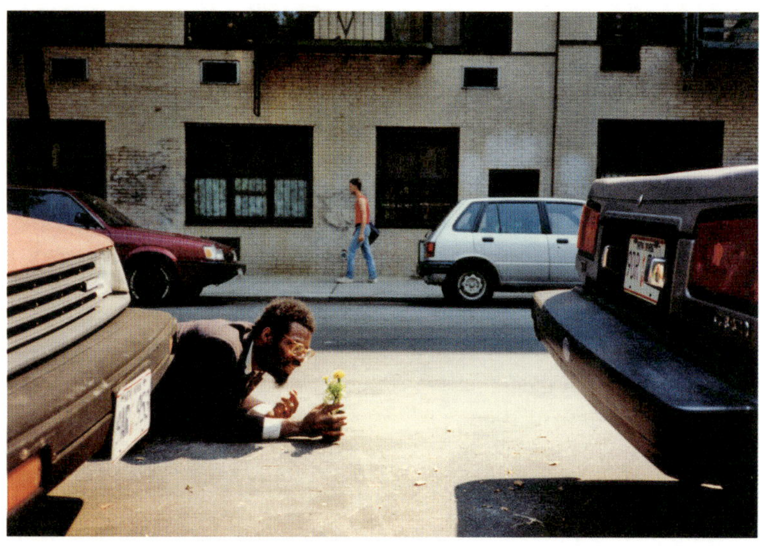

Page 62 and this page: *How Much Is That Nigger in the Window a.k.a. Tompkins Square Crawl*. Tompkins Square Park, New York, 1991. Inkjet prints, 15 × 10" (38.1 × 25.4 cm) and 10 × 15" (25.4 × 38.1 cm). The Museum of Modern Art, New York

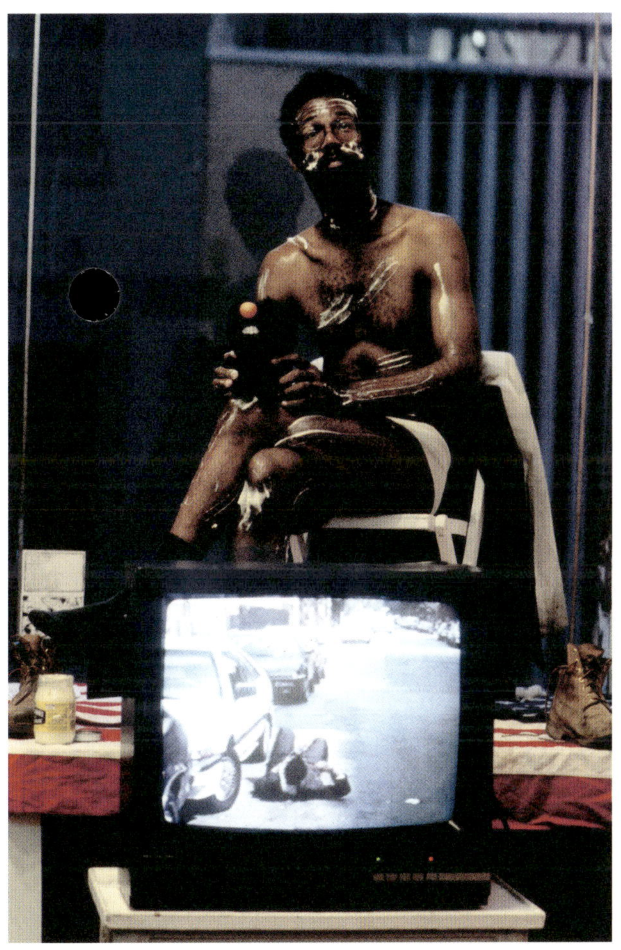

I Get Paid to Rub Mayo on My Body, Version 1. Part of *How Much Is That Nigger in the Window*, Franklin Furnace, New York, 1991.
Franklin Furnace Archive, Inc., New York

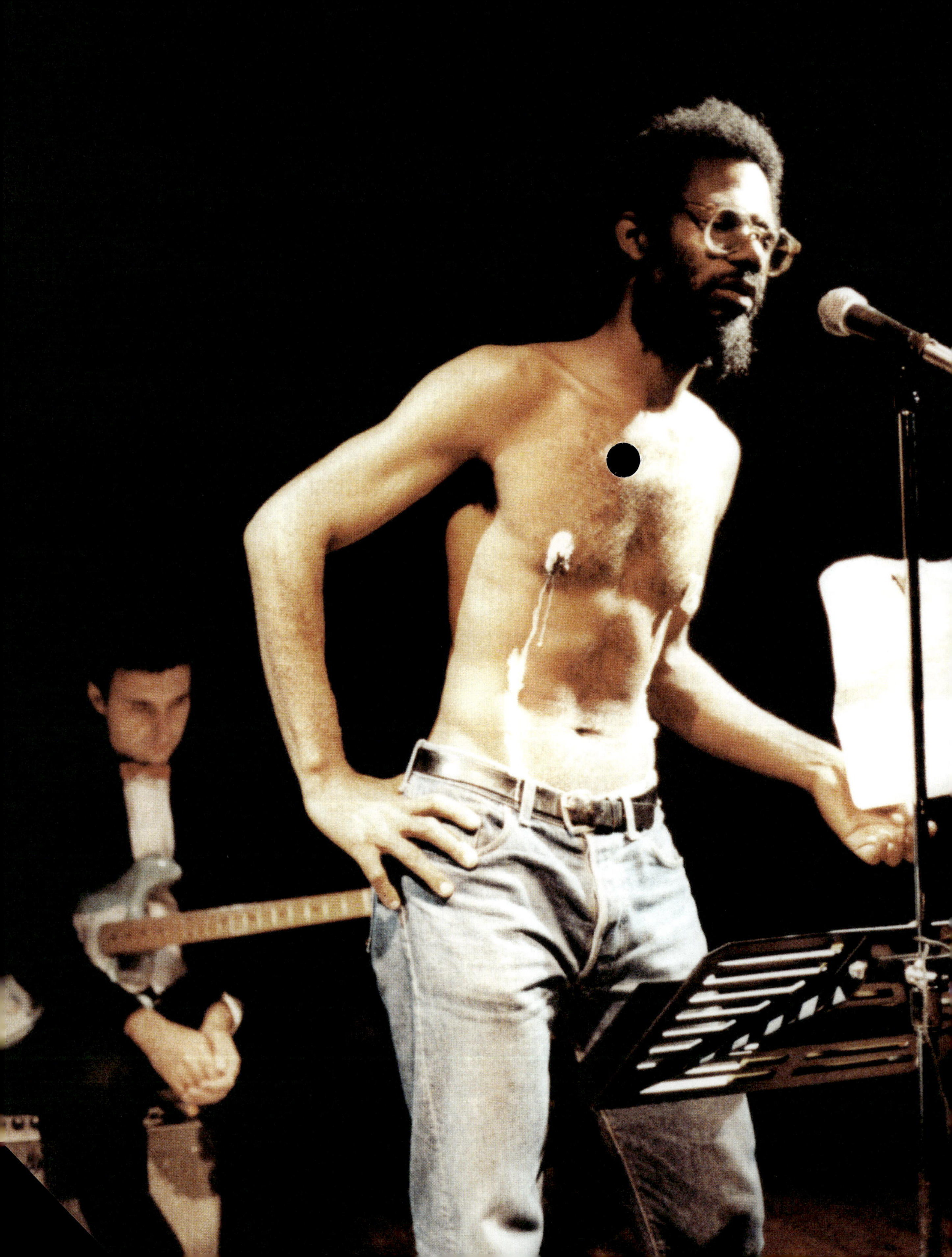

THE AUNT JENNY CHRONICLES
1990–91

Performance History

The Aunt Jenny Chronicles. Dixon Place, New York, June 8, 1990.

Looking for Aunt Jenny, audio installation. Art in General, New York, March 2–April 6, 1991.

The Aunt Jenny Chronicles/Journey to Incontinence. PS122, New York, October 3–6 and 10–13, 1991.

TRUTH TO POWER

MARK H. C. BESSIRE ON *THE AUNT JENNY CHRONICLES*

The theater-based performance *The Aunt Jenny Chronicles* (1990–91) is perhaps one of Pope.L's most personal pieces, part of the artist's ongoing effort to open difficult and important conversations about race, masculinity, family, and identity, in a trajectory that began in such works as *Times Square Crawl a.k.a. Meditation Square Piece* and *Thunderbird Immolation a.k.a. Meditation Square Piece* (both 1978). The three versions of *The Aunt Jenny Chronicles* reveal more about Pope.L's family and sense of self (in particular, with regard to his choice to become an artist) than any other of his performance works. In the piece, Pope.L illuminates crucial aspects of the addiction, incarceration, dependence, and love he experienced while growing up with three siblings, his mother, his Aunt Jenny, and an absent father. *The Aunt Jenny Chronicles* provides an insightful road map of the family relationships that impact Pope.L's practice and that he continues to express with subtle opacity through the present.

Today, we consider early 1990s New York a pivotal site for Pope.L's engagement with audiences in the street, gallery, and theater. In the wake of the go-go 1980s, *The Aunt Jenny Chronicles* opened up a new space, far away from the cultural excesses symbolized by Julian Schnabel, the clever commodification and commercialization of art by Jeff Koons, and the masterful appropriations of Sherrie Levine; far away as well from the ever-present NYC of white privilege and decadence illuminated in Jay McInerney's *Bright Lights, Big City* (1984) and Tom Wolfe's *The Bonfire of the Vanities* (1987). In 1990, with the art world and Wall Street still in the midst of a correction following the Black Monday stock-market crash of 1987, Pope.L highlighted the vulnerability of victimhood and recognized the raw power of channeling marginality into low-tech theater in an era of hype and spectacle. Whether working within the proscenium's frame, in the streets, or in alternative galleries, Pope.L had something to say. He crafted a practice melding life and art while focusing on social critique, giving little concern to his work's commercial value. It is during the early 1990s that we can begin to identify one of the artist's truisms as he expressed it through his artistic practice: "Lack is a value worth having," the subtitle to his 2002 retrospective *William Pope.L: Eracism*.[1] Or, as he stated in an interview in that exhibition's catalogue: "It's the lack in black that makes me what I am."[2]

Never afraid of taking risks, Pope.L channeled the story behind *The Aunt Jenny Chronicles* into two theatrical performances and one audio installation that were radical in the moment and, in hindsight, recalibrated our expectations of art. The work was informed by his experiences at the Whitney Independent Study Program with Yvonne Rainer, a Mabou Mines/Re.Cher.Chez intensive workshop, the MFA program at the Mason Gross School of the Arts at Rutgers University with Fluxus artist Geoffrey Hendricks, and a Franklin Furnace residency with Martha Wilson. In *The Aunt Jenny Chronicles*, Pope.L unveiled an expansive lexicon of symbolic content that the artist would explore for years to come—Reddi-wip, Alka-Seltzer, watermelons, cherries, baloney, fishing, holes, penis size, and Superman.

In a *Village Voice* review of the PS122 performance version of the work, *The Aunt Jenny Chronicles/Journey to Incontinence* (1991), the critic Joe Wood describes his experience of the work as follows: "Pope's twisty Clintonesque musings and rankings about (black) penis size, paternal absence, autobiography, etc. *did* engage those of us who stayed—even if the show did get too personal and inaccessible half the time."[3] The only existing footage of the staging, lasting some three minutes, presents us with an irreverent and subtly confrontational Pope.L behind a microphone and a music stand holding his script, which will fly into the air and land on the stage when he's done with it. A foreboding guitar chord lingers; Pope.L shakes a can of Reddi-wip and sprays it on each of his nipples, daring it to drip with a wiggle of his hips; the chord is hit again. Just as we might laugh or look away in amusement or embarrassment, Pope.L addresses the audience in a gruff voice: "Aunt Jenny died in the late '70s in a nursing home in Cliffwood, New Jersey."[4] In this and similar moments, one flinches at the raw expression of detached emotion in Pope.L's abstract dialogue with his aunt, mother, father, and siblings as he takes on Aunt Jenny, black male identity, his mother's addiction, and his own decision to become an artist.

Pope.L describes Aunt Jenny as "old South as they come . . . afraid of the modern world." She was "a mighty 5 foot amazon who caught possums at a single bound," the artist says, invoking that classic characterization of Superman, whom Pope.L invokes in his epic *The Great White Way: 22 miles, 9 years, 1 street* (2001–9)—and whom Aunt Jenny watched on television in her bedroom, "in the canyon of her belongings." Pope.L reveals that he wasn't present when Aunt Jenny died, implying that he failed to show up because he "was entering the white-biz. The showbiz of the art-biz. I had my toreador pants on in a corridor of projects. Always a lot of projects." He also implies a connection between his absence and the plight of the males in his family who were "afraid of their shadows," variously tormented: "Fear of self. Fear of life. Other puds. The same old penis barking up the same old rebus." Even though he was not there for Aunt Jenny's passing, the AJ whose initials are scrawled on his T-shirt during the piece (and who, Pope.L reveals, wasn't his biological aunt) is clearly the hero of this tale. She was the one who was present and helped keep the family together. Reading the handwritten *Aunt Jenny Chronicles* manuscript, I felt like an intruder, as if I were reading someone else's diary. Yet the "too personal and inaccessible" work to which Wood refers transcends these aspects via its depth, earnestness, and honesty to become a moment of family healing and an awakening for the audience. Or if not healing, an opportunity to broach a conversation.

In the program for the PS122 performance, Pope.L tell us: "[*The Aunt Jenny Chronicles*] was about me, my mistreatment of Aunt Jenny and my bias against uneducated southern blacks. I began to symbolize the young, leafless abrasive black north. I began to think about power, government, movies and image. . . . Eventually the combination of directions led to my family and bad faith as autobiography. . . . In addition, my mother wrote me, saying: though she'd learned to put the past behind her, she wasn't gonna stop me from putting it in front of you."[5] Pope.L has never stopped putting "it" in front of us, his audience, and leveraging his willingness to be simultaneously vulnerable, powerful, and funny to prepare us for a conversation. He's said as much about his intentions: "Artists don't make art, they make conversations. They make things happen. They change the world."[6] *The Aunt Jenny Chronicles* does precisely that, opening a dialogue that Pope.L continues to share in the hopes of making that change.

1. The exhibition took place at the Institute of Contemporary Art at Maine College of Art, Portland, then traveled to DiverseWorks, Houston, and the Portland Institute for Contemporary Art, Oregon. **2.** Lowery Stokes Sims, "Interview with William Pope.L," in *William Pope.L: The Friendliest Black Artist in America©*, ed. Mark H. C. Bessire (Cambridge, Mass.: MIT Press, 2002), 66. **3.** Joe Wood, "Cameos: *The Aunt Jenny Chronicles/Journey to Incontinence*," *Village Voice* 36, no. 42 (October 15, 1991), 130. **4.** All quotations from *The Aunt Jenny Chronicles/Journey to Incontinence* are taken from its performance manuscript (1991) in the collection of the artist. **5.** Program for William Pope.L, *The Aunt Jenny Chronicles/Journey to Incontinence*, October 3–6 and 10–13, 1991, PS122, New York. Fales Library and Special Collections, New York University, Martha Wilson Papers. **6.** Sims, "Interview with William Pope.L," 64.

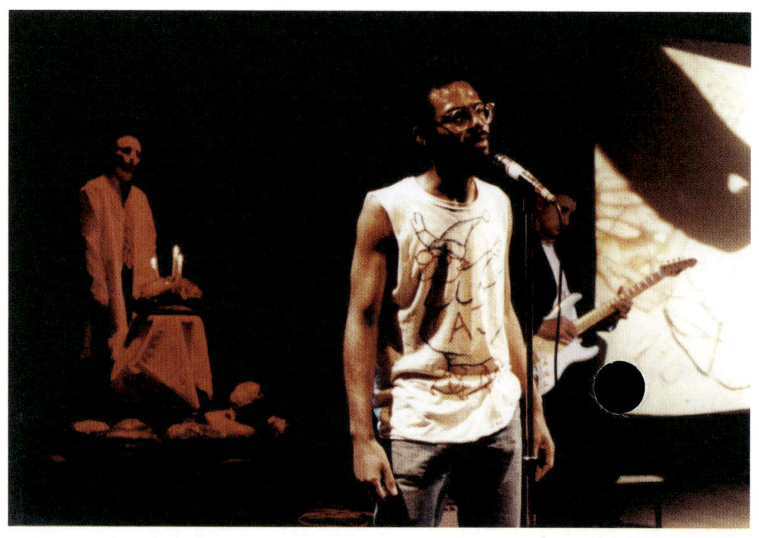

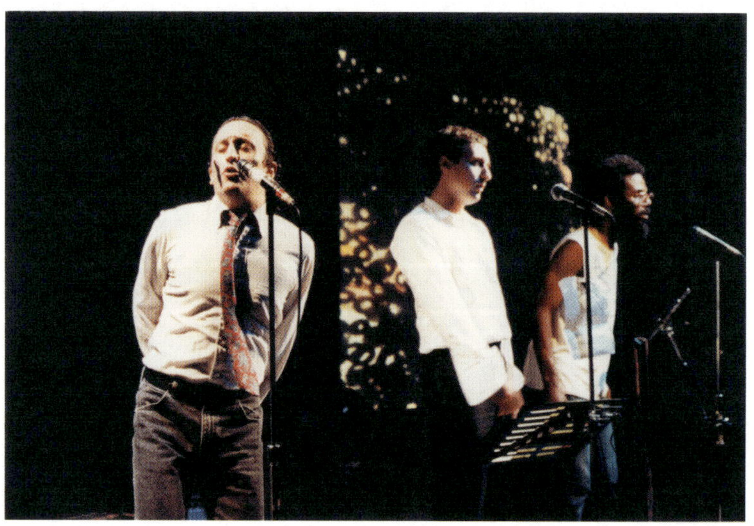

Page 68 and this spread: *The Aunt Jenny Chronicles*. PS122, New York, 1991. Inkjet prints, 15 × 10" (38.1 × 25.4 cm) and 10 × 15" (25.4 × 38.1 cm). The Museum of Modern Art, New York

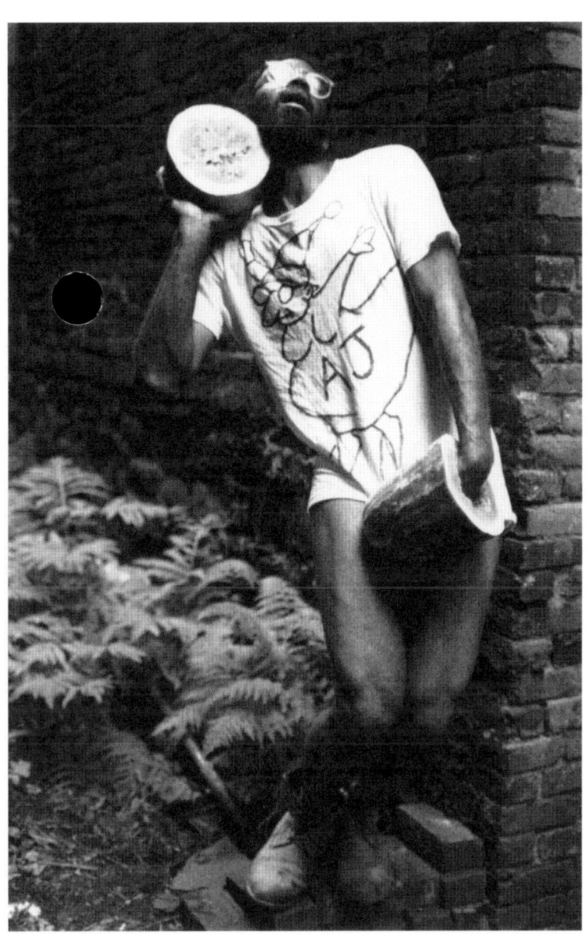
AJ

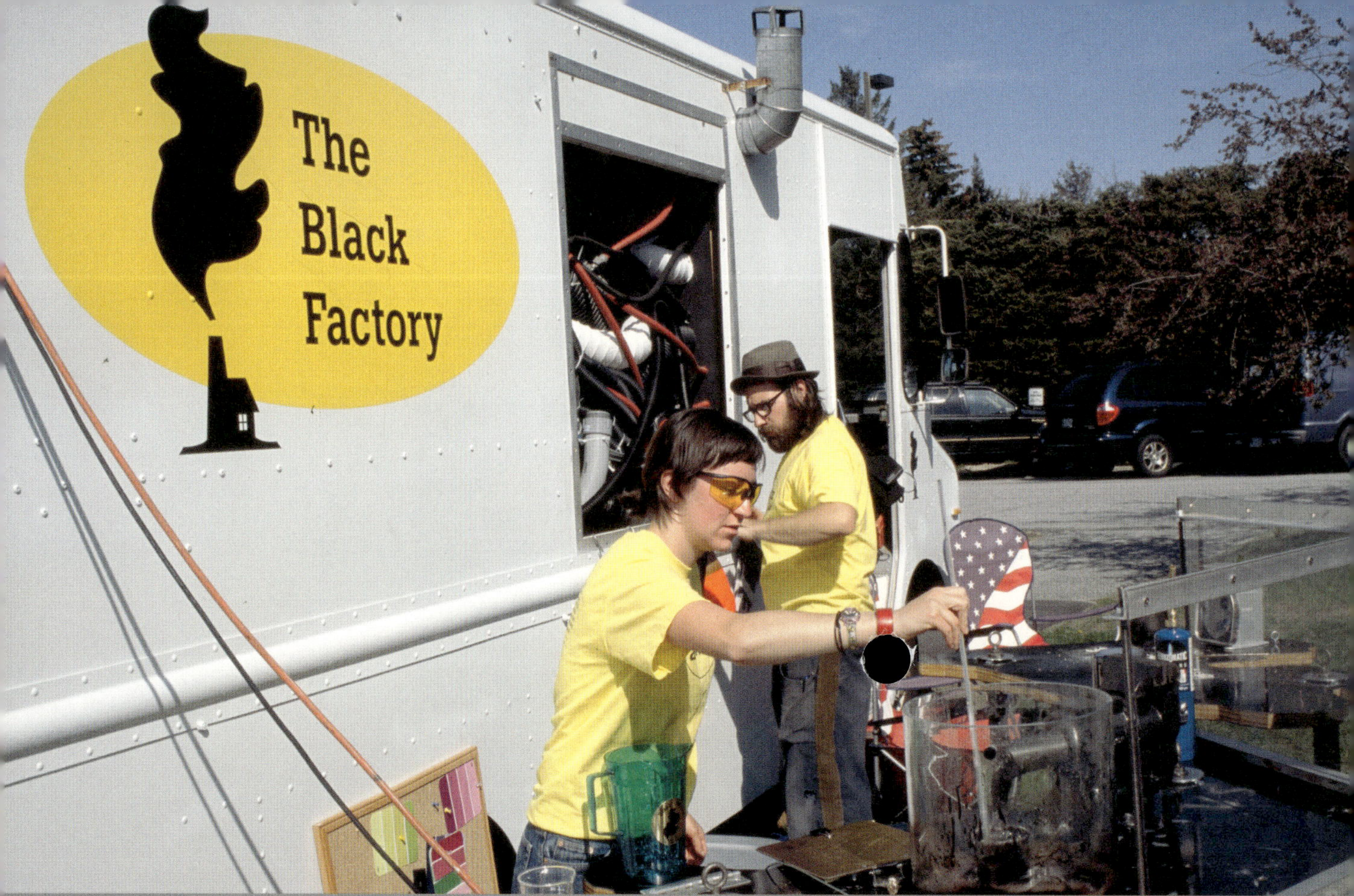

1.

What *is* the Black Factory (or the BF as we sometimes call it)?

http://www.theblackfactory.com/

What does *it* do?

And how can YOU get in on the action???

"What? A factory that makes blackness?"

Yes, finally! BUT The Black Factory does not make blackness. we make something *better*: opportunity.

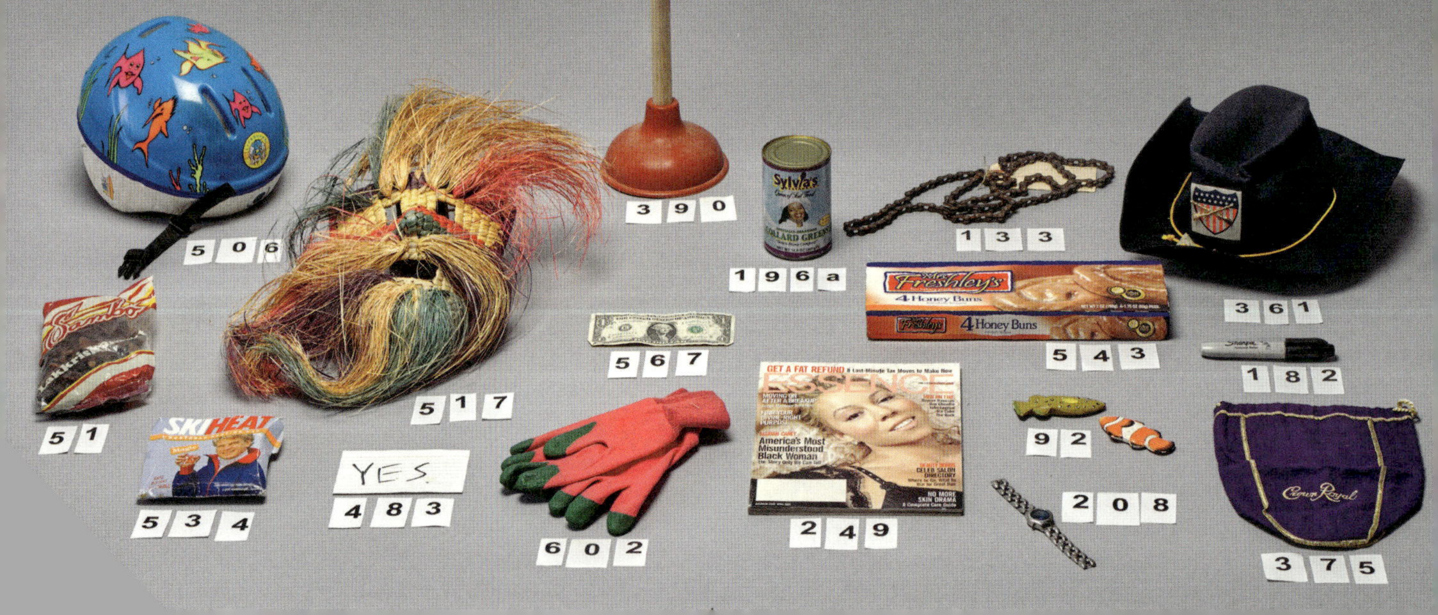

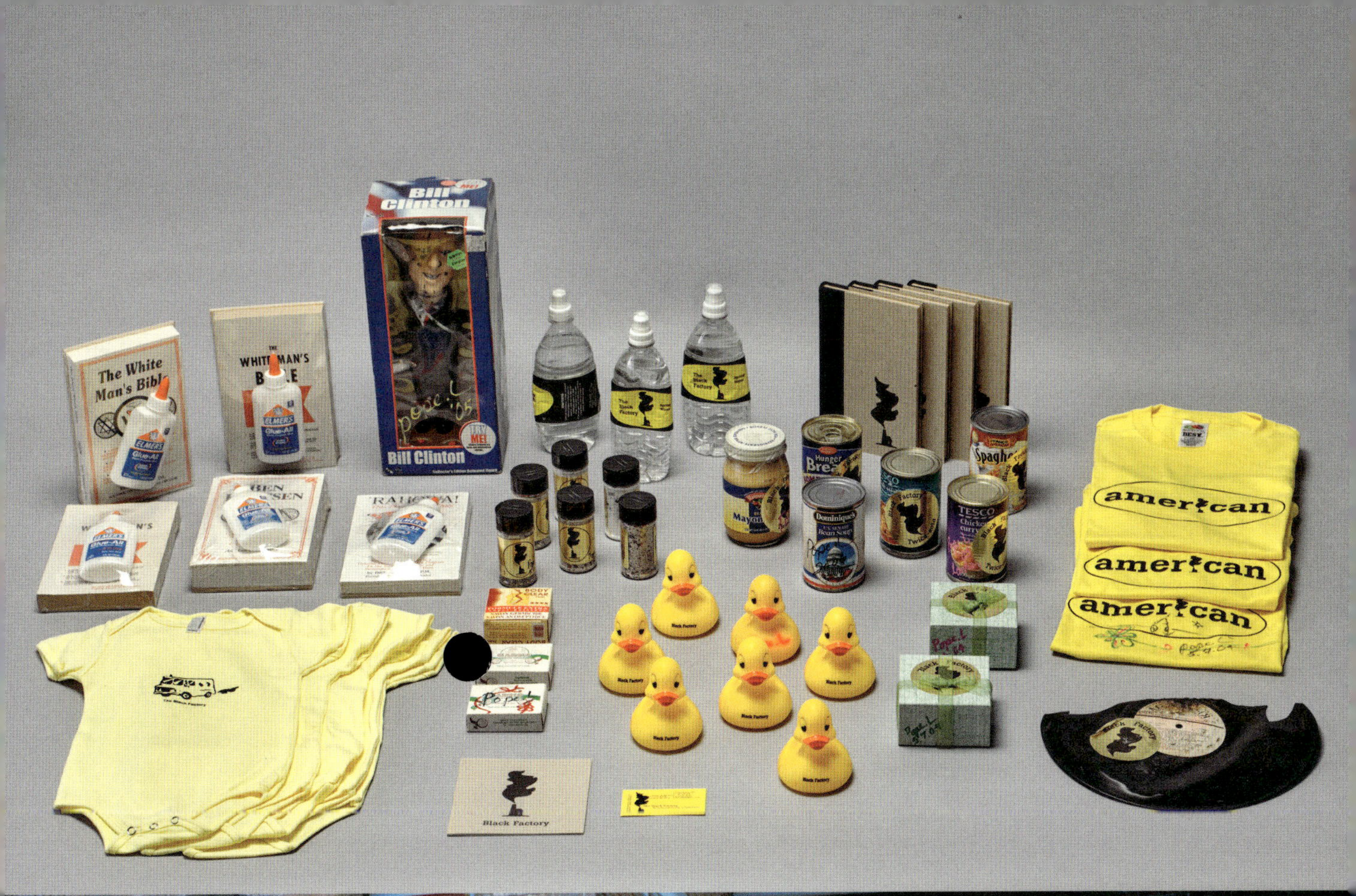

The White Man's Bible
Bill Clinton
Black Factory
american
american
american

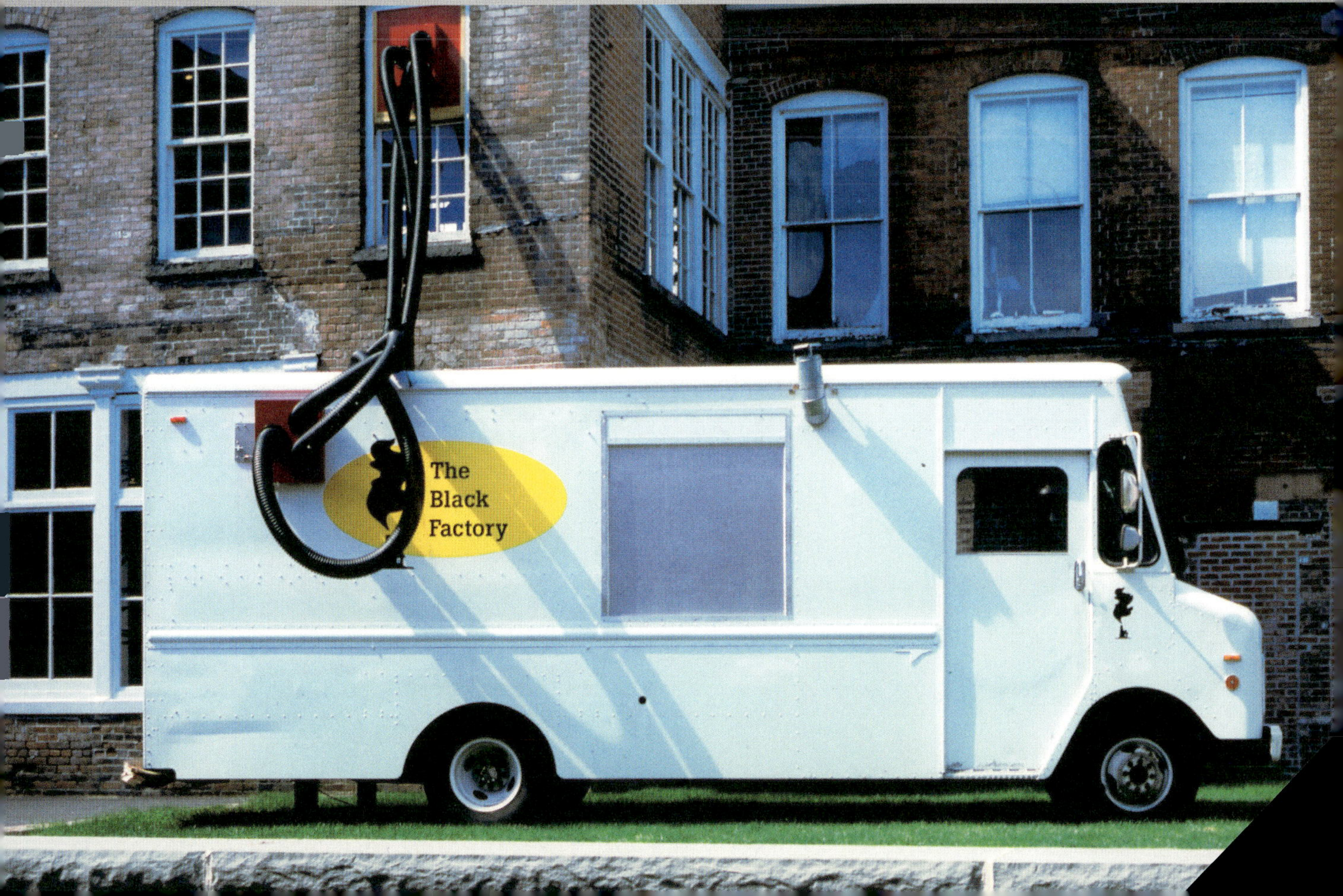

The Black Factory

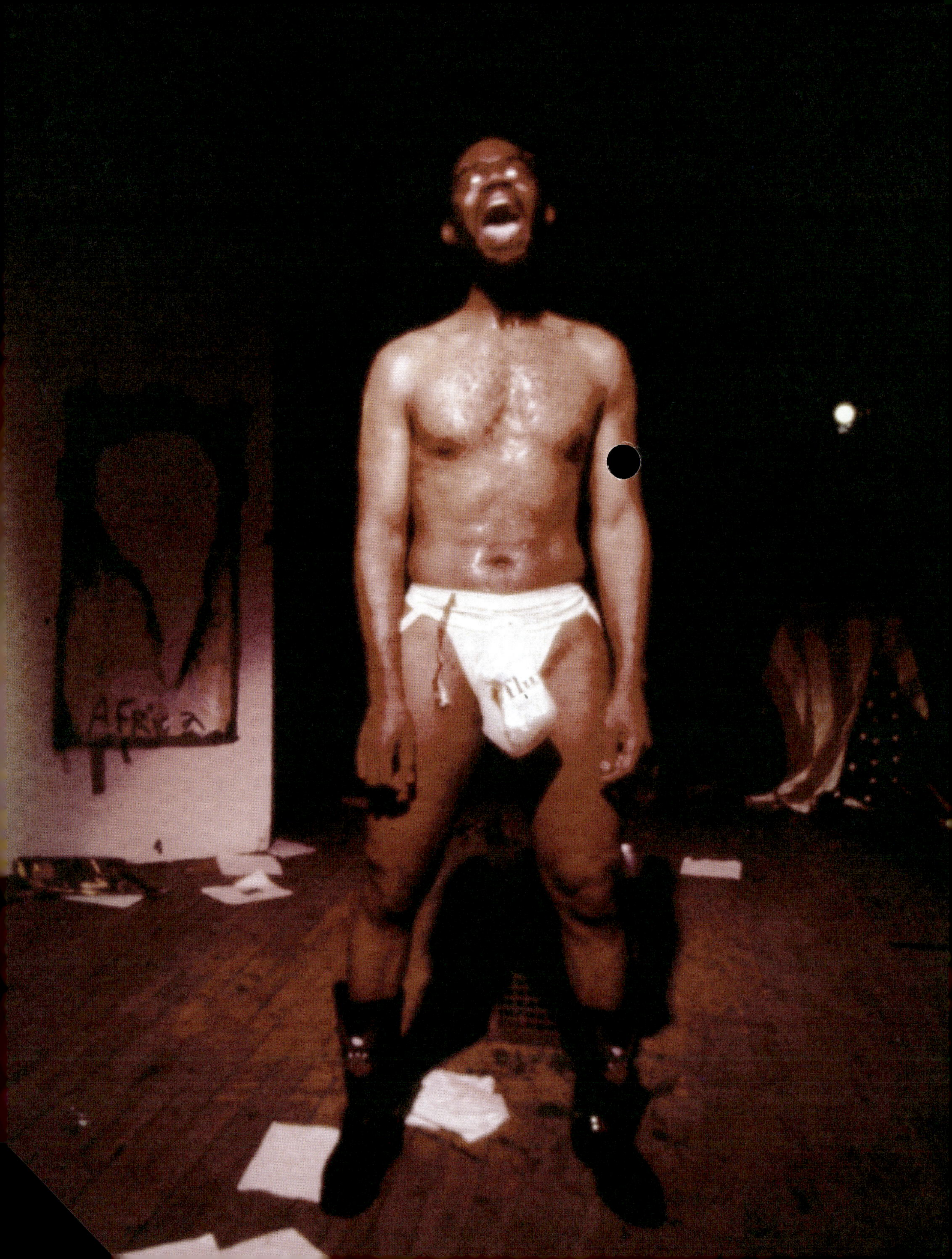

ERACISM
1992–2002

Performance History

Eracism, Version 1. Downtown Art Co., New York, February 20–March 1, 1992.

Eracism, Version 2. Drew University, Madison, N.J., January 29, 1993.

Eracism, Version 3. Hallwalls Contemporary Arts Center, Buffalo, N.Y., March 20, 1993.

Eracism, Version 4a, with golf demo. Yellow Springs Institute, Chester Springs, Penn., September 25, 1993.

Eracism, Version 4. Karamu House, Cleveland Performance Art Festival, February 25–26, 1994. Part of the exhibition *Outside the Frame: Performance and the Object: A Survey History of Performance Art in the USA since 1950*, Cleveland Center for Contemporary Art, February 11–May 1, 1994.

Eracism, Version 5. Snug Harbor Cultural Center, Staten Island, N.Y. Part of the exhibition *Outside the Frame*, Snug Harbor Cultural Center, February 26–June 18, 1995.

Eracism, Version 7. Ko Performance Festival, Amherst College, Mass., July 26–28, 1996.

Eracism, Version 7a. Performance Art, Culture, and Pedagogy Symposium, Pennsylvania State University, University Park, November 13–16, 1996.

Eracism, Version 7b. Mobius Experimental Theater Space, Boston, May 30–June 1, 1997.

Eracism, Version 8. 7a*11d Festival, Toronto, September 26, 1998.

Eracism, Version 8a/8b. Thread Waxing Space, New York, June 15, 2000.

Eracism, with Lydia Grey. Portland Stage Company, Maine, September 13–14, 2002. Part of the exhibition *William Pope.L: eRacism*, Institute of Contemporary Art at Maine College of Art, Portland, July 26–October 17, 2002.

BLACK MILK

ADRIAN HEATHFIELD ON *ERACISM*

If white perception were just a material—rather than the all-pervasive camouflaged eye of Western culture, its malignant and relentless machinery of violence—what substance would it be? Perhaps the contaminated tap water from Flint, Michigan, that Pope.L purchased, bottled, and resold (*Flint Water Project*, 2017), or the turbulent air that flayed and tore apart his altered American flag (*Trinket*, 2008), or the gloopy mayonnaise slathered over his skin as he performed in the window of Franklin Furnace (*I Get Paid to Rub Mayo on My Body*, part of *How Much Is That Nigger in the Window*, 1991). It would be an elemental or common material for sure, something encountered every day, a supposed sustenance that is in reality unbearable for black life. As Pope.L's famous "friendliest" moniker makes plain, almost everything in Western culture proceeds in relation to white perception: it is the jailhouse of black existences and yet the scene for subversive and excessive countertactics of play. Living in and creatively working through the consequences of this understanding takes a particular shape in *Eracism* (1992–2002), the scripted performance work Pope.L reiterated a dozen times over a ten-year period in distinct modulations. Typical of an oeuvre marked by formal promiscuity, degradable stuff, and immaterial actions, there is no stable, recoverable object called *Eracism*, though there are photos and videos of some enactments, its remaining props and other effects, and a published text. Rethinking the force of this performance, I can only write about it from the outside, as secondary witness, reading between its residual things.

As the "cover boy" of a 1997–98 issue of *P-Form*, a now-defunct Chicago performance zine in which a version of *Eracism*'s script is printed, Pope.L is a pearly white beaming smile. His body is already a historical artifact, judging by the monochrome, photocopied look of his skin, which humorously jars with the full-color brown of the baggy trench coat he wears. Glassy '70s-intellectual specs make for more laughs, as does the oversized plastic cow protruding from his crotch. Such ridiculous pride: an intelligence that doesn't see its own base absurdity. Or knows it well, of course, and revels in it. Pope.L holds out a glass of milk as if to toast something. "I drank the milk from my own fake cow-cock," he seems to say, "and man, was it a pleasure." A secret, animalized sexual self-relay surfaces in this photograph, some autonomous black male circuitry of pleasure you cannot touch—racist species degradation played out in visual reverb. I linger on this image because it crystallizes a subject that recurs throughout the language acts of Pope.L's performances of *Eracism*: black bodies as sites of contorted desire and fear, their paradoxical sexualization within white imaginaries. *Eracism* is a laying bare of the politics and carnal stakes of race relations but without the sweat or blood of endurance and body art.

Perhaps the most theatrical of Pope.L's enactments, performed in a ragtag set of venues on the East Coast and in Ohio, *Eracism* features a character called Mr. Poots, who delivers a wildly digressive monologue, in some versions with the help of a white female "servant" and musical accompaniment. As Poots, Pope.L appears in a femme tulle dress worn below the nipples and worker's boots; he sports a jockstrap-codpiece bodged together from a plastic bottle and some gaffer tape. Though Pope.L describes the work as a "solo art performance lecture,"[1] its genre is perhaps less stable than this categorization suggests, being simultaneously a work of theater, stand-up comedy, and warped didactics, interspersed with plain actions and poor song. When set against the testimonial, affirmative, and identitarian drives of much early-'90s solo performance, the standout aesthetic radicalism of Pope.L's "interbred" antigenre work[2] and "schizophrenic" voicings is clear. From the outset, Poots's monologue makes manifest its self-conscious address to black flesh, a subject whose necessity arises from the lived experience of its possession by the ideas of white others, its continuous accessibility to their violent incursions. This dispossession of bodies, of black life, is the erasure of which Pope.L speaks. In rhyming turns between anecdotes, disclosures of fake personal archives, social observations, paranoid fantasies, and speculative theorizations, Poots affirms inquisitive vulnerability and gendered dissonance as a response to a world that constantly wants to fuck with you. Recounting a pedestrian scene of childhood homophobia, Poots, or Pope.L, talks back to the bully boys across time: "I have a COCK which is a pussy and it's filled with DOUBT."

In *Eracism*, Pope.L deploys elaborate associative streams of language, aphorisms turned inside out, street poetics, and rambling analyses in order to speak another logic of experience. Language here is much like the materials in his more object-oriented visual work: it is the secondary, everyday, or degraded lingo, culture's waste material, that when re-treated can articulate the value of experiences deemed insignificant by that culture. Through this negated matter, Pope.L makes plain the operations of "the spectrum of hate, the spectrum of night, the spectrum of invisible light which is American racism."[3] When it comes to unpicking "the nexus of this business of race and sex,"[4] Pope.L's incantations dredge up its savage history: "Let's whisper to the stars made by our slave masters' whips on our ancestors' backsides. Let's listen to the love made by our ancestors' tits on our slave masters' insides. Let's whisper to the stars in our ancestors' wish as it scrapes against the teeth of our slave masters' genocide."[5] A sullied, hilarious, and acerbic sermon on violent sexual economies is spilled in the hope of communion.

In an interview with artist and curator Martha Wilson, founding director of Franklin Furnace, Pope.L laid out the genealogy of the affinity he sees between messy materials and babble, between altered experience and the imperative to negate reason:

> It goes back to my experiences . . . [of] how performance and culture was constructed in church. Visceral, visceral and more visceral. It works in your body as well as your soul. Language, voice is a part of it. The body. Dust to dust. Language is more than the intellectual. It orders your body. It writes. It has a rhythm: the way things are spoken; the choir comes in at certain points; people in the audience jump out of their seats and talk in tongues, sound surrounds, enters you. There's all of this, foaming, ranting and cacophony. Joyous noise. Uh huh. I want the visual to be more physical. The materials that I use oxidize and transform.[6]

Eracism convenes a temporary sacrilegious church for another kind of linguistic alchemy where "base" materials, a vernacular of pain, fear, and shame, turn into performative gold: shared joy at the limits of sense in a senseless world. Through this transformation, the contortions and impossibilities of living in the long night of the racial incarceration of culture are returned to those who choose to hear.

1. William Pope.L, introduction to "Eracism," *P-Form* 44 (Fall 1997/Winter 1998): 28. **2.** "Language, movement, images and songs are 'interbred' to create a new family of racial vision." Ibid. **3.** Pope.L, "Eracism," 28. **4.** Ibid., 29. **5.** *Eracism*, Version 8a/8b, performed at Thread Waxing Space, New York, June 15, 2000. **6.** Martha Wilson, "William Pope.L," *Bomb* 55 (Spring 1996), 53.

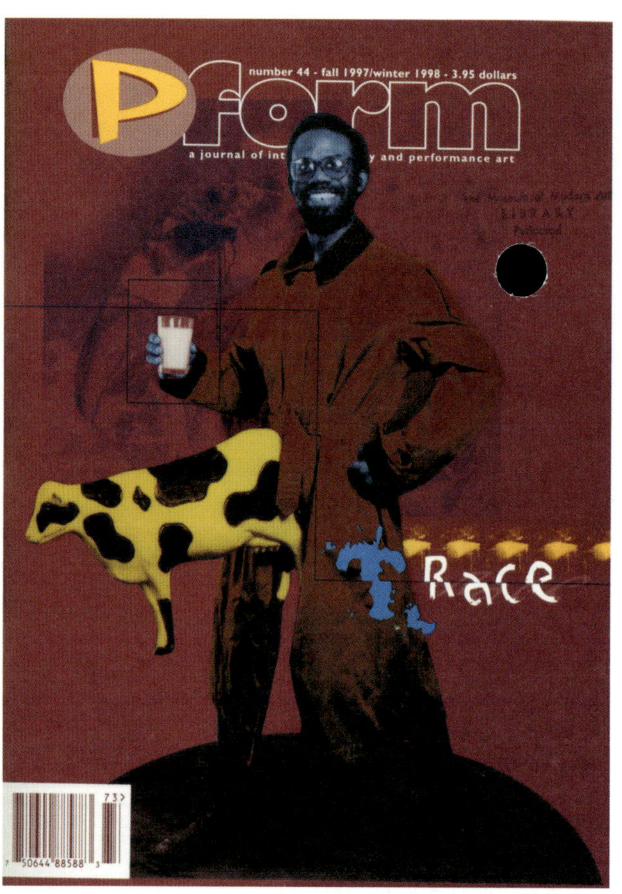

Page 76: *Eracism*, Version 7. Ko Performance Festival, Amherst College, Mass., 1996. Inkjet print, 10 × 15" (25.4 × 38.1 cm). The Museum of Modern Art, New York
This page: Cover of *P-Form* 44 (Fall 1997/Winter 1998). The Museum of Modern Art Library, New York

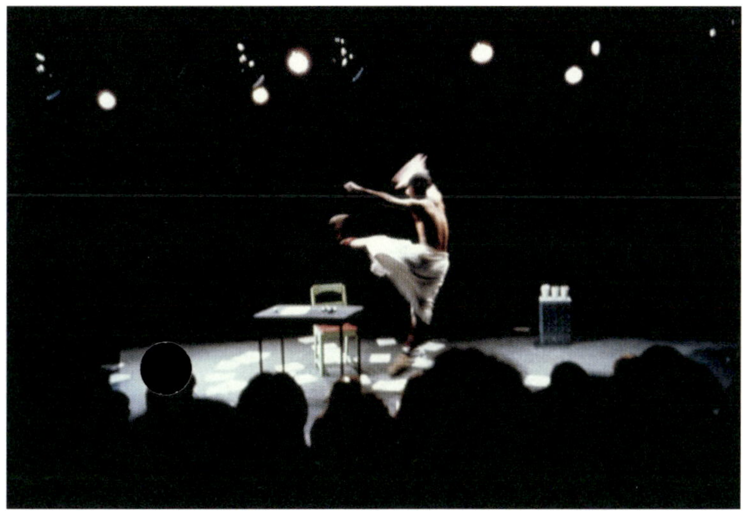

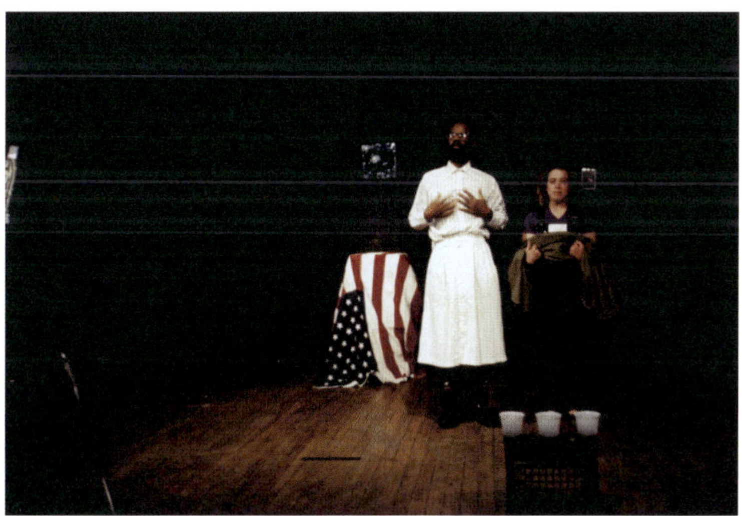

Top: *Eracism*, Version 2. Drew University, Madison, N.J., 1993. Inkjet print, 10 × 15" (25.4 × 38.1 cm). The Museum of Modern Art, New York
Bottom: *Eracism*, Version 7b. Mobius Experimental Theater Space, Boston, 1997. Inkjet print, 10 × 15" (25.4 × 38.1 cm). The Museum of Modern Art, New York

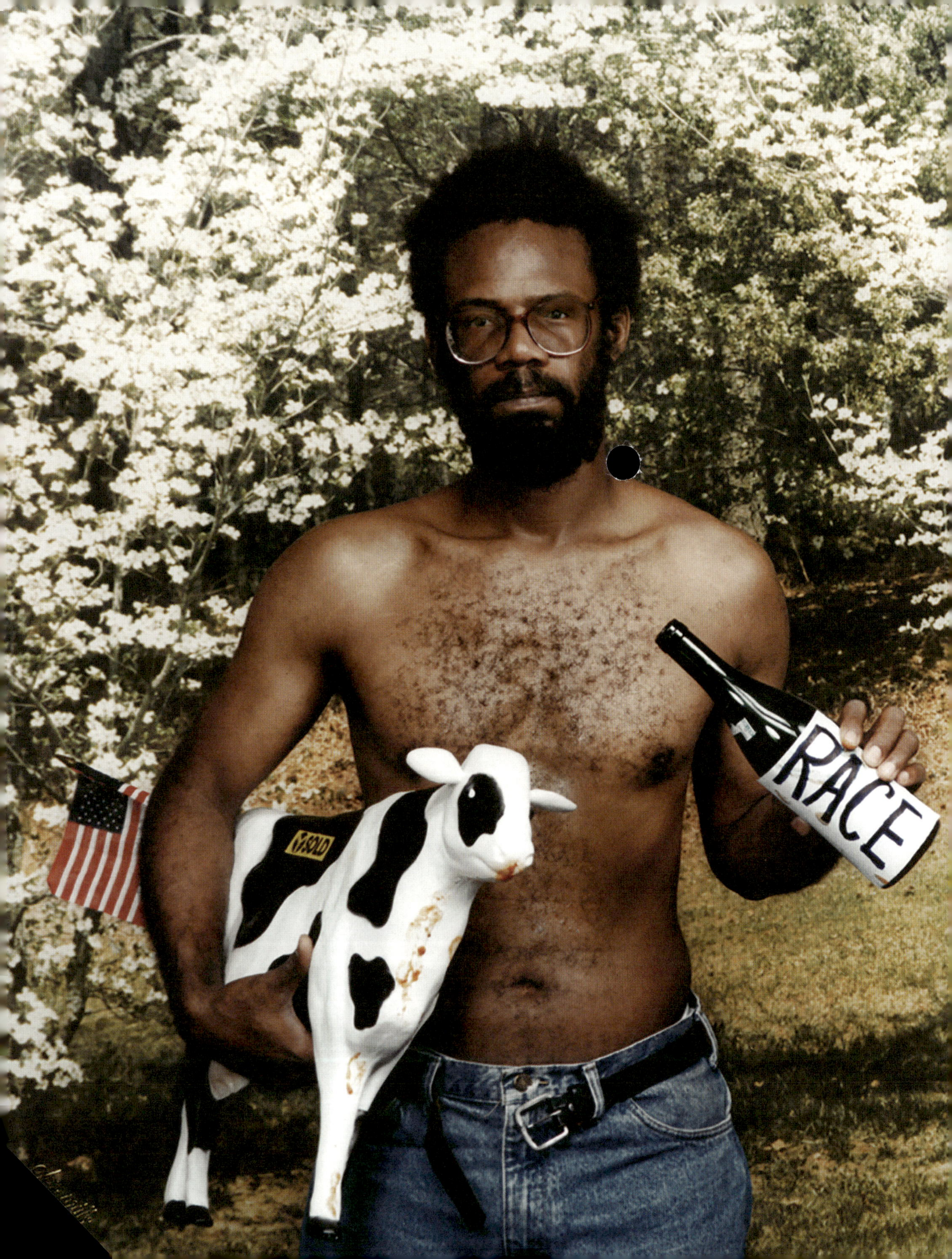
RACE

BLACK DOMESTIC
A.K.A. COW COMMERCIAL
1994

Performance History

Black Domestic a.k.a. Cow Commercial. Midtown, including a Banana Republic store, New York, August 17, 1994.

COY COMMODITIES AND PATRIARCHAL PROMISES

NAOMI BECKWITH ON *BLACK DOMESTIC A.K.A. COW COMMERCIAL*

Black Domestic a.k.a. Cow Commercial (1994) opens with a scene of our protagonist on top of New York City, perhaps even the world. “Looking down like a god,” he surveys Manhattan from the quiet rooftop terrace of a Midtown skyscraper, and we too are voyeurs, viewing the mass of the city with him from our perch on high: “An Icarus flying above these waters, he can ignore the devices of Daedalus in mobile and endless labyrinths far below.”[1] What has bestowed this godlike status? Cradled under our hero’s right arm is a toy cow marked SOLD. A prize he carries with him as he descends an elevator and onto the city’s streets. Here, our once voyeur, now pedestrian must navigate and negotiate the noisy and dangerous Midtown traffic, always clutching his newly acquired cow.

The Cow is the land; it is the promise, made flesh, in plastic.[2]

These Biblical tones imply that our hero has arrived, overcome even, acquiring his new Icarian status as a consumer through the purchase of the Cow. Yet on the street, it’s now clear that the Cow is both prize and responsibility. Is it bleeding, and leaving bloody tracks on the sidewalk? Is its mini American flag properly positioned up its ass? Is it being nurtured in the manner to which it’s become accustomed, as it suckles on a wine bottle labeled RACE? Is it trained? Is it literate? Can it eracism?

Despite *Cow Commercial*’s opening scene, Pope.L’s usual point of view is from the street. From *Thunderbird Immolation a.k.a. Meditation Square Piece* (1978) to the *Black Domestic* performative actions at locations including a Banana Republic store (1993–94) to the protestlike *ATM Piece* (1997) and *Shopping Crawl (crawl with balloon)* (2001), much of his performative work has been in publicly accessible yet commercially loaded sites in Manhattan and other cities. For his Crawls, Pope.L goes even lower than a pedestrian’s view: his perspective is that of the serpent rather than an angel. From physical debasements to metaphorical ones, his work generally insists on taking up the tawdry, the irrational, the pornographic, and the disreputable; it’s often downright nasty. He frequently discards the elevated and sublimated altogether, instead acting on a shrewd suspicion of the markers of Enlightenment: language, reason, respectability, private property, the patronymic, cleanliness.

If a black person owns the cow, does the meaning of the cow change?[3]

Cow Commercia[illegible] a part of Pope.L’s *Black Domestic* project, a set of performances, photographs, and at least one video in which our hero often plays a cheerful but wholly inappropriate domestic worker. In the photo works, he is often shirtless with pants undone, accompanied by the cow with the American flag planted firmly in its rear. The *Cow Commercial* video marks the entire suite as a marketing project: Pope.L is selling off a shiny new domestic worker. “It is a direct and confrontational critique of the manipulation of consumption, race, and the neatly packaged social ideas we are faced with everyday as consumers,” as one author has put it. “It is also a spoof of the ‘Got Milk’ campaign, which displayed a variety of celebrities (the epitome of American desire) consuming milk.”[4]

Marketing, consumerism, and the fungibility of the worthless sit at the center of Pope.L’s practice, yet these concerns have been thought of as parallel to his work with race. The *Black Domestic* project makes explicit that his commodity-culture critique and race-confounding works are one and the same practice, inextricably linked. Pope.L poetically proposes blackness as myriad things in his work, or oftentimes as nothing at all, but it is unquestionably a construct of capital: the result of the trade in African bodies and their consumption as commodities.

The black domestic laborer is such a common presence in the United States that we forget that such a worker is only a (slight) variation of the enslaved domestic. “Being a servant has been naturalized to the point of the unnatural being made natural," says Pope.L.[5] Thus he enacts a *détournement* of black servitude by branding a "goofy" version of this role. In *Cow Commercial*, Pope.L makes a macabre double entendre by alluding to the manner in which black bodies were often seared, or *cattle-branded*, by their owners. But why let a good pun go to waste when, in making it, one can unmask the continuous and unacknowledged relations between the historic trading of black bodies and contemporary American consumerist culture? As the new owner of the Cow and the promise, the Black Domestic has not so much arrived but become a caretaker of its own metonym.

The black male body is a lack worth having.[6]

The iconic image of a black domestic worker is that of a woman; consider, for instance, the enduring tropes of Aunt Jemimas and Mammies. Pope.L, cognizant of this gendered lineage, is encased in the feminine as he performs the consumer object that itself simultaneously performs consumption and caretaking. By aligning himself with women's work (as he did literally as a youth, often over summers, by helping his maternal grandmother do housekeeping work for her white clients), Pope.L further instantiates his suspicions of the mechanisms of capital and patriarchy. As his work pushes back against social norms, he also seeks to denature the very terms that establish those norms. This effort is no attempt to kill the father, however, as such rebellious moves are as juvenile as they are counterproductive: "When you banish the father, you banish yourself. My father is myself."[7] Yet Pope.L is interested in the possible inscription of the feminine onto the traditional masculine, what he terms "the father-ness begat by women."

Much has been made of the "pathological" and "matriarchal" African American family, most severely articulated in the Moynihan Report of 1965. Black families perpetually produce "notorious bastards" who are marked by lacking a father.[8] But how can a woman, who is historically a possession, a commodity, and who has no legal rights to her own offspring, be a matriarch? If this irony supposedly sits at the heart of the black family condition—and is seen as particularly deleterious for African American males—then Pope.L is keen to unmask the hypocrisy behind terming these conditions a "disadvantage" and upending this lack.

THIS IS A PAINTING OF MARTIN LUTHER KING'S PENIS FROM INSIDE MY FATHER'S VAGINA reads posters Pope.L plastered around Manhattan in 2001–2.[9] Let us attempt to grasp this series of inversions and sex-organ dysmorphia that disrupt agency and gender. Pope.L calls this condition "involution"; in the words of one observer, "The image (a father's vagina?) is more complicated than just turning something inside out. Pope.L describes it as involuting 'the inside inside another inside another.'"[10] Pope.L hypothesizes a nesting series of negations that don't cancel each other out like a double negative. Rather, they conjure a sense of being comfortably wrapped in and rapt to complete absurdities and paradoxes. It's like "a creature consuming its own kind. Very human. Very social. Very capitalist."[11] It is our contemporary consumer culture. It is a proposition for the condition of blackness. It's a lack worth having.

1. Michel de Certeau, *The Practice of Everyday Life*, trans. Stephen Rendall (Berkeley: University of California Press, 1988), 92. **2.** Pope.L, *Black Domestic a.k.a. Cow Commercial* (1994). **3.** Ibid. **4.** Mark H. C. Bessire, "The Friendliest Black Artist in America©," in *William Pope.L: The Friendliest Black Artist in America©*, ed. Bessire (Cambridge, Mass.: MIT Press, 2002), 30. **5.** E-mail to the author, December 31, 2018. **6.** Lowery Stokes Sims, "Interview with William Pope.L," in Bessire, *William Pope.L: The Friendliest Black Artist in America©*, 62. **7.** All quoted material this paragraph from "Interview between Pope.L and Hamza Walker," in *Pope.L: Showing Up to Withhold*, ed. Pope.L and Karen Reimer (Chicago: Renaissance Society at the University of Chicago and University of Chicago Press, 2014), 148. **8.** See Hortense Spillers, "Mama's Baby, Papa's Maybe: An American Grammar Book," *Diacritics* 17, no. 2 (Summer 1987): 65. **9.** This postering took place as part of Pope.L's project *distributingmartin* (2000–2008). For more information, see Rhizome's Net Art Anthology, https://anthology.rhizome.org/distributing-martin, which includes links to an archived version of the project on Pope.L's site The Black Factory, http://theblackfactory.com/. **10.** C. Carr, "In the Discomfort Zone," in Bessire, *William Pope.L*, 50. **11.** "Interview between Pope.L and Hamza Walker," 149.

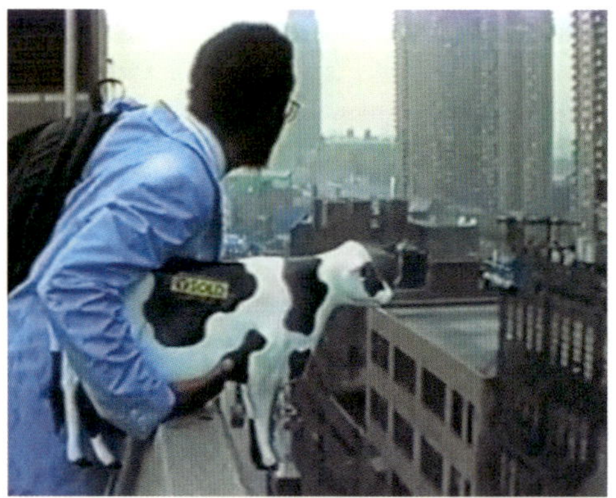

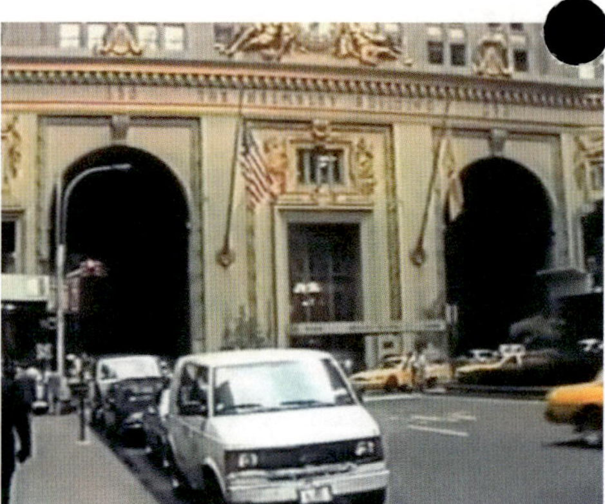

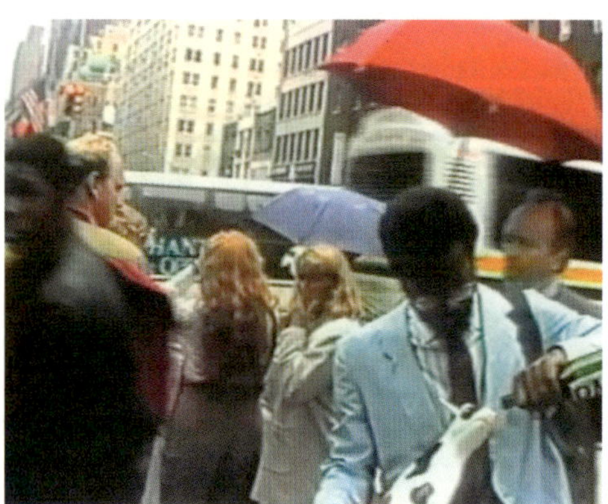

Page 82: Promotional photograph for *Black Domestic*. 1993–95
This spread: *Black Domestic a.k.a. Cow Commercial*. 1994. Video: color, sound; 2:49 minutes. The Museum of Modern Art, New York

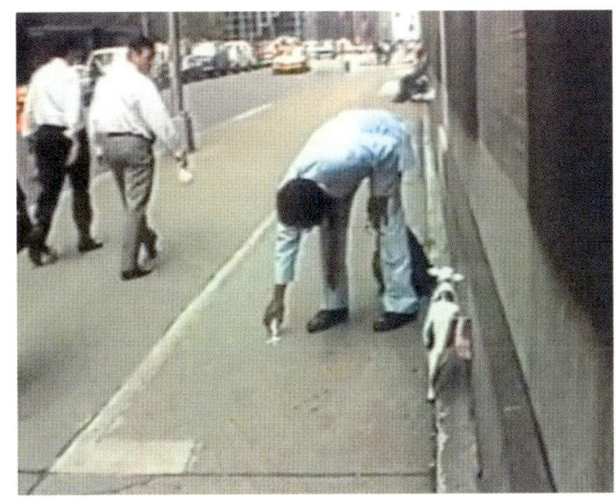

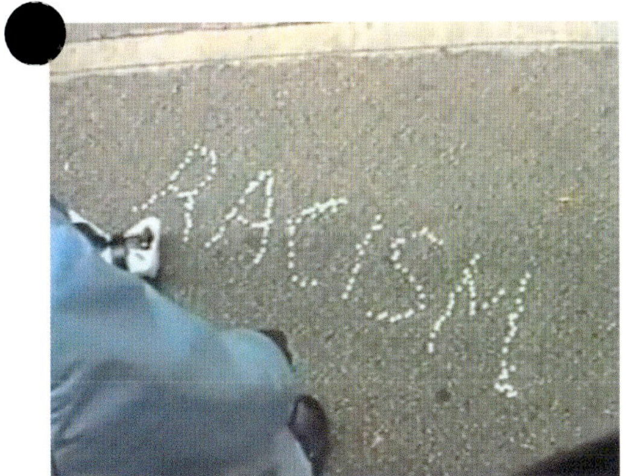
RACISM

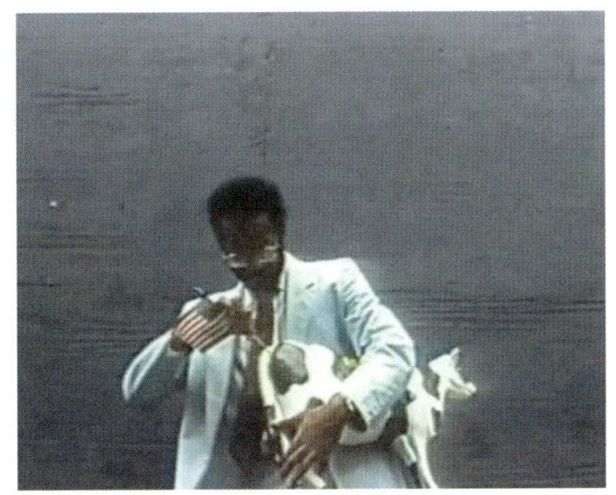

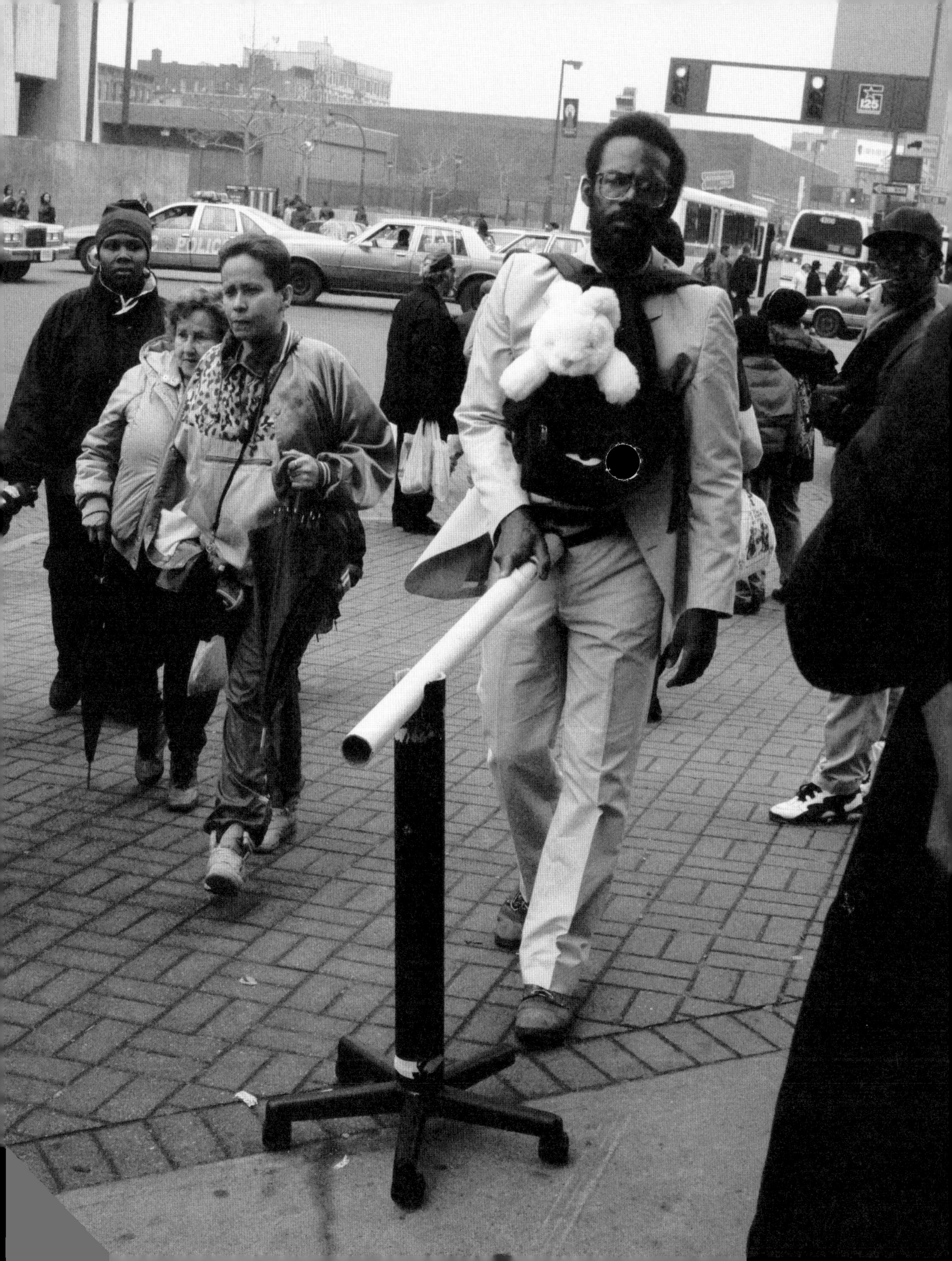

MEMBER A.K.A. SCHLONG JOURNEY
1996

Performance History

Member a.k.a. Schlong Journey. 125th Street, Harlem, New York, March 15, 1996.

POPE.L'S WHITE STUFF

THOMAS J. LAX ON *MEMBER A.K.A. SCHLONG JOURNEY*

On a mid-March day in 1996, Pope.L cruised down 125th Street in Harlem, aka the Mecca of the New Negro. Bearded, he wore a light blue suit, brown dress shoes, and round-framed glasses. He strapped a backpack across his chest in which he positioned a white stuffed animal like a newborn in a Snugli, poking out from a zippered cavity. And the coup de grâce: a long cardboard tube, painted white and harnessed to his midsection. Propped on the rolling base of an office chair, it moved freely, an extension of the artist's body. Occasionally, he interrupted his gait to insert a raw egg into the cylinder and watch it splatter on the sidewalk, or to cover his head with a latex glove that expanded and contracted with each breath. *Show you how the heart goes up and down*, an onlooker commented.

For the most part, the journey was uneventful. The video he later made—edited to three and a half minutes and interspersed with jump cuts, quick loops, and slow motion—is a mundane soundscape of black life. We hear a djembe drum circle in the distance, Ghostface Killah's "Winter Warz" (1996) playing from a boombox, and a car alarm sporadically going off, drowned out by screaming children and street traffic. A few passersby laugh and stare. Some inquired about what he was doing; others imitated his actions. One young man performed for the camera, the way people do for the local evening news. But for the most part, spectators paid Pope.L and his protrusion little mind: he was just another character on a street teeming with things to look at.

The work *Member a.k.a. Schlong Journey* (1996) met with a more emphatic reaction in the U.S. Congress, however, after a Maine newspaper detailing Pope.L's plan for his performance was faxed to the National Endowment for the Arts in Washington.[1] The apoplexy the rumor caused echoed the famous thwarting of the 1989 retrospective of Robert Mapplethorpe, who had himself pictured a black man's protruding penis in *Man in Polyester Suit* (1980). As many critics at the time noted, the fantasy of the big black dick has long been a disavowal of its obverse: whiteness's brutalizing force in the everyday lives of nonwhite people.[2] It was this power that Pope.L scrambled on his stroll, his admixture of an ambling black vagrant, a suited African-American professional, and a surveilling white cop an explicit commentary on "the supremacy of the white phallus."[3] Judging from the mostly unfazed Harlem onlookers at his performance, it seems that news of this condition was far less noteworthy for them than for the overwhelmingly white members of Congress.

Throughout Pope.L's work, whiteness has served as a binding agent, tethering aspects of culture that are intimately entangled yet often imagined to be separate. In *Member*, for example, the plush white rabbit in the handmade baby carrier and the raw eggs tie female fecundity to the hypermasculinity invoked by the rooster-comb glove and white schlong, an incongruous biomorphology at once sci-fi, lo-fi, and true to gender's unruliness. His Skin Set works on paper (1998–) also evoke white things in the form of declarations such as "White people are . . . ," "Black people are . . . ," "Green people are . . . ," so that variously shaded types are tagged with descriptions that slide between on-the-nose critiques and absurdist allusions. White people are described as kin (MUM, MY FAMILY, MY FATHER, MY SON); fragments (PARTS, THE BREAKING OF EVERYDAY THINGS); and memories of historical catastrophe (HOI VOC, VIETNAM 1965; THE FINAL SOLUTION; THE SMOKE FROM THE RUINS). That Pope.L uses white correction fluid—i.e. Wite-Out—in these drawings to create an impastoed surface emphasizes the visceral way in which language can name the disordering effects of race, imaging the disequilibrium experienced at the body's surface as an act of overwriting. These material passages, like his linguistic descriptors, conjoin nonsense with matters of fact, evoking objects from the real world but messing with them to the point of abstraction.

One signal precedent for Pope.L's conjunction of realism and abstraction are the paintings of Robert

Ryman. Pope.L has described Ryman as his "nemesis"—an epithet with an Oedipal panache structured by rejection and identification. On first glance, he and Pope.L don't share much except for a mutual interest in white, the pigments Ryman returned to across a six-decade career. But Pope.L is serious about the relation: "It almost seems that Ryman acts in my art-life as an absent father. Stern and unpredictable. Showing up with gifts unannounced. The gifts always too big or too small. A tee-totaled drunk on absence. A king of something that's a fantasy to the son but even more so to the father."[4] Competing mythologies can also produce affiliation. Ryman's expressive yet nearly mechanical sense of gesture rhymes with *Member*'s step-by-step procession. If Ryman's white rectangles were imagined to encourage a viewer's numinous perception of light or her contemplative relationship to the surrounding architecture, Pope.L's white stuff in *Member* might also be understood as simply drawing attention to what was already there: the scintillating presence of black people making their way down the street.

Since the 1960s, various artists have explicitly sent up the white phallus and its equation with creative genius.[5] In queer Canadian collective General Idea's 1969–70 film *God Is My Gigolo*, a large toy penis is discovered by a group of "natives" who celebrate the artistic license the fetish object offers them. For Scott Burton's 1970s performances, he wore splattered pants decorated with a long white dildo to mock the machismo he associated with Carl Andre's *Lever* (1966), 137 white firebricks set in a long line. In a well-known *Artforum* ad for a 1974 gallery show, Lynda Benglis also satirized Minimalism's masculinism, parodying its equivalence with plentitude and commercial success by posing cockily (shoulders back, mouth agape) and nude, except for white cat-eye sunglasses and a white, double-ended dildo. In Paul McCarthy's 1987 *Family Tyranny (Modeling and Molding)*, the contemporary artist guild is portrayed as a scene of father-son incest where, as in Pope.L's work, inanimate white shafts—a funnel, cooking spoon, and baseball bat—allow food to be substituted for pigments and collaborators to stand in for malleable materials. Together these artists offer spectacular and abject precedents for Pope.L's pageant of white manhood.

Now, seventy-some blocks away from the City of Refuge where it premiered, *Member* enters the ivory-toned holdings of The Museum of Modern Art, finding itself in the company of the white phalluses of yore. Will member-ship in the *patriarcat* offer the cover of profundity, severity, and spirit guaranteed other artworks in its care despite (or because of) his debased black materials? Can a son, dispossessed and dis-membered, still be protected by his white fathers, offering them another history, a different future, a way out? What can be re-membered from the 1996 stroll—by the two young boys, for example, who played around by ducking under Pope.L's appendage—during which he was just one of several people acting extra on a spring day? For an artist who has used wordplay as a second skin, taking his long white member for a walk is just another loop in his slippery knot.

1. Philip Kennicott, "William Pope.L Stands Up for His Art, Even When He's Crawling," *Washington Post*, January 6, 2002. **2.** See Kobena Mercer, "Skin Head Sex Thing: Racial Difference and the Homoerotic Imagination," in *Welcome to the Jungle: New Positions in Black Cultural Studies* (New York: Routledge, 1994), and Thelma Golden, "My Brother," in *Black Male: Representations of Masculinity in Contemporary American Art* (New York: Whitney Museum of American Art, 1994). **3.** Robin Pogrebin, "Arts Agency Delays Decision on Two Grants," *New York Times*, December 1, 2001, 15 and 20. Pope.L has further described *Member* as "a piece about trying to own whiteness, male whiteness." See Barbara Pollack, "Superman Enters the Culture Wars," *Village Voice* 57, no. 2 (January 14, 2002), 47. **4.** Mark H. C. Bessire, "The Friendliest Black Artist in America©," in *William Pope.L: The Friendliest Black Artist in America©*, ed. Bessire (Cambridge, Mass.: MIT Press, 2002), 25. **5.** On the other hand, Pope.L and other artists have also found creative possibility in the big black dick. Pope.L's interest includes his *Egg Eating Contest* (1990), *Quarter Section (Penis)* (2013), and *Syllogism (MIN version)* (1998–2018) and situates him within a genealogy that comprises works such as Adrian Piper's *The Mythic Being* (1973–75), David Hammons's *Untitled/Green Power* (1975), and Robert Colescott's *George Washington Carver Crossing the Delaware: Page from an American History Textbook* (1975).

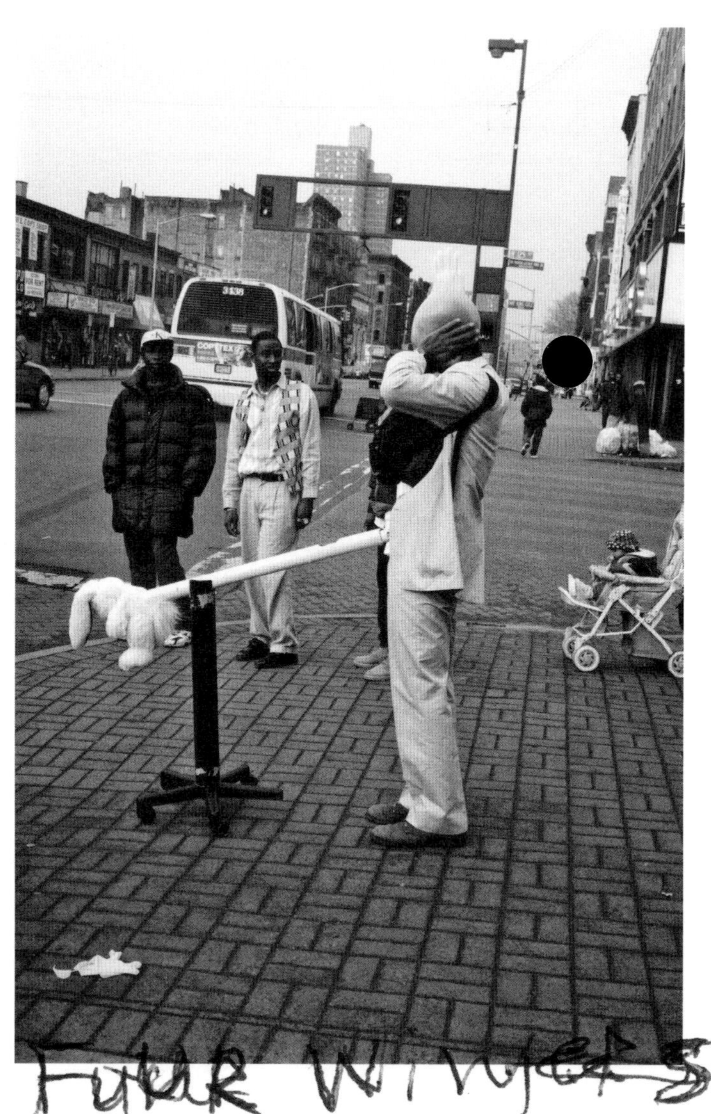

The Four Winters

one summer

Page 88 and this page: *Member a.k.a. Schlong Journey*. 125th Street, Harlem, New York, 1996. Inkjet prints, 15 × 10" (38.1 × 25.4 cm) each.
The Museum of Modern Art, New York

The Four Winters with their

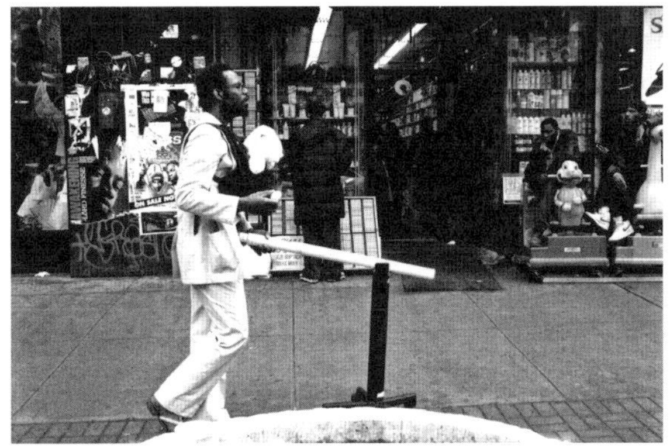

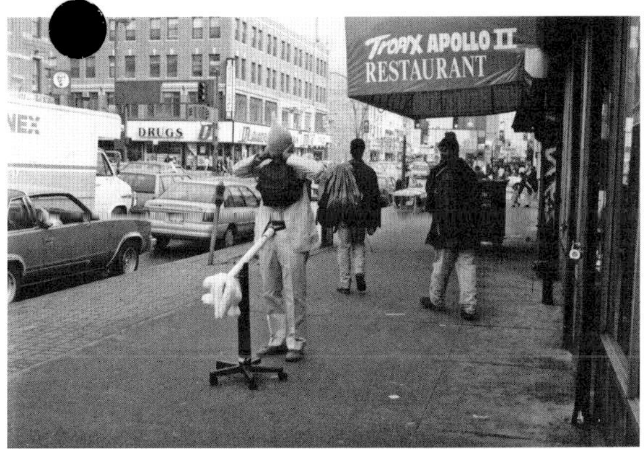

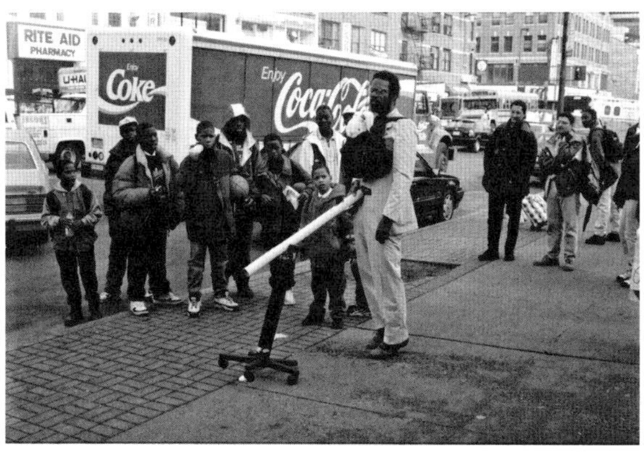

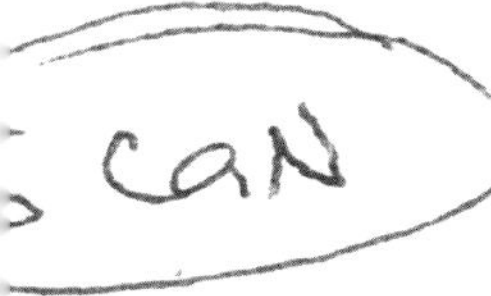

Member a.k.a. Schlong Journey. 125th Street, Harlem, New York, 1996. Inkjet prints, 10 × 15" (25.4 × 38.1 cm) each. The Museum of Modern Art, New York

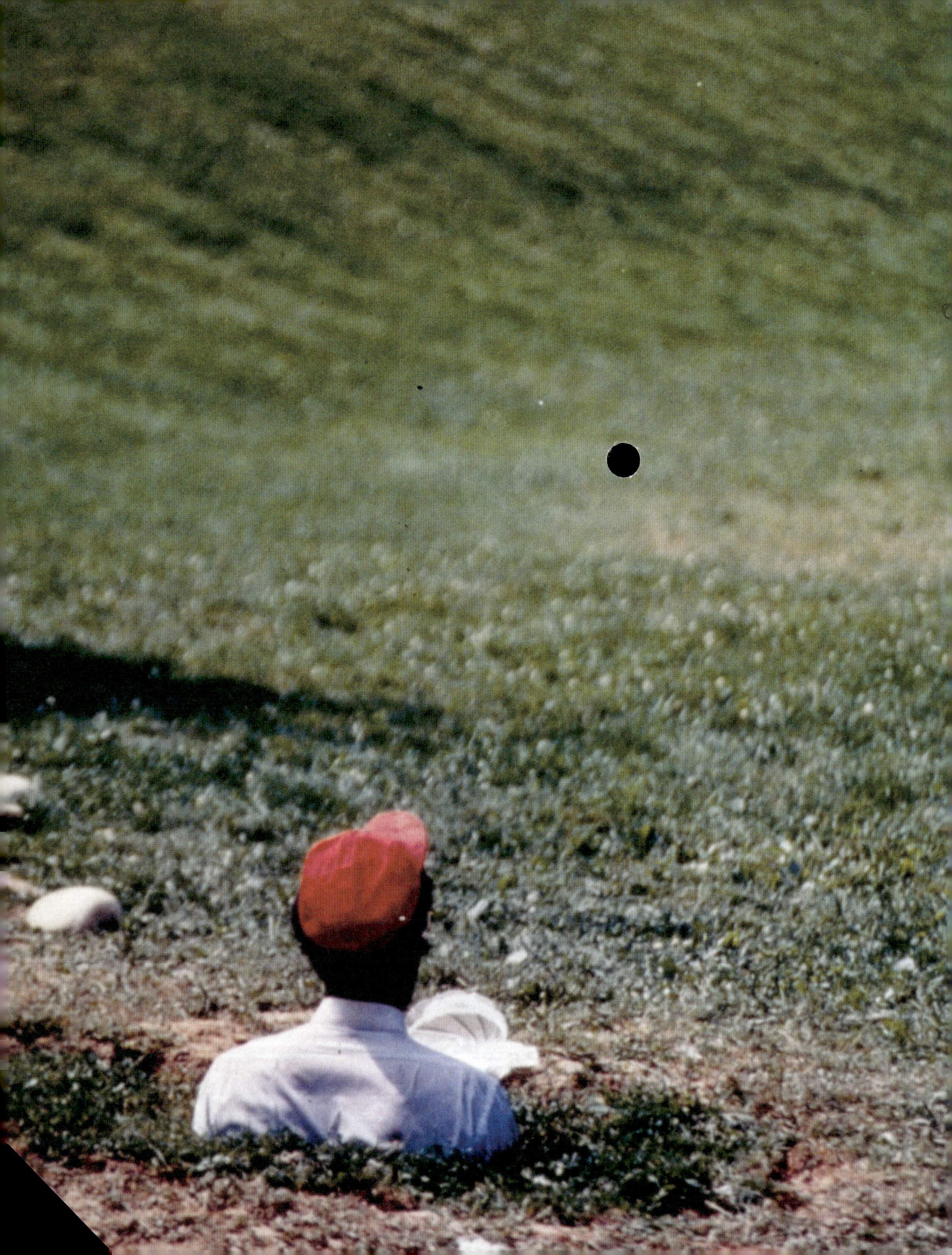

SWEET DESIRE A.K.A. BURIAL PIECE
1996–97

Performance History

Sweet Desire a.k.a. Burial Piece. Skowhegan School of Painting and Sculpture, Maine, August 1996.

Sweet Desire a.k.a. Burial Piece. Maine Arts Festival, Thomas Point Beach, Brunswick, July 1997.

HUMAN WITH A CAPITAL *B*

EJ HILL ON *SWEET DESIRE A.K.A. BURIAL PIECE*

When a seed is buried in the ground, the conditions necessary for it to sprout, grow, and survive depend on the needs of that particular plant. A hibiscus, with its own requisites for lushness, will not perform well in the bone-dry home of the cactus. The lily's and the ivy's success hinges on how staunch their climb toward or away from light. Proliferation—or at the very least, sustenance—is not promised under all suns. Though the same could be said of *us*, history has proved that even under the most dire of conditions, we have continued to bloom in spite of it all. Imagine the fruit we would yield if this land was truly made for us.

I am writing in 2019 America, where the political and cultural landscape is as fraught as it has always been. Sure, it can be argued that the current threats to our bodies are not as serious as they once were, as we have made much progress over the years, but I cannot attest to that. These are the times that I live in. And these times feel as lethal as ever.

If I had to guess, I would say that I have been asked to write about Pope.L's *Sweet Desire a.k.a. Burial Piece* because of my own relationship to Blackness, pain, struggle, and monumental feats of endurance within the context of performance art. Over the years, I have dragged, shaved, confined myself; licked walls, hung from ladders and scaffolding, pressed myself onto floors and against other bodies, jumped, and stood for hours on end to the point of literal sweat, tears, and yes, even blood within my own work. The question I am often asked is "Why do you do this to yourself?"

For almost two weeks during the summer of 2015, I did not leave my apartment out of crippling fear that I would be murdered. This was shortly after the highly publicized deaths of Sandra Bland, Freddie Gray, and Walter Scott. The year before that, it was Michael Brown, Eric Garner, and Tamir Rice. And in 2016, it would be Philando Castile and Alton Sterling. Black death spectacle was inundating contemporary visual culture in a way that I had not experienced in my lifetime. I was familiar with the lynching postcards of the early twentieth century, but I believed (perhaps naively) that it could never be that bad again. This terror, absolutely unwarranted, is buried deep within these soils. These lands hold our darkest bequests.

The relationship between our bodies and this land is not lost on someone like Pope.L, whose signature Crawl works anchor him sweating and purposeful onto the very grounds upon which our ancestors toiled.

In August 1996, Pope.L performed *Sweet Desire a.k.a. Burial Piece* for the first time while at Skowhegan School of Painting and Sculpture in Maine. He stood in a rectangular hole that had been dug in the ground while a team of assistants (presumably fellow residents) refilled it with the soil that had been extracted. They buried him up to his shoulders, rendering him completely immobile from the neck down. The area immediately surrounding his body was then laid with squares of fresh sod in order to, I imagine, provide visual continuity with the rest of the lawned area. He wore a neatly pressed, white collared dress shirt, a red logoless cap, and a red tie that lay aboveground, draped casually away from his chest. Finally, a glass bowl of white ice cream with a red-handled spoon was placed on the ground atop a white doily about twelve inches from his face. Here he stood, paralyzed in the earth, unshaded from the hot sun, as the ice cream melted before him. Beads of sweat dripped from his forehead onto his chin and his shirt. He remained in the ground for eight hours before being dug out. At some point during all of this, the artist Jacob Lawrence, then nearly eighty years old, stood witness to the performance, cane in hand and hovering closely to Pope.L as if guarding him—tending, quite knowingly, to the sprout.

One year after the original performance, Pope.L performed a second iteration of *Sweet Desire* at the Maine Arts Festival in the town of Brunswick, where he was buried in sand rather than dirt. The intended duration of this version was twelve hours; due to severe pressure on his spine and legs, however, he was dug out and pulled from the ground after only four. Pope.L was then rushed to the hospital and treated for dehydration and constricted blood vessels in his legs.

There are the obvious associations with death for *Sweet Desire*, but I also think of the promise of life—one that is intertwined with an endless chain of desires. As Pope.L has noted, bodies do stuff. But above all, bodies desire. Plainly put, desire is concerned with ownership—or at least, the prospect of it. Once a coveted object is attained, it is no longer desired; it is consumed. Desire only exists in the tension between the one that wants and the one that is wanted. Pope.L's interest in "lack" or "have-notness" is illustrated here in his perceived want for the ice cream, as well as in his inability to attain it. But desires are temporary, ultimately put to rest by the acquisition of what is desired or shunted by the appearance of another, more seductive something that comes along to distract from what attracted us in the first place. A newer, shinier, version. Out with the old and in with the same ol' shit we've been watching reformat itself in an attempt to siren-sing us into placation. The eternal carrot dangle. The illusion appears to be that if we can get close enough to it, then we can have it. But this tension that exists within the space between Pope.L and the ice cream is not a one-way street. Ice cream is designed to be eaten hurriedly before it changes form, before it melts and curdles, thus rendering it in fact undesirable. It *wants* to be consumed. Whether or not Pope.L wants to eat the ice cream is irrelevant. He doesn't, because he can't.

The video documentation for the August 1996 performance of *Burial Piece* is edited without sound and intercut several times with queries in all lower-case black text on a white background:

> *what do black people want?*
> *who do they want it from?*
> *why do they want it?*

I've mused on these questions for a while now, and I think I have finally come up with answers that speak to our desire—our need, rather—to mine the deepest parts of ourselves, exhume the heaviest loads, and share them alongside our most valuable treasures:

> We want to live, unobstructed.
> We want it from everyone.
> Because it is necessarily, without question, the sweetest and most human thing we can do.

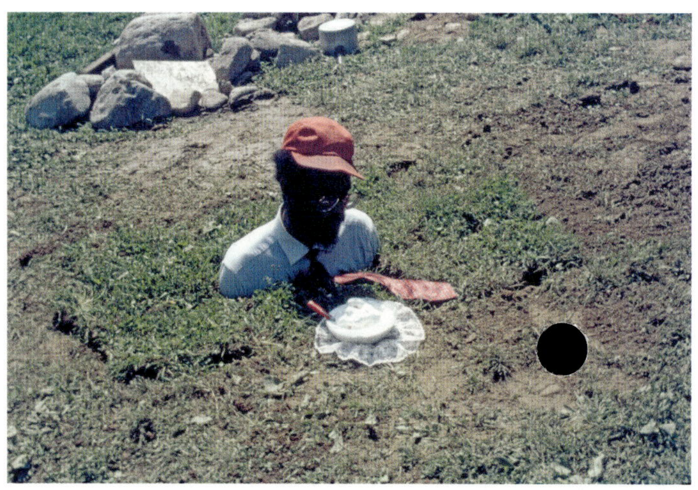

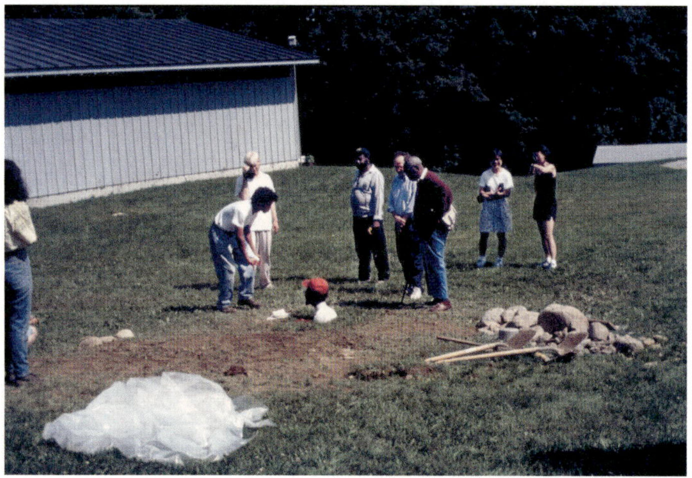

Page 94 and this spread: *Sweet Desire a.k.a. Burial Piece.* Skowhegan School of Painting and Sculpture, Maine, 1996. Inkjet prints, 10 × 15" (25.4 × 38.1 cm) and 15 × 10" (38.1 × 25.4 cm). The Museum of Modern Art, New York

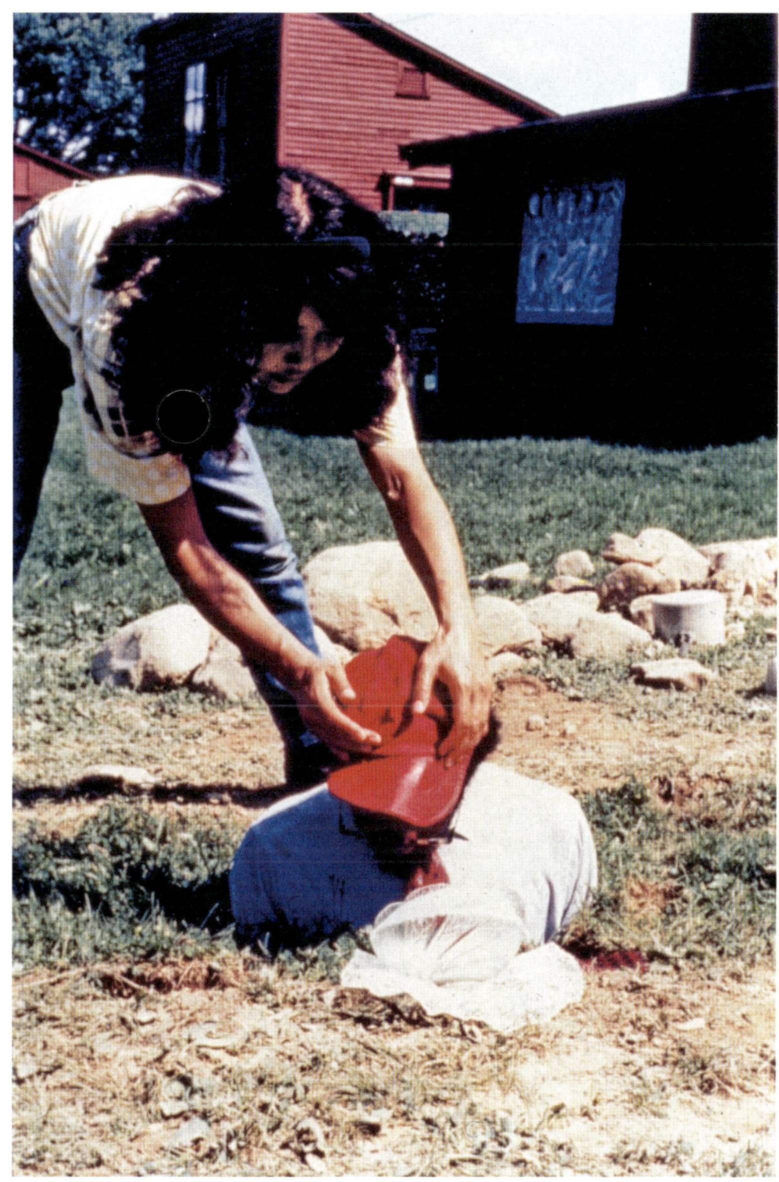

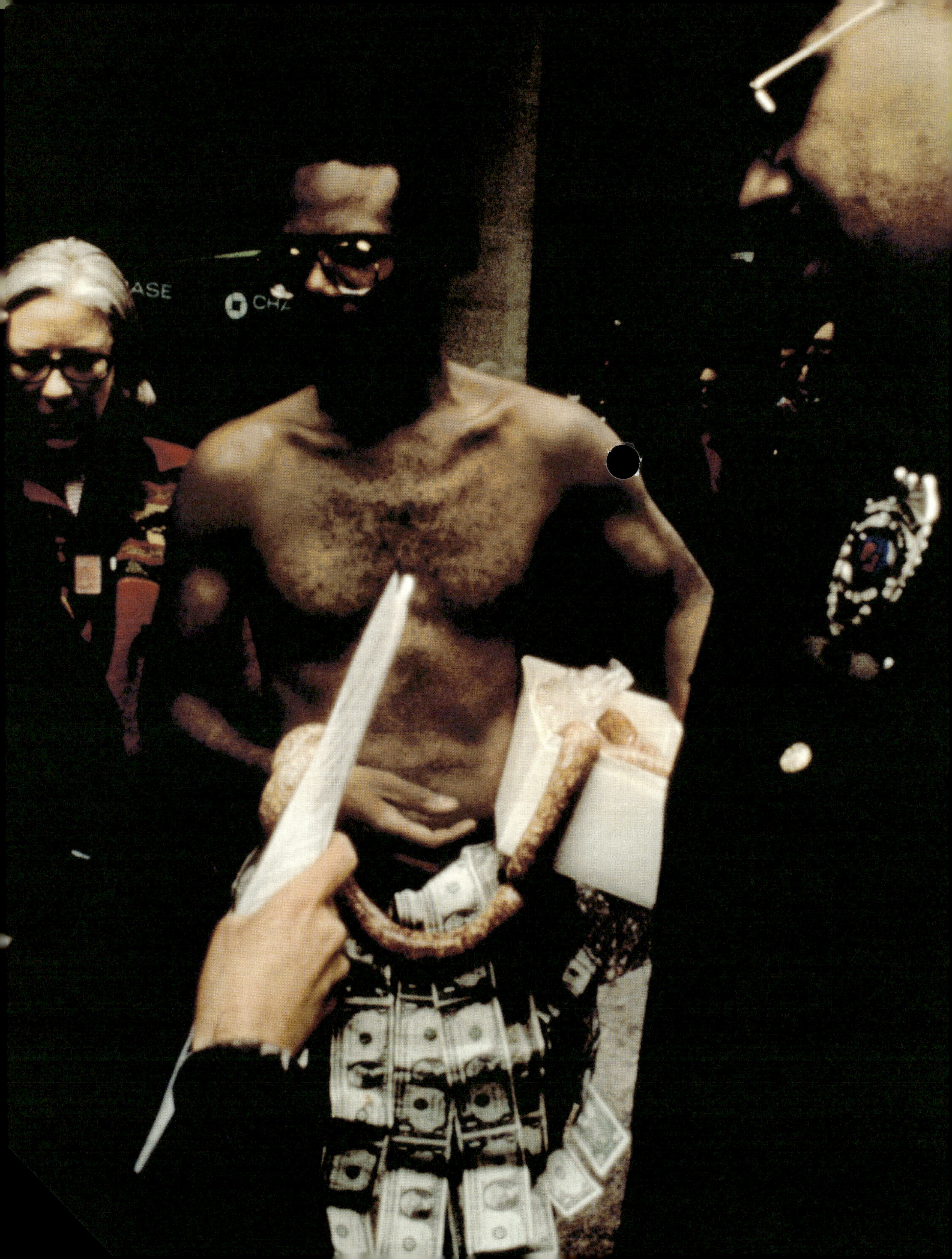

ATM PIECE
1997

Performance History

ATM Piece. Chase Manhattan Bank, Forty-Second Street, New York, February 19, 1997.

GIVING IT AWAY

CYNTHIA CARR ON *ATM PIECE*

Pope.L conceived of *ATM Piece* as "an attempt to bring fresh discomfort to an age old problem," he said in its press release—the relationship between haves and have-nots. He would chain himself to the door of a Chase 24-Hour Banking Center across the street from Grand Central Station while wearing a skirt made of money. He would position himself as street people often do, opening the door for those entering to use a cash machine. But instead of panhandling, he would tear the dollar bills from his skirt and give them away.

That was the plan, at least. He'd been ruminating on it for a couple of years by the time he carried it out on February 19, 1997.

Most of the artist's street performances are about the vulnerable black male body and what Pope.L describes as "lack," a sense of insufficiency and damage. His work combines identity politics with abjection in uniquely discomfiting ways. In his Crawls, his ingestions of newsprint, and his perambulating roach motels, he evokes what racism feels like: the anxiety, humiliation, and dyspepsia. *ATM Piece* would draw more on the other constant in Pope.L's work—his absurdist humor.

Like the Crawls, *ATM Piece* would also be very personal. "My family members have been on the street," he told me a couple of days beforehand. "I know there are white folks out there too, but mostly I see darker-skinned people. That really bothers me. It's like it enters your house. Sometimes I look at someone on the street and I wonder, Is that someone I know?" He considered the piece an act of civil disobedience aimed at a particular new law. Under New York Mayor Rudolph Giuliani's "quality of life" regime, panhandlers could not stand within ten feet of an ATM. Would the law apply to someone who was "reverse panhandling"? He had no idea.

But Pope.L knew he'd probably pick up some collaborators during *ATM Piece*, and he figured they'd be cops. What he'd observed about the police during other street performances was that they didn't intervene "if you just keep moving." This time he'd be stationary, and, as he put it, "It'll be a problem for them—being next to someone's property and not matching the property in terms of foreground and background." He'd be shirtless in February, wearing hiking boots and what he described as a "hula skirt" made of cash, the dollars sewn so they'd be easy to detach.

He had pondered every aspect of this little piece, from costume to the possibility of arrest. A man in a skirt is a man determined to challenge the status quo, and Pope.L likes to address gender expectations. In his multiversion monologue *Eracism* (1992–2002), for example, he sometimes wore a skirt, explaining to the audience: "People think if they know what's under your skirt, they know how your mind works." In case he went to jail, he would have a friend nearby holding bail money. He had consulted a lawyer and even considered asking the bank for permission. Briefly. "I didn't want the bank to be able to present a case. A too-ready response," he said. "I wanted them to deal with it as it was." His appearance would be an insult to the bank's image, but he wasn't going to modify his look. He decided, however, "I can modify how I attach myself to their property. I *did* modify that."

He would be using a material other than metal. "I'm not going to say now what it is," he chuckled when we spoke. "But I think it will reduce their feeling that I'm impinging on their property in some quote terrorist sense."

So a few days later, at the appointed hour of noon, I watched Pope.L walk to the door of the banking center, where he quickly removed his pullover and jean shorts to reveal the skirt circling his waist, three dollar bills long. From a plastic bag, he withdrew his nonthreatening chain: an eight-foot length of Italian sausages.

This would be the shortest performance of his career. In the video documentation of the work, he finishes tying the slippery sausage at 0:23 and the first security guard gets to him at 1:12.

At that point, the artist was standing there expectantly, holding the first dollar to hand to someone, but no customer approached. Instead everyone stood in an arc as if waiting for Pope.L to burst into song. The guard can be heard on the tape saying, "I got an EDP over here." (That's police jargon for "emotionally disturbed person.") At 1:35, Pope.L offers that guard the dollar, but he demurred, hands out. Freeze frame. It was over.

Not included in the video documentation is the security guard's deadpan radio call: "We have a black male tied to the door with sausage links." Four policemen materialized almost instantly. Pope.L untied his sausage chain, and the security guard talked into his walkie-talkie again: "He is being dispersed. He is being dispersed right now."

One of the policemen spoke to Pope.L: "We've got pedestrian traffic here. They'll walk in the street. It's unsafe. Okeydokey?"

Then he wanted to know what it all meant. A protest? I couldn't hear what Pope.L told him, but the cop replied, "OK. OK. Gotcha. Have a good day."

Untethered and standing a little away from the door, the artist began to hand out the eighty or so dollars that made up the skirt. "He's giving out money!" yelled a kid. From young black men to old white ladies, folks darted for the green. Within about thirty seconds, Pope.L was standing there, sans culottes, in his blue denim shorts. He looked slightly shell-shocked.

"Clear the sidewalk!" a cop screamed. When I approached, the artist mused, "The people taking the money looked like they needed it."

The next day on the phone, Pope.L seemed disappointed. When your work comes out of the fantasy that you can make things better, he told me, you risk having your fantasy erode when the piece doesn't work. Yet I didn't think the piece had failed. I think that, just briefly, "fresh discomfort" had been achieved on Forty-Second Street.

Unless otherwise noted, all quotes from the artist: interview with the author, New York, February 17, 1997.

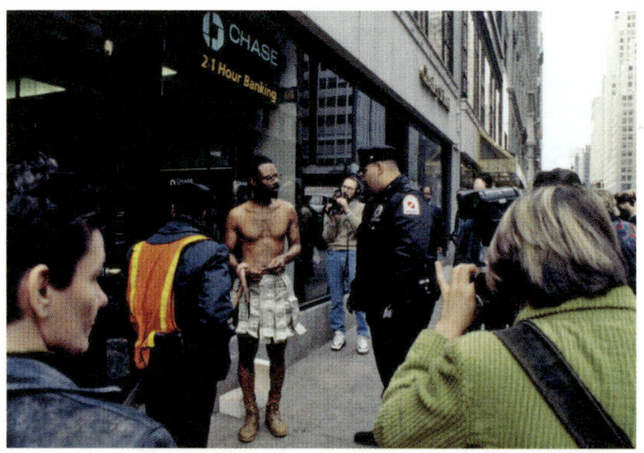

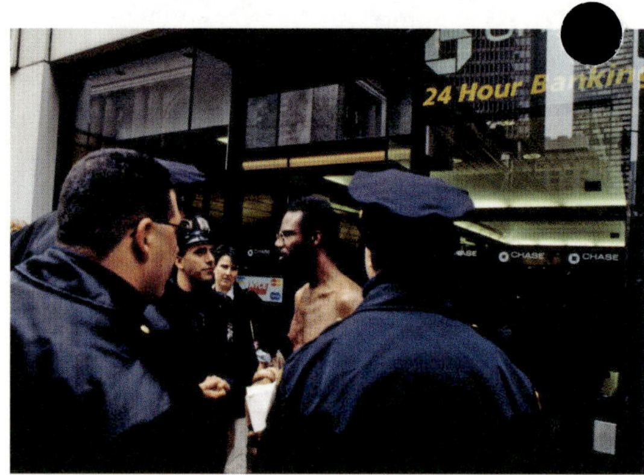

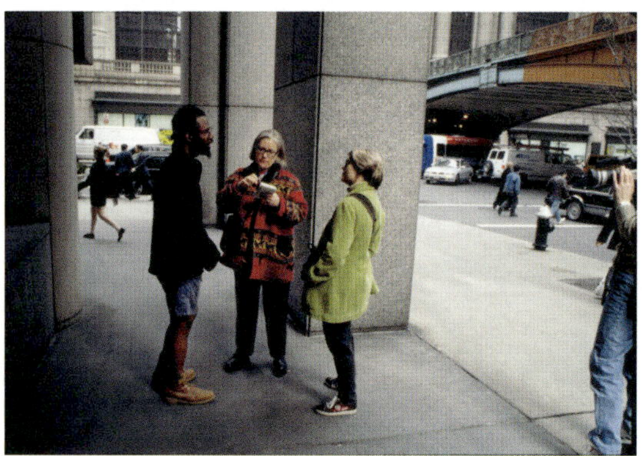

Page 100 and this page: *ATM Piece*. Chase Manhattan Bank, Forty-Second Street, New York, 1997. Inkjet prints, 15 × 10" (38.1 × 25.4 cm) and 10 × 15" (25.4 × 38.1 cm). The Museum of Modern Art, New York

William Pope.L NEWS RELEASE
102 Nichols Street, Apt. 2, Lewiston, ME 04240 • 207-786-6378

February 1, 1997
FOR IMMEDIATE RELEASE CONTACT: WILLIAM POPE.L
(207)786-6378

THEATRE/PERFORMANCE ART LISTINGS

'ATM' PIECE

a street performance work
WILLIAM POPE.L
FEBRUARY 19, 1997

What: William Pope.L will chain himself to the door of an **ATM** wearing a skirt made of money. As people enter the **ATM** he will remove bits of the skirt and hand it to them.

'ATM' PIECE is an attempt to bring fresh discomfort to an age old problem: *The haves* and *the have not* and what they have to do with each other.

Where: The **ATM** entrance of Chase Bank on 42nd Street and Vanderbilt Place (across from the southwest corner of Grand Central Station).

Who: **William Pope.L**, performance artist, worker, teacher.

When: **February 19, 1997, 12 noon.**

Admission: **Free.**

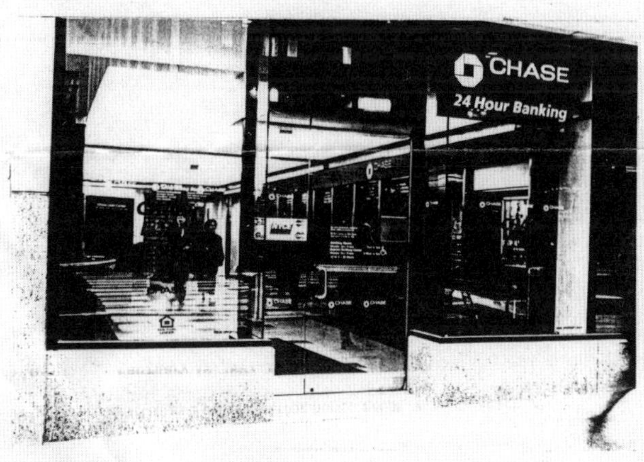

Press release for *ATM Piece*. 1997. Fales Library and Special Collections, New York University. Martha Wilson Papers

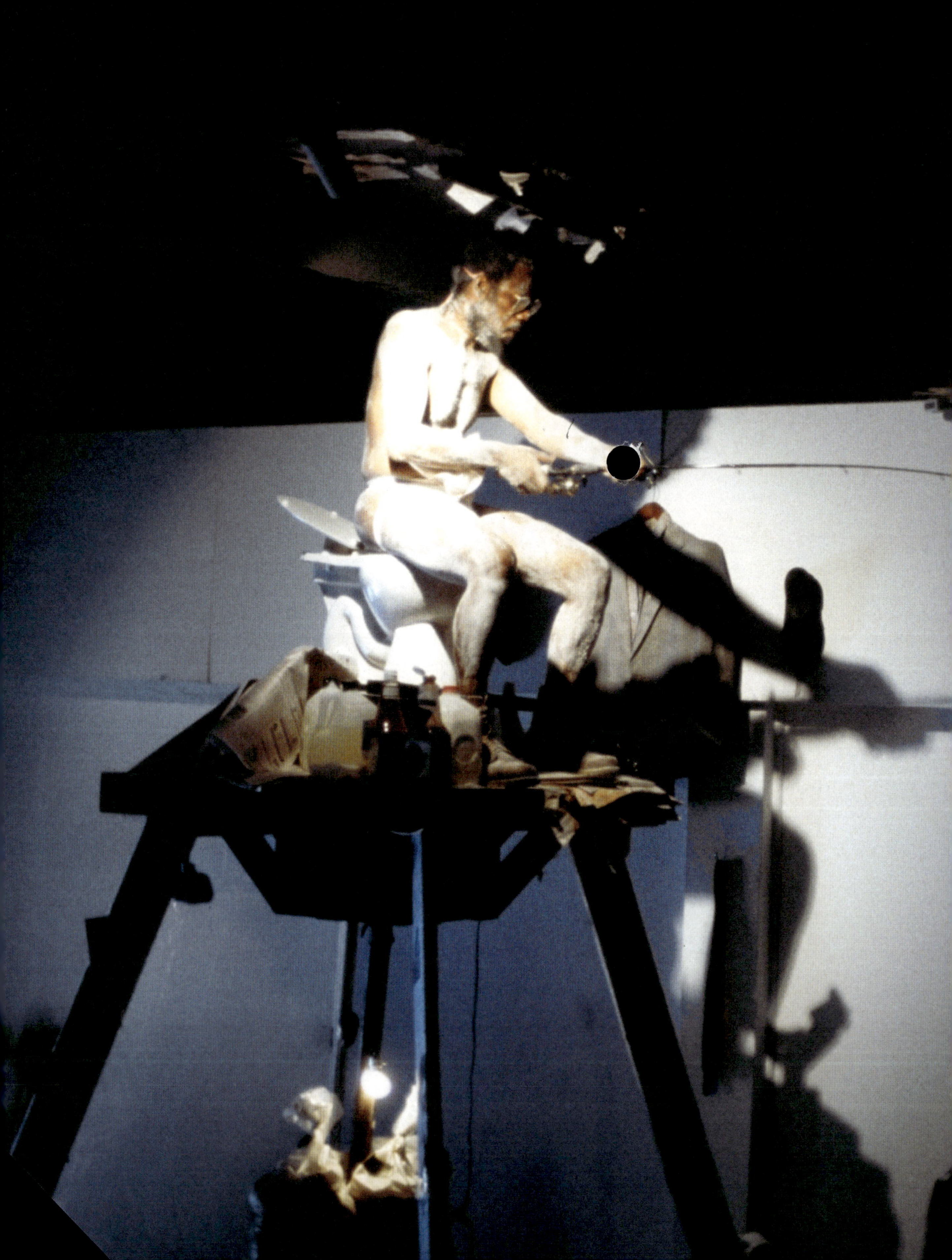

EATING THE WALL STREET JOURNAL
1991–2020

Performance History

Eating the Wall Street Journal, early street version. Part of *How Much Is That Nigger in the Window*. New York, July 1991.

Eating the Wall Street Journal, Version 2. Boston. Organized by Mobius Experimental Theater Space, January 15, 2000.

Eating the Wall Street Journal, Version 3. Sculpture Center, New York, June 22–24 and July 15, 2000.

Eating the Wall Street Journal, new millennium version. New Museum, New York. Part of the exhibition *The Last Newspaper*, New Museum, October 6, 2010–January 9, 2011.

Eating the Wall Street Journal, flag version. The Museum of Modern Art, New York, November and December 2019 and January 2020. Part of the exhibition *member: Pope.L, 1978–2001*, The Museum of Modern Art, October 21, 2019–February 1, 2020.

CANONIZING THE CANNIBAL

VALERIE CASSEL OLIVER ON *EATING THE WALL STREET JOURNAL*

"Our consumer society promises power and wealth simply by owning certain objects," Mr. Pope.L said, "which harks back to primitive magic and voodoo. I figured if I also eat it, just imagine how much power I can drain from this fetishized object!"
—Michael Rush, "Performance Hops Back into the Scene," 2000[1]

Pope.L's performance actions can best be described as existential spectacles of absurd anxiety. His works are arduous; with their physical demands, they feel like relentless assaults on both the artist and those who witness his discomfiting feats. Whether staged in a gallery to engage audiences there or performed in the streets for unsuspecting passersby, Pope.L's works demand to be seen and deeply felt. His telegraphic messages speak to the heart of issues such as mental illness, homelessness, disparaging ideas about blackness and especially black men, and the inequities in our society as they relate to the economic poor. The work is less social elixir than an attempt to dispel the mythology of the other through corporeal engagement. Pope.L places himself on the line in acts of endurance, making the artist's body at once an agent of resistance and an act of defiance. In this way, he gives promise to an awareness of social struggle and the potential for societal catharsis that may one day heal us of the trauma caused by our self-destructive tendencies.

Pope.L's crusade to save humanity is at its core an effort to save himself. Coming of age in the 1960s, the artist was no stranger to the social and political disparities that left an indelible impression on the lives of many in that era. His own upbringing reads like fiction, as the chronology in his 2002 exhibition catalogue *William Pope.L: The Friendliest Black Artist in America©* attests.[2] His presence, his work, even his embodiment of "blackness" have been shaped by myriad encounters over a lifetime. In turn, his works make for challenging encounters, with the artist acting as both provocateur and instigator. Their overt politics are inherent in the demand to be seen—and seen on the artist's terms. It is perhaps for this reason that Pope.L is unapologetic about the intensity of his performances and unfazed by the audience's response to their disturbing aspects. A student of experimental theater and visual art including Fluxus and Neo-Dada, he creates scores for actions as well as producing objects out of said actions. Objects become tools, residuals, or byproducts—as well as autonomous things—as he effortlessly seams together objects born out of action and objects that stage action. This fluidity resonates with the artist's practice of forging into everyday objects and consumables as proxies for race.

Pope.L first staged *Eating the Wall Street Journal* in 1991 on the street in New York as part of his larger ensemble of works *How Much Is That Nigger in the Window*. In the years since—prior to its inclusion in *member* at The Museum of Modern Art—the piece had been reiterated only three times. In the third version, which appeared at Sculpture Center in New York in 2000, the artist created a stage of sorts where, over the course of five days, for three to four hours each day, he engaged audiences from a kind of throne, a four-legged apparatus rising ten feet from the ground holding a makeshift toilet. The platform was also set with several gallons of whole milk and a large bottle of ketchup, a substance that appears frequently in Pope.L's work. The two items are a throwback to his childhood, when milk and condiments were often all that were to be found in the refrigerator and with which he would sustain himself.

And then there is the newspaper. Seated on the toilet, Pope.L cannibalized power from what he deemed a fetish object, the *Wall Street Journal*—not just any daily, examiner, or chronicle but an indicator of wealth and power. At Sculpture Center, the scaffold's base was surrounded by scattered pages and ordered stacks of the paper, there for the artist to consume and expel, as well as by wads of pulp generated by the artist's chewing of them.

In video documentation of the piece, Pope.L enters covered in white flour, signifying the way whiteness obscures his black body. He is nude save for a white jockstrap that not only holds his manhood but also, with its allusion to athletics, prefaces the exertions to come. Mounting a series of precarious steps, the artist reaches the platform, positions himself on the toilet, and begins reading. This act evokes the daily upkeep of one's constitution as well as ritual—Pope.L's own brand of meditative scatology. As minutes turn to hours, he rocks back and forth as far as his seat will allow, creating a sense of rhythm and timing. He reads with great concentration, sealing the "fourth wall" between himself and his voyeurs—until it is necessary to eject what has been ingested. After a period of intense mental consumption of the printed word, he begins the act of physical consumption. Tearing strips from the page, Pope.L inserts the printed matter into his mouth, adding milk or ketchup to aid in creating a pulp. Once chewed, the artist spews the liquid and macerated matter onto the floor in front of the audience below, breaching the fourth wall. We are not privy to what has been consumed, only that it has been, and that now it has been reconstituted by a black man doused in flour sitting atop a toilet high aloft in a room reserved for art. It is here where the absurdity of Pope.L's work intersects with the absurdity of life's realities of disenfranchisement, violence against black bodies, and the inequities that have shaped his life and the lives of others. His act can be seen as a means of opening the wounds of his reality and allowing all the toxic waste to spew from his corporeal self.

Having been made aware of the danger of ingesting bleached paper and chemical-laden ink in the early 1990s, Pope.L has rarely restaged *Eating the Wall Street Journal* and since then has avoided actual swallowing of pulp during it. He performed the piece in two versions in 2000 and then again in 2011 at the New Museum in New York. Now it appears at MoMA. Pope.L's willingness to occasionally re-create the work underscores his determination to bring attention to the fallacies of success, the nauseating effects of financial excess, and the ways that money shapes power. In 2012, Pope.L staged the piece as an installation for the exhibition *Radical Presence: Black Performance in Contemporary Art*, which I organized for the Contemporary Arts Museum Houston.[3] The artist was fastidious in replicating the environment of the performed action, complete with copies of *Wall Street Journal* and containers of ketchup and milk. In that staging, he entered a second order of performance: creating pulp with water, instead of saliva, to set the scene of an immediate aftermath of performing the work. Macerated paper and liquid dotted the walls and the pages from the *Journal* were strewn about the sculpture's base.

In its presentation at The Museum of Modern Art, Pope.L continues in this vein, restaging the performance's environment. Instead of the structure being erected, it will live first disassembled as fragmented relics of action to be re-realized during the course of the exhibition. The curatorial decision to allow the piece to evolve honors the artist's practice while giving viewers insight into how art can be altered to speak to specific moments in time. *Eating the Wall Street Journal* stands as a testament to the artist's understanding of the persistence of financial inequities and its linkages to race and proximity to power. The artist continues to cannibalize that power via proxy. It is fitting that his steadfast intention be celebrated and, as such, canonized.

1. Michael Rush, "Art/Architecture; Performance Hops Back into the Scene," *New York Times*, July 2, 2000, National edition. **2.** See Mark H. C. Bessire, ed., *William Pope.L: The Friendliest Black Artist in America*© (Cambridge, Mass.: MIT Press, 2002). **3.** The exhibition had three additional showings, at the Grey Art Gallery, New York University, and the Studio Museum in Harlem, New York; at the Walker Art Center, Minneapolis; and at Yerba Buena Center for the Arts, San Francisco.

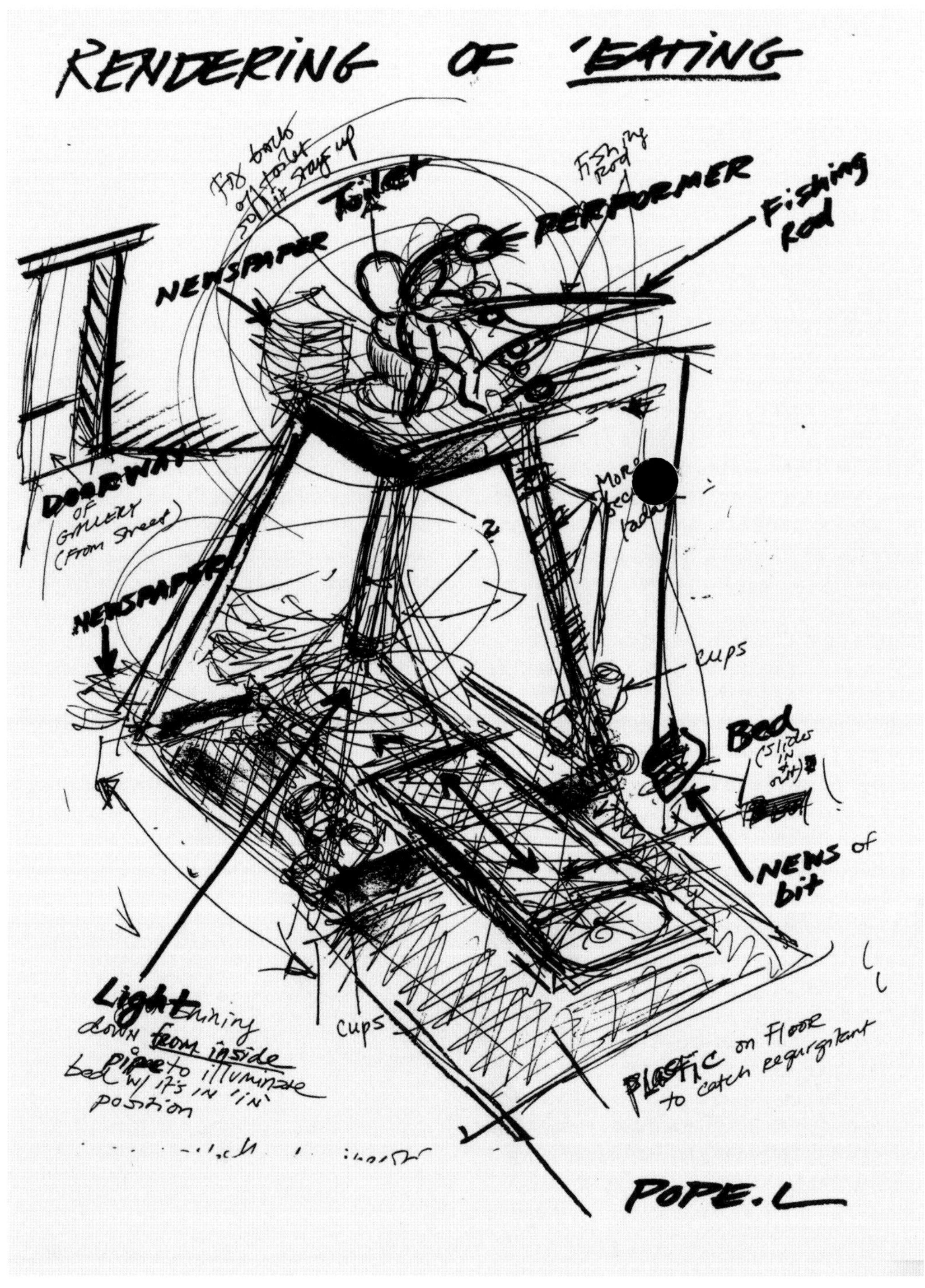

Page 106: *Eating the Wall Street Journal*, Version 3. Sculpture Center, New York, 2000. Inkjet print, 10 × 15" (25.4 × 38.1 cm). The Museum of Modern Art, New York
This page: Sketch for *Eating the Wall Street Journal*. 2000. Ink on paper, 8½ × 11" (21.5 × 27.9 cm). Franklin Furnace Archive, Inc., New York

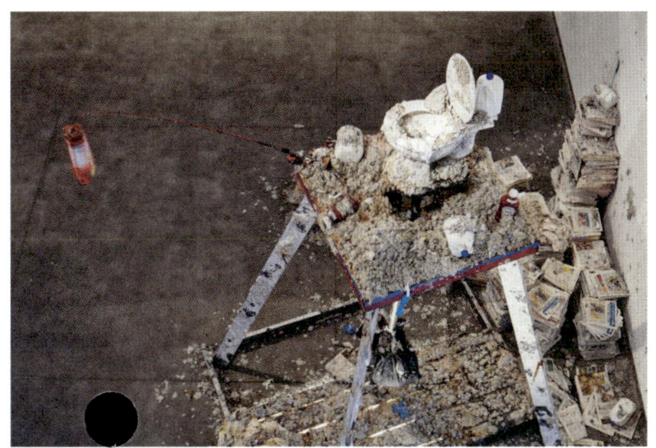

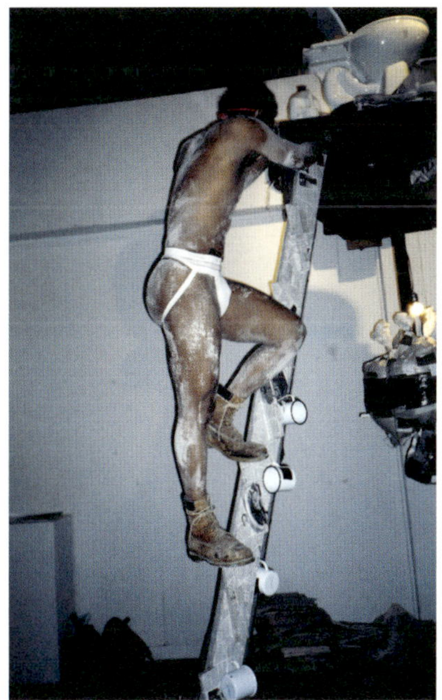

Top: *Eating the Wall Street Journal*. 2000. Wood-and-metal structure, toilet, newspaper, fishing pole, Heinz Ketchup bottles, and milk cartons, dimensions variable. Installation view: *Radical Presence: Black Performance in Contemporary Art*, Yerba Buena Center for the Arts, San Francisco, June 13–October 11, 2015
Bottom: *Eating the Wall Street Journal*, Version 3. Sculpture Center, New York, 2000. Inkjet print, 15 × 10" (38.1 × 25.4 cm). The Museum of Modern Art, New York

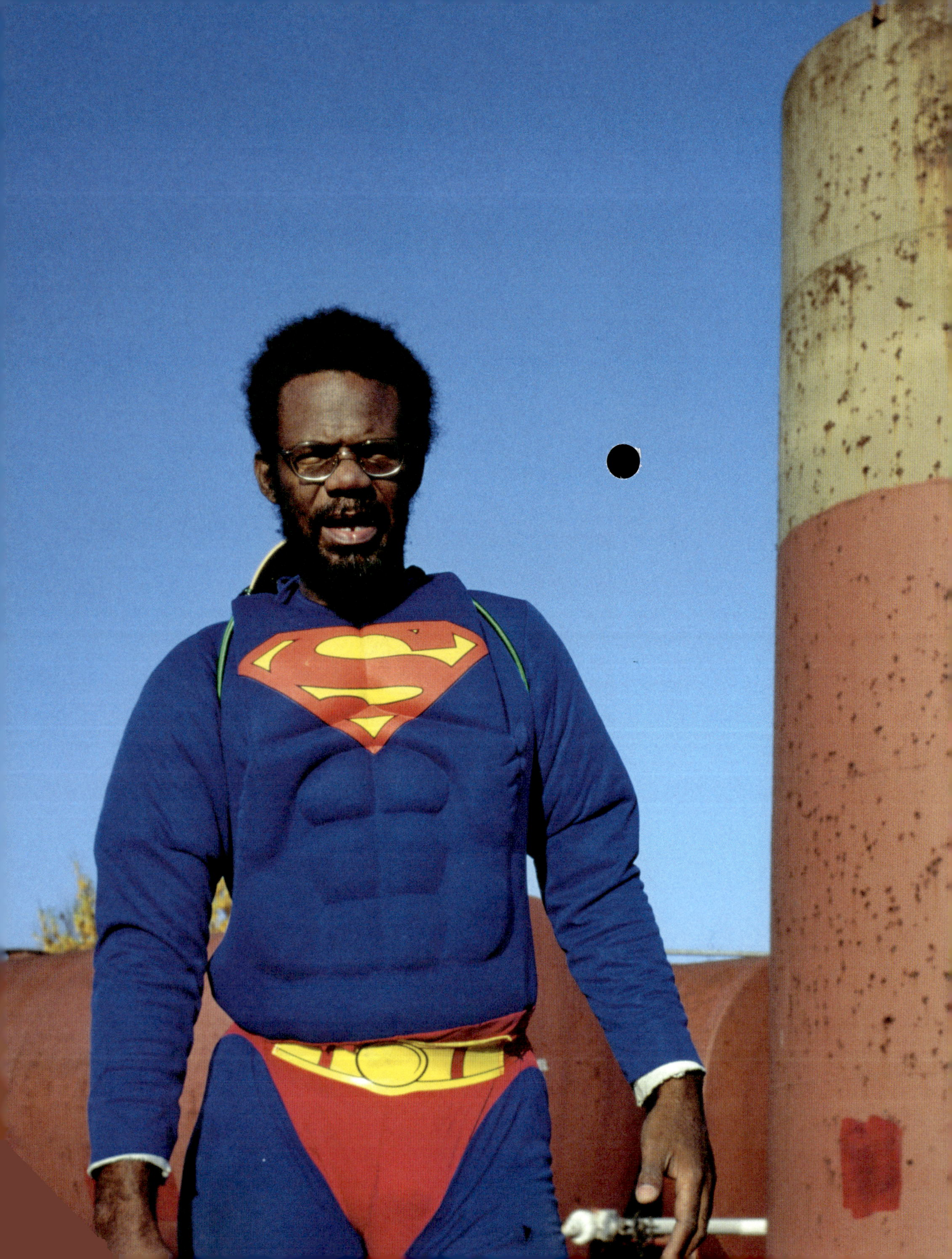

THE GREAT WHITE WAY: 22 MILES, 9 YEARS, 1 STREET 2001–9

Performance History

The Great White Way: 22 miles, 9 years, 1 street. Broadway, New York, 2001–9.

MAKING WAYS

ANDRÉ LEPECKI ON *THE GREAT WHITE WAY: 22 MILES, 9 YEARS, 1 STREET*

I get down on my belly and crawl till I'm reality.
—Pope.L, "Notes on *Crawling Piece a.k.a. How Much Is That Nigger in the Window*," 1991[1]

Since *Times Square Crawl a.k.a. Meditation Square Piece* (1978), Pope.L has engaged in more than thirty individual and collective crawling pieces in different cities across several continents. In 1991, in one of his most iconic Crawls, *Tompkins Square Crawl* (part of the work *How Much Is That Nigger in the Window*), Pope.L donned a brown suit and crawled past Tompkins Square Park in New York's East Village while holding a small flowerpot containing a little yellow flower. Commenting retrospectively on those early works, Pope.L invoked his motivation as a "response to the steady increase of street people occupying the sidewalks of New York City, the community's refusal to recognize this calamity, and my coming to terms with this lifestyle as an ongoing problem within my immediate family."[2]

As his practice of "giving up verticality" progressed,[3] however, the times changed. As Pope.L's own embodied knowledge of crawling evolved, other elements, which were already implicated in the Crawls from the start, became increasingly prominent. Those elements stretch the paradoxes of Pope.L's particular way of crawling to its limits. Already in his 1997 "Notes on *Crawling Piece*," Pope.L outlined one of those crucial paradoxes propelling his practice: "The real question / Lies in the juxtaposition / of destitution and plenitude."[4] To acknowledge this complex and counterintuitive juxtaposition is to reveal the reality informing Pope.L's Crawls: crawling makes way for a mode of being whose full potentiality (plenitude) emerges only after going through the lived experience of existing *in* and *as* absolute lack (destitution). The latter is a condition Pope.L has often associated with blackness. "The black body is a lack worth having,"[5] he told an interviewer shortly after he had embarked on his most epic crawl, *The Great White Way: 22 miles, 9 years, 1 street* (2001–9).

In *The Great White Way*, Pope.L donned a party-store Superman outfit, replaced the superhero's red cape with a red skateboard (with a yellow Superman shield at its center) strapped to his back, and began to crawl in segments of about six city blocks at a time for the entire length of Broadway, New York City's longest and most famous street, from its southernmost tip to its end in the South Bronx. The first installment of *The Great White Way*, from December 2001, began on Liberty Island and was documented in a six-and-a-half-minute video of the same title. The video opens with a shot of the American flag waving in the wind, followed by a close-up of the Statue of Liberty's face. The cameraman pans down the height of the statue, and reveals Pope.L already in the process of crawling, belly against the ground, pulling his body with his elbows, moving painstakingly away from the foot of Lady Liberty with two black mittens protecting his hands from the frost.

Pope.L has barely begun the almost decade-long project before his movement is arrested. Almost immediately as he inches toward the water's edge, two National Park troopers confront him and his cameraman. One of them orders Pope.L to immediately stop what he is doing and "get back to the boat." On the video, we can hear the cameraman, James Pruznick, explaining to that officer that they have a permit to film. "Not for this," the trooper replies. "He can't do this. He has to get back on the boat. He can crawl back to the boat, I don't care, but he has to leave."

Being the "Friendliest Black Artist in America©," Pope.L crawls to board the ferry, but just slowly enough so that the officer's refrain, "He has to get back to the boat," can be reuttered, so as to be relistened to, re-recorded, redocumented, and therefore rewritten, resignified. In this process, a police semantics is revealed, one that articulates that even with a permit, even with proper paperwork, even under the guise of art, on Liberty Island a black man cannot and will not perform an "aberrant movement," to use David Lapoujade's expression.[6] On Liberty Island, no juxtaposition of black destitution and black plenitude, no paradoxical, counterdoxical, "anachoreographic" black movement is to be allowed.[7] A black man's proper place is back on the boat. He may even crawl back to it, as long as he gets back on it.

This incident is more than enough for the artist to extract, for the record, a scene of racial choreopolicing.[8] That's why Pope.L makes his art: to "make things happen," as he once said;[9] to create "discomfort zones," as Cynthia Carr once described his work;[10] and to turn performance not into an object for spectatorship but into the *occasioning of an event*—a disruptor of quotidian habits that makes and unmakes subjects and their freedoms, subjects and their acquiescence, subjects and their movements, subjects and their (counter)powers.

Up the gangway and back on the boat, Pope.L finds a corner on the upper deck, where he remains still, in a semicrouched position, left hand holding the white railings, waves shimmering before him, cresting against the ferry's hull in rapid succession. The camera lingers on Pope.L's back to produce the longest shot of the video. Slowly zooming away, the camera shows us a black body being shipped between two islands, facing the open waters ahead, bobbing up and down according to the rhythms of the Atlantic Ocean as it meets the Hudson River, a rhythm cut only by the ferry's prow slicing the waves and the resulting wake. Why is it that a six-and-a-half-minute video aimed at documenting a twenty-two-mile crawling performance on Broadway's asphalt dedicates a two-minute shot to the artist sitting still, contemplating the water from the deck of a moving boat? And why is it that more than half of the footage revolves around Pope.L crawling in, staying on, and crawling out of a boat?

There is something of the oceanic informing *The Great White Way*. The video suggests a kinetic unconscious of black movement in the wake of the Middle Passage, one where the particular kind of crawling Pope.L executes—with its micromovements of bobbing the body up and down as it inches along—becomes the kinetic echo, the kinesthetic residue, the moving afterlife of oceanic turbulence, the movement *in* and *of* "the wake," to use Christina Sharpe's extraordinary expression and affective-political concept: "and while the wake produces Black death and trauma . . . we, Black people everywhere and anywhere we are, still produce in, into and through the wake an insistence on existing: we insist Black being into the wake."[11] We can transpose Sharpe's analysis of Black "existence in the wake" into this scenario of whiteness and its racial policing arresting black movement and dispatching yet another black body onto a boat. In *The Great White Way* video, just as in Sharpe's analysis of the images of "boat people" around the world, "one of the larger questions that arises from the image is how does one mark someone for a space—the ship—who is already marked by it?"[12]

The Great White Way, both as video and as performance, rechoreographs and resemanticizes the word *crawl*. It regrounds Pope.L's Crawls as black oceanic events. Within the turbulent pull of the wake, to crawl gains a kinetic-political-affective meaning: to insist on surviving and not being dragged into the great white pit. These are Sharpe's and Pope.L's theories of blackness transmogrifying into performance: to realize that living in the wake of the Middle Passage is to discover that American soil is but a bottomless, turbulent whirlpool, always about to drag down and drown those whose lives matter nothing, or close to nothing, to the great white way of power. If Pope.L *crawls* on asphalt, belly on the ground, it is because black life still *swims* in the wake. Thus the task at hand: to painstakingly make way on one's belly until a better, more joyful, and freer ground for living is made a reality.

1. William Pope.L, "Notes on *Crawling Piece a.k.a. How Much Is That Nigger in the Window?* (Summer 1991/Streets of New York City)," *Art Journal* 56, no. 4 (Winter 1997): 66. **2.** Alisia Chase, "Learning to Be Human: An Interview with William Pope.L," *Afterimage* 33, no. 4 (January/February 2006): 21. **3.** C. Carr, "In the Discomfort Zone," in *William Pope.L: The Friendliest Black Artist in America©*, ed. Mark H. C. Bessire (Cambridge, Mass.: MIT Press, 2002), 49. **4.** Pope.L, "Notes on *Crawling Piece a.k.a. How Much Is That Nigger in the Window?*" 65. **5.** Lowery Stokes Sims, "Interview with William Pope.L," in Bessire, *William Pope.L: The Friendliest Black Artist in America©*, 62. **6.** David Lapoujade, *Aberrant Movements: The Philosophy of Gilles Deleuze* (South Pasadena, Calif.: Semiotext[e], 2017), 23. **7.** Stefano Harney and Fred Moten, *The Undercommons: Fugitive Planning and Black Study* (Wivenhoe, UK: Minor Compositions, 2013), 50. **8.** See André Lepecki, "Choreopolice and Choreopolitics: or, The Task of the Dancer," *TDR: The Drama Review* 57, no. 4 (Winter 2013): 13–27. **9.** Sims, "Interview with William Pope.L," 64. **10.** Carr, "In the Discomfort Zone," 48. **11.** Christina Sharpe, *In the Wake: On Blackness and Being* (Durham, N.C.: Duke University Press, 2016), 11. **12.** Ibid., 48.

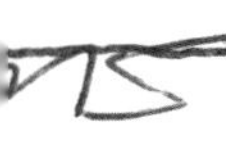

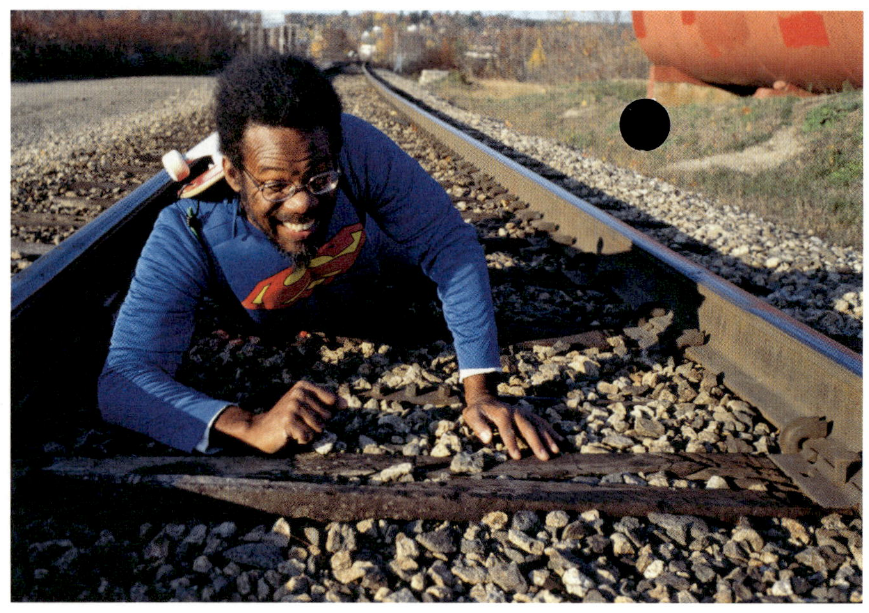

Page 112 and this page: *Training Crawl (for The Great White Way: 22 miles, 5 years, 1 street).* Lewiston, Maine, 2001. Inkjet prints, 10 × 15" (25.4 × 38.1 cm) each. The Museum of Modern Art, New York

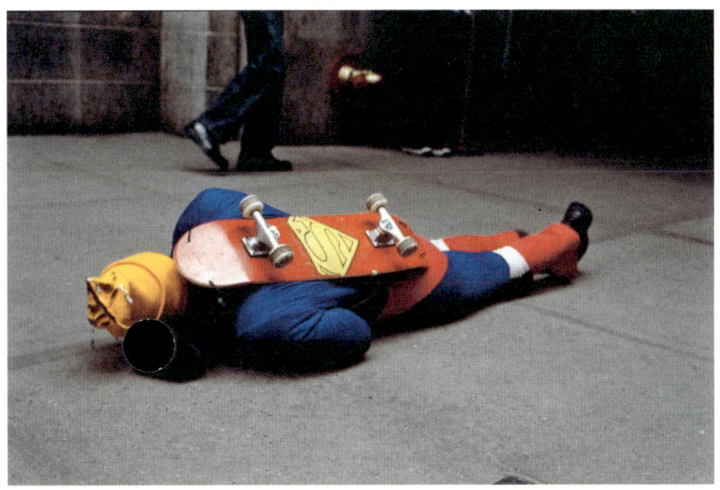

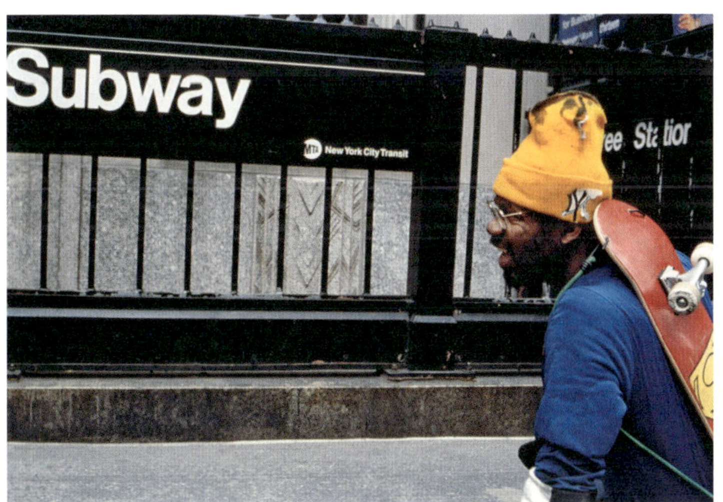

The Great White Way: 22 miles, 9 years, 1 street. Broadway, New York, 2002. Inkjet prints, 10 × 15" (25.4 × 38.1 cm) each. The Museum of Modern Art, New York

SOME QUESTIONS AND OBSERVATIONS FOR POPE.L

From a formerly secret admirer regarding an individual act causing physical discomfort only to the artist/actor and not to inadvertent onlookers

What are you doing?

What injustice are you trying to invoke or redress?

Are you accusing anyone?

Whom do you think you are impersonating? Whose real-life pain? For whose benefit?

Why am I looking? Because you are black? Because I am white? Because of the nasty narrative in which we both live?

The metaphors and questions morph into explicit alarms: You spell RACISM on a public sidewalk with white pills; you squeeze white goo onto your bare nipples. After you have tied yourself to the glass door of a bank, the cop who has been called spreads his hands in refusal of your offer of what looks like a mes[illegible] on a piece of paper.

Am I assuming too much when the thought crosses my mind that you are accusing ME?

In that I am an atheist, how should your Jesus thing affect me? What effect would you like your transcendence and catharsis to have on me?

Do you expect your enactment of deprivation and self-punishment to seduce me?

After all, you are nothing but/if not an artist.

After all, have you imagined that if I read in the *New York Times* tomorrow that you froze to death the previous night and no one came to your aid, THEN would I feel different?

How can an individual act stand for all others?

As an individual artist, do you expect to provide much needed diversion, even entertainment via this “performance”?

As a borderline crazy lawbreaker, are you trying to set yourself up as a sorry reminder of social inequities? It takes courage to do what you have done in teeming outdoor public spaces. Performing in theatrical venues is so much less dangerous and takes less courage—

Moments that stand out for me: your *Snow Crawl* in the Superman outfit in a spectacular winter landscape, ending with your cuddling a gleaming, snow-white cat; crawling around the Statue of Liberty in *The Great White Way;* your conversation in *Eracism* with your white gloved hand—“You’re my hand”; “No, I’m white”—while dressed in a strapless gown.

Do your endurance and abjection justify my attention?

Does my race matter to you?

Do my liberal, so-called progressive politics make a difference to you?

Whom are you addressing? Artists, passersby, racists, academics, gallerists, children, black people, white people, museum curators, guilty liberals, fucking morons, art critics, all the preceding?

Do you expect your self-humiliation and abnegation to create a field for self-reflection in your spectators? Like this one? Or is that irrelevant?

What's in it for me? Or do you care? (I doubt if you're interested in "self-expression.")

From the perspective of someone skeptical of metaphor, does the all-too-real outcome of your three-quarter body-burial stunt—i.e., your hospitalization—bring its meaning home more acutely than the act itself?

What are some personal implications of self-immolation? Sensationalism, exhibitionism, challenge, animosity, anger, pride, alienation, martyrdom?

Again, your act and its relationship to me, also to paraphrase John Cage: "If I can stand it for two minutes, should I try it for four?" Should I try to engage you with any of these questions during your "act," or, if you prefer, hold off and congratulate you afterwards by email?

You may use materials that decay and cause you to smell but you do not cause yourself to bleed, as some of your peers have done. What are your limits? A cleaner's bill? The cost of another suit? A shower?

In planning *Sweet Desire*, did you anticipate the effects on your body beforehand?

During *Sweet Desire*, did you speak to anyone? Did you make sure one or more assistants stayed nearby? Did you fall asleep? What induced you to end the event? Pain? Boredom?

The racial/racist implications of *Sweet Desire* are clear: the confined black man unable to reach the reward of the white ice cream that is available to others more privileged. Why the extended duration that produces such punishment on your body when, say, a series of photos or a ten-minute video might have a comparable effect?

Somewhere in all the enactments and condensations of rage there is room for tenderness, as in *The Aunt Jenny Chronicles*, in which you lament, "I didn't allow myself to like her. . . . Love takes time. . . . Her sexuality scared me. It was so alive, so ancient."

Again: Why the self-immolation risking physical damage (a dancer's question)?

Related: Why must your art cause you physical pain? Does your pain make a difference to the spectator? Is it your challenge to cause revulsion in your audience, or is that just a side effect of the main message? Have you anticipated that it will either alienate me or draw me in? Do you care which?

You may remember when you were a student in the Whitney Independent Study Program around 1975 and I was teaching there a couple of times a week. One day you invited Ron Clark and me into your studio and screened a pornographic video. After five minutes I got up and left, leaving Ron to deal with your discomfort. I would like to think that my abrupt exit contributed even a tiny bit to your later work!

No need to answer any of the above questions, which you've probably already encountered many times over. After reading your words in Martha Wilson's interview with you in *Bomb*, I tend to be more impressed with your ideas as manifest in language than with your solo performance work. I can identify with that pickle. But on further thought, I must admit that your solitary acts are meaningful, perhaps even indispensable insofar as they engender such provocative analysis and interpretation. If you want to bounce your future multiple heterogeneous "acts" off an aged white female art worker, or need a willing participant, count me in.

Yvonne Rainer, October 30, 2018

PERFORMANCE AND EXHIBITION CHRONOLOGY, 1977–2001

Compiled by Kaegan Sparks

During the years 1977–2001, Pope.L's performance pra[illegible] *involved a variety of roles and situations: writing, dire*[illegible] *performing, collaboration, solo work, and performances on stage, in the street and on sidewalks, and in art institutions and other spaces. This chronology attempts to capture that variety. The designation* proscenium *indicates works that closely align with Pope.L's theater practice, meaning that they may have involved a script, multiple performers, rehearsals, and props, whether or not they were performed on a traditional stage.*

Pope.L was known professionally as William Pope.L during the years covered by the chronology. During his time teaching at Bates College, starting in 1990, his students began to call him Pope.L. The name stuck and quickly became part of his creative identity outside school.

Descriptions are excerpted from archival documents related to the performances, including press releases, calendars, flyers, and performance programs. Idiosyncrasies of capitalization and punctuation have been preserved. Where the first person appears, the voice is that of Pope.L.

■ Street performance
▲ Proscenium performance
● Outdoor performance
★ Gallery performance
⬟ Solo/two-person exhibition
▮ Group exhibition

1977

Happening. Painting studio, Montclair State College, N.J.

Jon Wayne. Band. Multiple venues. Through 198[illegible]ormers: Steve Davison, Ellen Laforge, Brian McCormack, Franc Palaia, and Pope.L.

1978

■ ***Singing in the Rain a.k.a. Meditation Square Piece [a.k.a. Gutter Piece]***. Third Street Men's Shelter, New York.

■ ***Thunderbird Immolation a.k.a. Meditation Square Piece [a.k.a. Gutter Piece]***. West Broadway, New York.

■ ***Times Square Crawl a.k.a. Meditation Square Piece [a.k.a. Gutter Piece]***. Times Square, New York.

1982

▲ ***First Soap Opera (with butter)***. Written and directed by Pope.L. Mason Gross School of the Arts graduate and undergraduate graduation ceremony, Rutgers University, New Brunswick, N.J. Performers: Jody Clowes, Fico Montoya, Kathleen Smith, et al.

1983

★ ***Anxiety Speaks***. Written and directed by Pope.L. American Dreams Festival, Just Above Midtown, New York. Performers: Steven Davidson and Pope.L.

▲ ***Christ and Freedom***. Written and directed by Pope.L. Douglas College Cabaret, Rutgers University, New Brunswick, N.J. Performers: Jody Clowes, Lydia Grey, and Kathleen Smith.

▮ ***Rutgers Invitational***. Rutgers University, New Brunswick, N.J.

1984

▮ ***Found Language***. Franklin Furnace, New York. April 19–July 31.

▲ ***A Communications Device; An Exercise: 8 Part Soap Opera, Section 5A/ My BROTHER/MYSELF***. Written and directed by Pope.L. Found Language Performance Night and Benefit, Night Gallery, New York. May 30. Performers: Lydia Grey, Garrett Chingery, Pope.L, and Vivian Vassar; music: Gary Quasar.

▲ ***8 Part Soap Opera*, Section 2: The Son Is Shining: She Plays Golf.** Written and directed by Pope.L. Workshopped at Re.Cher.Chez, New York. Traveled to Darinka: A Performance Studio/Club, New York. December 15. Performers: Ledlie Borgerhoff, Jim Calder, Garrett Chingery, and Pope.L; music: Tom Miller; lighting: Jai Zion; costumes/ sets: Lydia Grey; sound: Anna Fuhr.

▲ ***At the Foot of the Grenade***. Written and directed by Pope.L. International Mime and Movement Festival, Davis and Elkins College, Elkins, W.Va. Performers: Jim Calder, Joe Daly, and Pope.L.

▮ ***Radical Culture***. Fashion Moda Gallery, Bronx, N.Y.

1985

★ ***Christ and Freedom***. Written and directed by Pope.L. Art Galaxy Gallery, New York. Performers: Lydia Grey, Pope.L, and Kathleen Smith.

1986

▲ ***Okee-La-Homa***. Written and performed by Jim Calder, Joe Daly, and Pope.L as members of Tesla Linkum Theater Collective. Workshopped at Re.Cher.Chez, New York. Traveled to Fringe Festival, BACA Downtown, Brooklyn, N.Y. October 24–November 1.

"A musical dialectic that pits the ebullience of American musical comedy against a stark depiction of frontier econopolitics."

▲ ***8 Part Soap Opera, Sections 1, 2, 5A, and 7***. Written and directed by Pope.L. Tweed Gallery, New York. Traveled to Re.Cher.Chez, New York; BACA Downtown, Brooklyn, N.Y.; WFMU/Upsala College (adapted for radio), East Orange, N.J.; Gerdes Folk City, New York. Performers: Ledlie Borgerhoff, Jim Calder, and Pope.L; music: Tom Miller.

1987

▲ ***Loco-Motives***. Written and directed by Pope.L as a member of Tesla Linkum Theater Collective. Workshopped at Re.Cher.Chez, New York. Traveled to PS122, New York. January 9–31. Performers: Ledlie Borgerhoff, Jim Calder, Catherine Coray, Joe Daly, Carl Schnedeker, et al.; music: Tom Miller.

"*An anti-soap opera* about a black family that mistakes the Oedipus myth for their own reality. *T.V. Guide is the Oracle*, and murder is the result."

▲ ***Anna and Paul***. Written by Pope.L. BACA Downtown, Brooklyn, N.Y. Traveled to Chameleon Bar, New York. Director: Catherine Coray; performers: Bill Castle and Holly Hughes.

★ ***Gen. George at Valley Forge***. Written and directed by Pope.L. Longwood Arts Gallery, Bronx, N.Y. Performers: Jessie Allen, Ledlie Borgerhoff, Joe Daly, Barbara Hiesiger, Tom Miller, et al.

▲ ***Opie in the Desert***. Chameleon Bar, New York. Performers: Garrett Chingery et al.

1988

▲ ***Bombs: Three Ordnances***. 1. *Anna and Paul*: Written by Pope.L. 2. *Jhampa*: Written by Joe Daly. 3. *At the Foot of the Grenade*: Written and directed by Jim Calder, Joe Daly, and Pope.L. Franklin Furnace, New York. January 8–9. Performers: Bill Castle and Holly Hughes (*Anna and Paul*); Barbara Benary, Ledlie Borgerhoff, Jim Calder, Catherine Coray, Joe Daly, Joan Harmon, Pope.L, and Carl Schnedeker (*Jhampa*); Jim Calder, Joe Daly, and Pope.L (*At the Foot of the Grenade*).

"1. *Anna and Paul*: A story of a man and a woman in love. 2. *Jhampa*: A musical-puppet horror chorus. 3. *At the Foot of the Grenade*: Three men who never quite grew up explore weapons for their beauty, soldiering for its glamour, and destruction for the hell of it."

1989

▲ ***George Is in the Lake***. Written by Pope.L, directed by Jim Calder and Pope.L. Franklin Furnace, New York. January 13–21. Performers: Ledlie Borgerhoff, Robert Caccomo, Chris Lanier, Pope.L, Carl Schnedeker, and A. Gordon Smith; music: Tom R. Miller and Pope.L; slides: Pope.L and Gwyneth Thomas; stage manager: Lydia Grey.

"A seriously funny feminist fairy tale, *George Is in the Lake* asks the question 'What if George Washington had not crossed the Delaware?' The answer is found in this anti-war, pro-gay, deconstructionist musical theater."

▲ ***The Nigger and the Narcissist***. Written, directed, and performed by Pope.L. Cleveland Performance Art Festival, Cleveland Public Theater. April 21.

▲ ***Candide***. Adaptation by Pope.L. Touchstone Theater, Bethlehem, Pa. April. Director: Jim Calder; performers: Bill George, Jennie Gilrain, Mark McKenna, and Sara Zielinska; costumes: Barbara Seyda; sound design: John Calder.

▲ ***Mindhouse a.k.a. Anxiety Speaks***. Rutgers University, New Brunswick, N.J.

Uncle Remus in Hell. Radio play. Written and directed by Pope.L. WFMU/Upsala College, East Orange, N.J.; WBAI, New York; WFMU, New York; WKNJ, Kean College, Union, N.J.; WKFJ, San Francisco; WZSC, San Francisco; CKLN, Toronto; WERU, East Orland, Maine. Performers: Joe Daly, Barbara Heisiger, Melinda Levokove, Pope.L., and Carl Schnedeker.

1990

▲ ***Egg Eating Contest***, basement version. Written, directed, and performed by Pope.L. East Orange, N.J. May 30.

"A solo performance lecture which attempts a vaudevillian deconstruction of the myth of the Black American Male and Patriarchy in general."

▲ ***The Aunt Jenny Chronicles***. Written, directed, and performed by Pope.L. Dixon Place, New York. June 8. Slide projection: Sue Bowman; music: Pope.L and Rich Robinson.

"A music-performance-revelation based upon the personal, political, and mythological dynamics of my relationship with my 114-year-old Aunt Jenny."

▲ ***Egg Eating Contest***, ensemble version. Written and directed by Pope.L. BACA Downtown, Brooklyn, N.Y. October 18–27. Performers: Pope.L, Richard Robinson, and Carl Schnedeker; music: Pope.L and Richard Robinson; lighting: Carise Skinner; slides: Lydia Grey, Pope.L, and Marlan Proctor.

▲ ***Egg Eating Contest***, ensemble version. Written and directed by Pope.L. Dixon Place, New York. Performed by Pope.L et al.

▲ ***Egg Eating Contest***, ensemble version. Written and directed by Pope.L. Painted Bride Arts Center, Philadelphia. Performed by Pope.L et al.

▲ ***Egg Eating Contest***, solo version. Written, directed, and performed by Pope.L. Cone Art Gallery, University of North Carolina, Greensboro.

▲ ***Egg Eating Contest***, solo version. Written, directed, and performed by Pope.L. Franklin and Marshall College, Lancaster, Pa.

▲ ***Egg Eating Contest***, solo version. Written, directed, and performed by Pope.L. Knitting Factory, New York.

▲ ***Egg Eating Contest***, solo version. Written, directed, and performed by Pope.L. Movement Research, New York.

▮ ***Action and Artifact***. Weatherspoon Gallery at the University of North Carolina, Greensboro.

■ ***Selling Mayonnaise for 100 Dollars a Dollop***. East Seventh Street and Cooper Square, New York.

■ ***Writing/Sleeping/Living on the Flag***. New York.

1991

⬟ ***Looking for Aunt Jenny***. Audio installation. Elevator shaft, Art in General, New York. March 2–April 6. Sound: Thomas R. Miller.

▲ ***Egg Eating Contest***, solo version. Written, directed, and performed by Pope.L. Cleveland Performance Art Festival, Cleveland Public Theater. March.

▲ ***S.T.U./I.R.*** Adaptation of Lorraine Hansberry's play *A Raisin in the Sun*. Written, directed, and performed by Pope.L. Bates College, Lewiston, Maine. March.

⬟ ***How Much Is That Nigger in the Window***. Franklin Furnace, New York. June 15–July 30.

"In this complex 4-part work [street performances, gallery installation, gallery performances, and an artist's book], Pope.L is Mr. Poots, a hybrid nigger-character who is a cross between a black militant, a preacher, a street-crazy and a Buppie (Black Upwardly-Mobile Professional)."

▲ ***Suck Harder***. Part of *How Much Is That Nigger in the Window*. Written, directed, and performed by Pope.L. Knitting Factory, New York. July 23.

■ ***Eating the Wall Street Journal***, early street version. Part of *How Much Is That Nigger in the Window*. New York. July.

■ ***Selling Mayonnaise for 100 Dollars a Dollop***. Part of *How Much Is That Nigger in the Window*. East Seventh Street and Cooper Square, New York. July.

■ ***Tompkins Square Crawl***. Part of *How Much Is That Nigger in the Window*. Tompkins Square Park, New York. July.

■ ***Writing/Sleeping/Living on the Flag***. Part of *How Much Is That Nigger in the Window*. New York. July.

★ ***I Get Paid to Rub Mayo on My Body***, Version 1. Part of *How Much Is That Nigger in the Window*. Written, directed, and performed by Pope.L. Franklin Furnace, New York. July 30.

▲ ***The Aunt Jenny Chronicles/Journey to Incontinence***. Written and directed by Pope.L. PS122, New York. October 3–6, 10–13. Performers: John Cyril Brooks, John Aloysius Patterson, Pope.L, and Richard Robinson; slide projections: Lydia Grey; overhead projection: John Aloysius Patterson; music: Richard Robinson; visuals: Gwyneth Thomas; lighting: Jan Bell-Newman.

"Voice, text, shaving cream, electric guitar, tar-and-feathered watermelon, absurd dance and live-action larger-than-life visual projections using Alka-Seltzer, gummy bears, freeze-dried coffee and images of Michael Landon and Al Sharpton combine to create evocative, rhythmical, poetic collisions of image and meaning. The piece explores the tensions between the fascism of youth and the wisdom of the aged, Black Matriarchy and the rainy day Patriarchy it nurses to power, older Southern Black Culture (patience, Freedom Rides and Aunt Jenny), and the newer Northern tradition (Nikes, the '60s riots and Patriarchy à la Bill Cosby and Jell-O pudding.)"

■ ***The Public Life of the Secret Writer***. Philadelphia. October.

● ***Snow Crawl***. Lewiston, Maine. Through 2001.

1992

▲ ***Eracism***, Version 1. Written, directed, and performed by Pope.L. Downtown Art Co., New York. February 20–March 1.

■ ***Murray Hill Road Street Intervention***. Cleveland Performance Art Festival, Murray Hill Road. March 27.

■ ***Cleveland Group Crawl***. Cleveland Performance Art Festival. March 28.

★ ***White Baby (a.k.a. How Much Is That Nigger in the Window)***. Written, directed, and performed by Pope.L. Cleveland Performance Art Festival, Cleveland State University Art Gallery. March 28.

▲ ***The Vulture Speaks.*** Written by Pope.L. Downtown Art Co., New York. May 28–June 7. Traveled to CoMotion Theater, Lancaster, Pa.; Touchstone Theater, Bethlehem, Pa., October 22–November 3. Director: Jim Calder, art direction: Joan Harmon, movement/image: Sigfrido Aguilar; sound and lighting: Tim Frey.

"A new interdisciplinary collaboration featuring an eccentric mix of commedia dell'arte, deadpan humor, and visual wit to mark the conquest of the Americas."

▲ ***The Death of the Last Black Man in the Entire World.*** Adaptation of Suzan-Lori Parks's play *The Death of the Last Black Man in the Whole Entire World*. Written and directed by Pope.L. Bates College, Lewiston, Maine. May.

★ ***Levitating the Magnesia.*** Horodner Romley Gallery, New York. December 15–19.

"I will sit in a chair for 3 days (from Thursday to Saturday) and attempt to levitate a bottle of Milk of Magnesia. On Saturday at 5:30 I will stand up."

1993

⬟ ***William Pope.L.*** Horodner Romley Gallery, New York. January 4–February 5.

⬟ ***William Pope.L: Recent Objects.*** Drew University, Madison, N.J. January 28–February 4.

▲ ***Eracism***, Version 2. Written, directed, and performed by Pope.L. Drew University, Madison, N.J. January 29.

▲ ***Eracism***, Version 3. Written, directed, and performed by Pope.L. Hallwalls Contemporary Arts Center, Buffalo, N.Y. March 20.

"In . . . a 'solo trickster performance piece' featuring his character Mr. Poots, . . . Pope.L examines 'the Crayola understanding of racism.'"

❚ ***Transient Décor.*** Roger Smith Hotel, New York. May 12–26.

★ ***I Get Paid to Rub Mayo on My Body***, Version 2. Written, directed, and performed by Pope.L. Roger Smith Hotel, New York. May.

■ ***A House Is a Home with a Hole in the Middle.*** Olney Branch, Philadelphia Free Library. June 18. Organized by COSACOSA art at large, Inc.

▲ ***Eracism***, Version 4a, with golf demo. Written, directed, and performed by Pope.L. Yellow Springs Institute, Chester Springs, Pa. September 25.

"A solo trickster art performance lecture which takes us on an evocative journey through the wilderness of our racial selves. . . . Using high-speed contrasting narratives of rapping and preaching, ecstatic hippo-dancing, jokes, ice, onions, maps, black coffee and the hurling of erasers into the audience, I attempt an agit-poetic exploration of American racial Co-dependence."

❚ ***The Return of the Cadavre Exquis.*** Drawing Center, New York. November 6–December 18. Traveled to Corcoran Gallery of Art, Washington, D.C., February 5–April 10, 1994; Santa Monica Museum of Art, Calif., July 9–September 6, 1994; F[illegible]n for Contemporary Art, Saint Louis, September 30–November 12, 1994, [illegible]can Center, Paris, December 1994–January 1995.

■ ***Black Domestic a.k.a. Roach Motel Black.*** New York.

❚ ***Various Objects.*** Rutgers University, New Brunswick, N.J.

1994

❚ ***Outside the Frame: Performance and the Object: A Survey History of Performance Art in the USA since 1950.*** Cleveland Center for Contemporary Art. February 11–May 1. Traveled to Snug Harbor Cultural Center, Staten Island, N.Y., February 26–June 18, 1995.

▲ ***Eracism***, Version 4. Written, directed, and performed by Pope.L. February 25–26. Part of the exhibition *Outside the Frame: Performance and the Object*, Karamu House Theater, Cleveland Performance Art Festival. February 11–May 1.

▲ ***Uncle Vanya.*** Adaptation of Anton Chekhov's play *Uncle Vanya*. Written and directed by Pope.L. Bates College, Lewiston, Maine. March.

■ ***Black Domestic a.k.a. Cow Commercial.*** Midtown Manhattan, including a Banana Republic store, New York. August 17.

▲ ***The Buddy Performance.*** Written, directed, and performed by Jim Calder and Pope.L. PS122, New York. November 17–18.

"*The Buddy Performance* is a two-man theatre work which utilizes the lecture format, the conventions of contemporary 'Buddy' movies such as *Lethal Weapon*, and the world of the male-dominated professional milieu, special gynecology, to explore the American psyche in relation to race and gender."

1995

▲ ***Eracism,*** Version 5. Written, directed, and performed by Pope.L. Part of the exhibition *Outside the Frame: Performance and the Object*, Snug Harbor Cultural Center, Staten Island, N.Y. February 26–June 18.

▮ ***Satellite Choice: Young Curators Explore Diversity.*** Artists Space, New York. May 20–July 15.

▲ ***Hair.*** Adaptation of James Rado and Gerome Ragni's musical Hair. Written and directed by Pope.L. Bates College, Lewiston, Maine. May.

▮ ***Dysfunctional Art.*** Tomkins Cove Art Center/Hudson Arts at Franklin Furnace, New York. July 28–August 27.

1996

▲ ***The Buddy Performance.*** Written, directed, and performed by Jim Calder and Pope.L. Touchstone Theatre Comedy Festival, Bethlehem, Pa. February 20–24.

⬟ ***Buddy Performance Objects.*** Created by Jim Calder and Pope.L. Touchstone Theatre, Bethlehem, Pa. February.

■ ***Member a.k.a. Schlong Journey.*** 125th Street, Harlem, New York. March 15.

▲ ***The Buddy Performance.*** Written, directed, and performed by Jim Calder and Pope.L. Here Performance Space, New York. June 10–12. Performers: Jim Calder and Pope.L; lighting: Charles Cameron and Frank DenDanto III; music: George Griggs and Eric Willis.

▲ ***The Buddy Performance***. Written, directed, and performed by Jim Calder and Pope.L. Ko Performance Festival, Amherst College, Mass. July 26–28.

▲ ***Eracism***, Version 7. Written and directed by Pope.L. Ko Performance Festival, Amherst College, Mass. July 26–28. Performers: Michelle Hendricks and Pope.L; music: Dustin Bowlin and Erik Noonan; lighting: Sabrina Hamilton.

● ***Sweet Desire a.k.a. Burial Piece***. Skowhegan School of Painting and Sculpture, Maine. August.

▲ ***Eracism,*** Version 7a. Written, directed, and performed by Pope.L. Performance Art, Culture, and Pedagogy Symposium, Pennsylvania State University, University Park. November 13–16. Music: Bryn Manion and band.

▮ ***Exquisite Corpse.*** Danforth Gallery, Portland, Maine.

▲ ***Raymond***. Written, directed, and performed by Pope.L. Barn, Skowhegan School of Painting and Sculpture, Maine.

1997

■ ***ATM Piece***. Chase Manhattan Bank, Forty-Second Street, New York. February 19.

"William Pope.L will chain himself to the door of an ATM wearing a skirt made of money. As people enter the ATM he will remove bits of the skirt and hand it to them. *ATM Piece* is an attempt to bring fresh discomfort to an age-old problem: *the haves and the have nots* and what they have to do with each other."

▲ ***Romeo vs. Juliet.*** Adaptation of William Shakespeare's *Romeo and Juliet*. Written and directed by Pope.L. Bates College, Lewiston, Maine. March.

▲ ***Raymond***. Written, directed, and performed by Pope.L. Galapagos (former factory), New York. May 3.

▲ ***Eracism***, Version 7b. Written, directed, and performed by Pope.L. Mobius Experimental Theater Space, Boston. May 30–June 1.

● ***Sweet Desire a.k.a. Burial Piece.*** Maine Arts Festival, Thomas Point Beach, Brunswick, Maine. July.

▮ ***Available Culture.*** Here Art Gallery, New York.

▮ ***Birdhouses***. Robin Hutchins Gallery, Maplewood, N.J.

▮ ***Birds of a Feather.*** Newark Museum, N.J.

▮ ***Habitat for Humanity: (bird)Houses.*** New Jersey Performing Arts Center, Newark.

▮ ***Out on a Limb***. Midland Gallery, Montclair, N.J.

1998

▮ ***Out of Actions: Between Performance and the Object, 1949–1979.*** Museum of Contemporary Art, Los Angeles. February 8–May 10. Traveled to MAK, Vienna, June 17–September 6; Museu d'Art Contemporani, Barcelona, October 16, 1998–January 6, 1999; Museum of Contemporary Art, Tokyo, February 11–August 11, 1999.

▲ ***Eracism***, Version 8. Written, directed, and performed by Pope.L. 7a*11d Festival, Toronto. September 26. Music: Justin Anders.

■ ***My Niagra #1 (Paint)***. Corner of Broadway and Lancaster Street, Fells Point, Baltimore. October 19.

"I will pour a great quantity of thick white liquid over my body. You will recognize me by my fine suit, overcoat, hat, and black skin."

▲ ***The Buddy Performance***. Written, directed, and performed by Jim Calder and Pope.L. College of the South, Sewanee, Tenn. Fall.

⬟ ***Recent Work***. The Project, New York. December 3, 1998–January 23, 1999.

★ ***My Niagra #2 (Bed)***. The Project, New York. December.

▮ ***Apocalypse Now.*** Here Art Gallery, New York.

▮ ***Freedom, Liberation and Change: Revisiting 1968***. Longwood Art Gallery, Bronx, N.Y.

● ***A Negro Sleeps beneath the Susquehanna.*** Cowan Compound, Bucknell University, Lewisburg, Pa.

"In this work, a black man comes awake on the banks of a river. He has been asleep on the bottom of the river for many years. When he awakens he fills his lungs with sweet air and speaks. When done, he returns to the river, carrying his image into the deep."

▮ ***Peek***. Here Art Gallery, New York.

▮ ***warming.*** The Project, New York.

1999

▮ ***Paradise 8***. Exit Art, New York. January 16-April 3.

▲ ***Raymond,*** Version 2. Written, directed, and performed by Pope.L. Barn, Southern Illinois University, Carbondale. February 2.

My Niagra #3 (Paint). College Art Association annual conference, Los Angeles Convention Center. Between February 10 and 13.

■ ***The Black Body and Sport***. Tauentzienstrasse near Kaiser Wilhelm Gedächtniskirche, Berlin. July 15.

■ ***The Black Body and Sport***. Highway, Budapest. Summer.

■ ***The Black Body and Sport***. Outdoor shopping mall, Madrid. Summer.

■ ***The Black Body and Sport***. Charles Bridge, Prague. Summer.

▲ ***The Buddy Performance***. Written and directed by Jim Calder and Pope.L. Here Performance Space, New York. November 27–December 19. Music: George Griggs and Justin Lander; lighting/sets: Felice Berna and Diane D. Fairchild.

■ ***Milk Pour***. Downtown, near West Side Highway, New York.

★ ***The White Mountain (Wonder Bread)***. Written, directed, and performed by Pope.L. Postmasters Gallery, New York.

2000

⬟ ***Eating the Wall Street Journal and Other Current Consumptions***. Mobius Experimental Theater Space, Boston. January 12–February 5.

●■ ***Eating the Wall Street Journal***, Version 2. Mobius Experimental Theater Space and Financial District locations, Boston. Circa January 15.

"The Mobius performance consisted of me sitting on a 'throne' of *Wall Street Journals* on the sidewalks in various locations within the Boston financial district. While there I attempted to ingest a stack of newspaper on which I was sitting while drinking milk (to coat my stomach and to dilute the poisons of the paper). At spontaneous intervals during the performance I made phone calls to the senior vice presidents of the district office of the *Wall Street Journal* in Boston. I invited each vice president to lunch with me at the particular location of the performance. I did this work once a day for five days calling one senior vice president a day."

■ ***Boston Common Group Crawl***. Boston Common. Organized by School of the Museum of Fine Arts, Boston. January.

★ ***The Hole inside the Space inside Yves Klein's Asshole***. VAV Gallery, Concordia University, Montreal. February 11.

"Two-hour ritual exotic dance performance with live ass printing."

▲ ***The Colored Museum.*** Adaptation of George C. Wolfe's play *The Colored Museum*. Written and directed by Pope.L. Bates College, Lewiston, Maine. March.

▮ ***Friendships in Arcadia: Writers and Artists at Yaddo in the 90s***. Art in General, New York. April 15–May 20. Traveled to Hyde Collection, Glens Falls, N.Y., May 28–September 4.

⬟ ***Eracism: White Room***. Thread Waxing Space, New York. June.

▲ ***Eracism***, Version 8a/8b. Written, directed, and performed by Pope.L. Thread Waxing Space, New York. June 15. Music: Richard Robinson. Commissioned by Yaddo.

▮ ***Söma Söma Söma***. Sculpture Center, New York. June 20–July 15.

★ ***Eating the Wall Street Journal***, Version 3. Sculpture Center, New York. June 22–24, July 15.

"Television ads for the *Wall Street Journal* promise: if you buy this paper then you will gain knowledge. This is a very old, almost medieval idea. So in *Eating* I decided to push this promise to its absurd [illegible]usion: 'Well, what if I not only buy it (consume it) but I eat it. I'll have [illegible]more knowledge.'"

▮ ***Pix***. Lance Fung Gallery, New York.

● ***Selling My Grandmother***. Yard sale. Lab School, New York.

2001

■ ***Bringing the Homeless Back to Shinjuku***. Shinjuku Station South Exit, Tokyo. March 14.

■ ***Shopping Crawl (crawl with balloon)***. Yoyogi Park, Shibuya, Tokyo. March 17.

★ ***I Love Japan and It Loves Me***. Nishiogi Wenz studio, Tokyo. April 9.

⬟ ***Hole Theory***. The Project, New York. May 13–June 30.

■ ***The Great White Way: 22 miles, 9 years, 1 street***. Broadway, New York. Through 2009.

■ ***Training Crawl (for The Great White Way: 22 miles, 5 years, 1 street)***. Lewiston, Maine.

▮ ***Video Jam***. Palm Beach Institute of Contemporary Art, Fla.

Sources

In order of first citation

Promotional mailer for Loco-Motives at PS122 and other Tesla Linkum productions, 1987. Fales Library and Special Collections, New York University.

Press release for *Bombs*, Franklin Furnace, New York, 1987. Franklin Furnace Archive, Inc., New York.

Press release for *George Is in the Lake*, Franklin Furnace, New York, 1988. Franklin Furnace Archive, Inc., New York.

Application submitted to Yellow Springs Institute for Contemporary Studies and the Arts, 1992. New York Public Library Archives and Manuscripts.

Press release for *How Much Is That Nigger in the Window*, Franklin Furnace, New York, 1991. Franklin Furnace Archive, Inc., New York.

Press release for *The Aunt Jenny Chronicles*, PS122, New York, 1991. Fales Library and Special Collections, New York University.

Downtown Art Co. calendar, 1992. Fales Library and Special Collections, New York University.

Poster for *Levitating the Magnesia*, 1992. Fales Library and Special Collections, New York University.

Hallwalls Contemporary Arts Center newsletter, March 1993. Available at https://www.hallwalls.org/pubs/1993_3.RFS.pdf.

The Buddy Performance descriptive document, 1994. Franklin Furnace Archive, Inc., New York.

Artist-produced press release for *ATM Piece*, 1997. Fales Library and Special Collections, New York University.

Grant proposal submitted to Franklin Furnace, ca. 2000. Franklin Furnace Archive, Inc., New York.

Document relating to *William Pope.L: eRacism* exhibition at Institute of Contemporary Art at Maine College of Art, 2002. Fales Library and Special Collections, New York University.

SELECTED BIBLIOGRAPHY

Writings and Books by the Artist

"Performance Manifesto #78." *The Act* 1, no. 1 (Winter/Spring 1986): 4.

William Pope.L's "How Much Is That Nigger in the Window": Rap Street Journal. New York and Lewiston, Maine: self-published, 1992.

"Forum: On Creativity and Community." In *M/E/A/N/I/N/G* 15 (May 1994): 14–16.

"Anti-Autobiography." *Global City Review* 8 (Fall 1996): 69–78.

"Notes on *Crawling Piece a.k.a. How Much Is That Nigger in the Window?* (Summer 1991/Streets of New York City)." *Art Journal* 56, no. 4 (Winter 1997): 65–66.

"*Eracism*." *P-Form* 44 (Fall 1997/Winter 1998): 28–34.

Eat Notes: "Eating the Wall Street Journal." Self-published, 2000.

"Beyond the Proscenium." In "How Do You Make Social Change?" a portfolio by Tony Kushner, Linda Frye Burnham, Doug Paterson, et al. *Theater* 31, no. 3 (Fall 2001): 92–93.

Hole Theory. Self-published, 2002.

"Sandwich Lecture #8." In *Live: Art and Performance*, edited by Adrian Heathfield, 228–31. New York: Routledge, 2004.

"The 'Looking for Miss Black Factory' Contest." *Art Journal* 64, no. 1 (Spring 2005): 50–58.

Untitled. In *Letters to a Young Artist*, edited by Peter Nesbett, Sarah Andress, and Shelly Bancroft, 71–73. Los Angeles: Darte Publishing, 2006.

"Crawling in Public." In *Intersection: Sidewalks and Public Space*, edited by Marci Nelligan and Nicole Mauro, 73–86. New York: ChainLinks, 2008.

"Canary in the Coal Mine." *Art Journal* 70, no. 3 (Fall 2011): 55–58.

Untitled. In *Draw It with Your Eyes Closed: The Art of the Art Assignment*, edited by Dushko Petrovich and Roger White, 81–86. Brooklyn, N.Y.: Paper Monument, 2012.

"The Limner Performance." With Anthony Adcock, Effie Bowen, Thad Kellstadt, Stephen Bartell, Lo Jan, Ja Zou Hon, Zhou Hai Hua, and Xiang Yue. *Triple Canopy*, November 20, 2014. https://www.canopycanopycanopy.com/contents/the-limner-performance.

Introduction to "H+G." *South as a State of Mind* 8 (Fall/Winter 2016): 157.

"The Cypress." *X-TRA* 20, no. 4 (Summer 2018): 4–21.

Solo Exhibition Catalogues and Brochures

Bessire, Mark H. C., ed. *William Pope.L: The Friendliest Black Artist in America©*. Cambridge, Mass.: MIT Press, 2002.

——. *William Pope.L: Snow, Spraypaint, Hair, Sperm & Baloney.* London: Kenny Schachter/ROVE, 2007.

Dirié, Clément, ed. *Black People Are Cropped: Skin Set Drawings, 1997–2011.* Zurich: JRP/Ringier, 2012.

Dorin, Lisa, and Darby English. "William Pope.L: Drawing, Dreaming, Drowning." Chicago: Art Institute of Chicago, 2008.

Melandri, Lisa, ed. *William Pope.L: Art after White People: Time, Trees and Celluloid.* Santa Monica, Calif.: Santa Monica Museum of Art, 2007.

Pope.L: Proto-Skin Set. New York: Mitchell-Innes & Nash, 2017.

Pope.L and Nicholas Bourriaud, eds. *Pope.L: One Thing after Another.* Montpellier, France: La Panacée; New York: Mitchell-Innes & Nash, 2019.

Pope.L, William, and Karen Reimer, eds. *Showing Up to Withhold.* Chicago: Renaissance Society at the University of Chicago and University of Chicago Press, 2014.

Pope.L, William, and Bennett Simpson. "William Pope.L: Trinket." Los Angeles: The Museum of Contemporary Art, 2015.

Pope.L, William, Nato Thompson, and Elizabeth Bard, eds. *William Pope.L: Some Things You Can Do with Blackness . . . .* London: Kenny Schachter/ROVE, 2005.

Roelstraete, Dieter, ed. *Pope.L: Campaign.* Milan: Mousse, 2019.

Walker, Hamza. "Double Consciousness, Squared." In "William Pope.L: Forlesen." Chicago: The Renaissance Society, 2013.

Academic Books and Dissertations

Cappelli, Maria Ghira. "Schlong Journey on the Great White Way: Pope.L's Spectacular Masculinity" and "Epilogue: To Demand and to Give." In "Inadmissible Presence: Objecthood, Spectacle, and the Theatricality of Race," 120–60. PhD diss., University of California, Berkeley, 2007. ProQuest (AAT 3306081).

Cervenak, Sarah Jane. *Wandering: Philosophical Performances of Racial and Sexual Freedom*, 22–23, 149–56. Durham, N.C.: Duke University Press, 2014.

English, Darby. "The Aesthetics of Dispossession: William Pope.L's Performance Interventions." In *How to See a Work of Art in Total Darkness*, 255–312. Cambridge, Mass.: The MIT Press, 2007.

——. "Differing, Drawn." In *To Describe a Life: Notes from the Intersection of Art and Race Terror*, 42–85. New Haven, Conn.: Yale University Press, 2019.

Gleisser, Faye Raquel. "Disorderly Conduct: Tehching Hsieh, William Pope.L, and the Policing of Resourcefulness, 1978–1982." In "Guerrilla Tactics: Performance Art and the Politics of Identity in American Visual Culture, 1967–1983," 159–210. PhD diss., Northwestern University, 2016. ProQuest (AAT 10117335).

Jackson, Shannon. "Staged Management: Theatricality and Institutional Critique." In *Social Works: Performing Art, Supporting Publics*, 104–43. New York: Routledge, 2011.

Jones, Amelia. "Witness, 1991–1996." In *Seeing Differently: A History and Theory of Identification and the Visual Arts,* 98–102. London: Routledge, 2012.

Laynor, Gregory. "Coda: William Pope.L's *Another Kind of Love: John Cage's 'Silence,' By Hand*." In "The Making of Intermedia: John Cage to Yoko Ono, 1952 to 1972," 121–26. PhD diss., University of Washington, 2016. ProQuest (AAT 10138634).

Lepecki, André. "Stumbling Dance: William Pope.L's Crawls." In *Exhausting Dance: Performance and the Politics of Movement*, 87–105. New York: Routledge, 2006.

Pittman, Alex. "Abandoned Futures: Urban Sensoria of Speculation and the Disappointments of William Pope.L." In "Dispossessive Acts: Aesthetics of Accumulation," 98–155. PhD diss., New York

University, 2014. ProQuest (AAT 3635291).

Stiles, Kristine. "*Thunderbird Immolation*: William Pope.L and Burning Racism (2002)." In *Concerning Consequences: Studies in Art, Destruction, and Trauma*, 244–50. Chicago: University of Chicago Press, 2016.

Thompson, Chris. "Afterbirth of a Nation: William Pope.L's *Great White Way*." *Women and Performance* 14, no. 1 (2004): 63–90.

Other Books

Munson, Lynne. *Exhibitionism: Art in an Era of Intolerance*, 83–85. Chicago: Ivan R. Dee, 2000.

Nelson, Maggie. *The Art of Cruelty: A Reckoning*, 199–204. New York: W. W. Norton, 2011.

Schotzko, Nikki T. *Learning How to Fall: Art and Culture after September 11*, 187–200. Oxford: Routledge, 2015.

Touré. *Who's Afraid of Post-Blackness?*, 26–31. New York: Free Press, 2011.

Interviews

Antebi, Nicole, Colin Dickey, Robby Herbst, and Gabriela Jauregui. "Thoughts on Failure, Idealism, and Art: A Symposium." In *Failure! Experiments in Aesthetics and Social Practice*, edited by Antebi et al., 54–65, 142–48, 174–88. Los Angeles: Journal of Aesthetics and Protest Press, 2006.

Barone, Mary. "William Pope.L, Yard by Yard." *Art in America*, October 6, 2009. https://www.artinamericamagazine.com/news-features/interviews/william-pope-l-allan-kaprow/.

Bradley, Rizvana. "An Interview with Artist, Pope.L." *Women and Performance* 24, nos. 2–3 (2014): 220–23.

Cahill, Zachary. "William Pope.L." Artforum.com, February 20, 2015. https://www.artforum.com/interviews/william-pope-l-discusses-his-upcoming-exhibition-at-la-moca-50371.

Chase, Alisia. "Learning to Be Human: An Interview with William Pope.L." *Afterimage* 33, no. 4 (January/February 2006): 20–23.

Huffman, Jibade-Khalil. "Slaves to Meaning: Jibade-Khalil Huffman in Conversation with Pope.L." *Flash Art* 315 (June/July/August 2017): 63–69.

Jablon, Samuel. "William Pope.L on 'Acting a Fool' and Alternative Futures." *Hyperallergic*, July 10, 2015. https://hyperallergic.com/221452/william-pope-l-on-acting-a-fool-and-alternative-futures/.

Lachance, Jonathan. "Inside the Black Factory: William Pope.L on Art and Race." *KGB Bar Lit Magazine*, June 2008. http://kgbbar.com/lit/columns/inside_the_black_factory_william_popel_on_art_and_race.

Laster, Paul. "Write Turn." *Time Out New York* 1093 (May 24–30, 2017): 56.

Locks, Mia. "Americanismo." *Mousse* 57 (February/March 2017): 100–109.

Osei-Bonsu, Afua. "The Art of Contraries: William Pope.L." McLir Blog. June 18, 2005. http://mclir.blogspot.com/2005/06/art-of-contraries-william-popel.html. Originally published in *Afrique News Magazine* (Chicago), May 2002.

Simonini, Ross. "William Pope.L." *Interview* 43, no. 1 (February 2013): 44.

——. "Pope.L in Conversation with Ross Simonini." *The Believer* 116 (December/January 2018): 87–92.

Thompson, Chris. "America's Friendliest Black Artist." *PAJ: A Journal of Performance and Art* 24, no. 3 (September 2002): 68–72.

Wilson, Martha. "William Pope.L." *Bomb* 55 (Spring 1996), 50–55.

Articles, Essays, and Reviews

Angeleti, Gabriella. "William Pope.L Tackles Race as a 'Daily Haunting.'" *Art Newspaper* November 2015, 8.

Anstead, Alicia. "Art That Pops—A New Installation by William Pope.L Transforms Carpenter Center into a Playground for Challenging Ideas." *Arts Spectrum* (Cambridge, Mass.), February 2009. https://sites.fas.harvard.edu/~spectrum/2008-09/Spring 2009/pops.html.

Banai, Nuit. "Reviews: William Pope.L at the Carpenter Center for the Visual Arts." *Artforum* 47, no. 9 (May 2009): 242.

Barliant, Claire. "Reviews: The Last Newspaper." *Time Out New York* 788 (November 4–10, 2010): 41.

Battista, Kathy. "*eRacism* and *Only Skin Deep*." *Third Text* 70, no. 5 (September 2004): 523–28.

Buckley, Annie. "William Pope.L." *Art in America*, May 28, 2015. https://www.artinamericamagazine.com/reviews/william-pope-l/.

Bucknell, Alice. "Renaissance Society Gets a Rise Out of Pope.L's New Exhibit." *Chicago Maroon*, April 30, 2013.

Burns, Charlotte. "William Pope.L Wants to Bring Down the House." *Art Newspaper*, March 16, 2015. http://79.125.124.178/articles/William-PopeL-wants-to-bring-down-the-house/37266.

Campbell, Andrianna. "Whitney Biennial." *Mousse* 58 (April/May 2017): 210.

Caniglia, John. "'Pull!' Offers City a Labor of Art as It Rolls through Cleveland Streets." *Plain Dealer* (Cleveland), June 9, 2013.

Carr, C. "Some Kind of Protest." *Village Voice* 42, no. 9, March 4, 1997: 52.

——. "The Generation Gap: Three Performers and a Waterbed." *Village Voice* 45, no. 28 (July 18, 2000): 55.

——. "The Fiery Furnace: Performance in the '80s, War in the '90s." *TDR: The Drama Review* 49, no. 1 (Spring 2005): 19–28.

Connors, Philip. "The Man Who Ate the Wall Street Journal—A Performance Artist Has an Appetite for Spectacle; Next Up: A 22-Mile Crawl." *Wall Street Journal*, April 9, 2002.

Cotter, Holland. "Art in Review; William Pope.L." *New York Times*, June 8, 2001.

——. "Little-Known Laureate of Performance Artists." *New York Times*, January 1, 2002.

——. "Art/Architecture; Never Mind the Art Police, These Six Matter." *New York Times*, May 5, 2002.

——. "Art Review; Tombs, Pop Tarts and Parties." *New York Times*, August 23, 2002.

——. "The Topic Is Race; the Art Is Fearless." *New York Times*, March 30, 2005.

——. "Art in Review: William Pope.L." *New York Times*, October 2, 2009.

Crawford, Cair. "William Pope.L at The Project, New York." *Nka: Journal of Contemporary African Art* 10 (Spring/Summer 1999): 67.

Dailey, Meghan. "William Pope.L." *Artforum* 42, no. 8 (April 2004): 162.

Dischinger, Mark. "The United Colors of America." *Riverfront Times* (Saint Louis), June 15, 2005.

Donovan, Thom. "The Hole (Notes): William Pope.L's Hole Theory." *Harriet*, April 30, 2010. https://www.poetryfoundation.org/harriet/2010/04/the-hole-notes-william-popels-hole-theory.

Duncan, David. "William Pope.L." *Art in America* 98, no. 8 (September 2010): 128–29.

Duray, Dan. "William Pope.L Discusses His Artforum Cover at CAA: 'Leave Me Out of It.'" *Art News*, February 17, 2015. http://www.artnews.com/2015/02/17/william-pope-l-discusses-his-artforum-cover-at-caa-leave-me-out-of-it/.

Edwards, Adrienne. "The Will to Exhaust." *Spike* 45 (Autumn 2015): 118–22.

Fateman, Johanna. "Rights and Privileges: Johanna Fateman on the 2017 Whitney Biennial," *Artforum* 55, no. 9 (May 2017): 296–302.

Fiduccia, Joanna. "Lacks Worth Having: William Pope.L and Land Art." *Shift* 8 (2015): 6–22.

Finkel, Jori. "Pronouncements from the Fringes." *New York Times*, March 22, 2015.

Firstenberg, Lauri. "Profile, Tapping the Energy of Predicament." *Contemporary Magazine* 69 (2005): 23–27.

Flautz, John. "Bethlehem Show Lets You Buddy Up to a Bruising Good Time." *Morning Call* (Allentown, Pa.), February 22, 1996.

Freeman, Nate. "Careful Whisper: Pope.L Discusses His Documenta Sound Work, Hidden across Kassel." *Art News*, June 8, 2017. http://www.artnews.com/2017/06/08/careful-whisper-pope-l-discusses-his-documenta-sound-work-hidden-across-kassel/.

Garza, Evan J. "Review: William Pope.L at Samson." *Flash Art* 272 (May–June 2010): 115.

Gerwin, David. "Deconstructing an Artist's Dubious Claim." *Hyperallergic*, August 14, 2014. https://hyperallergic.com/143477/deconstructing-an-artists-dubious-claim/.

Gilbert, Alan. "William Pope.L: *Proto Skin Set*." *Brooklyn Rail*, July 14, 2017.

Greenberger, Alex. "Pope.L's Bologna-Filled Whitney Biennial Installation Stinks—and Then Some." *Art News*, March 17, 2017. http://www.artnews.com/2017/03/17/pope-ls-bologna-filled-whitney-biennia-installation-stinks-and-then-some/.

Griffith, Phillip. "Pope.L, Will Boone." *Brooklyn Rail*, March 4, 2016.

Harcourt, Glenn. "William Pope.L at Geffen Contemporary, Los Angeles." *Artillery*, June 30, 2015. https://artillerymag.com/william-pope-l/.

Horodner, Stuart. "William Pope.L." *Zing Magazine* 3 (Autumn/Winter 1996): 171–73.

Johnson, Steve. "'Pope.L: The Escape' Reworks a Slavery Play as Performance Art and Dares You to Wonder What to Think about It." *Chicago Tribune*, November 16, 2018.

Joselit, David. "Material Witness: Visual Evidence and the Case of Eric Garner." *Artforum* 53, no. 6 (February 2015): 202–05.

Joselit, David, and Malik Gaines. "Exemplary Discussion." *Artforum* 53, no. 9 (May 2015): 52.

Junkermeier, Jennifer. "William Pope.L Navigates the Flint Waterways." *Bomb*, October 12, 2017. https://bombmagazine.org/articles/william-pope-l-navigates-the-flint-waterways/.

Hawbaker, KT. "Glass Curtain Takes on the Brain, Logan Center Visits Notions of Home." *Chicago Tribune*, December 1[illegible]7.

Knight, Christopher. "[illegible]am Pope.L Sets the U.S. Flag Waving at the MOCA/Geffen." *Los Angeles Times*, March 24, 2015.

Lax, Thomas J. "Previews: *William Pope.L: Forlesen*." *Artforum* 51, no. 9 (May 2013): 156.

Lennard, Debra. "The Radical Boundaries of African-American Performance." *Hyperallergic*, November 25, 2013. https://hyperallergic.com/95314/the-radical-boundaries-of-african-american-performance/.

Levin, Kim. "Reviews: New York, William Pope.L at Mitchell-Innes & Nash." *Art News* 107, no. 11 (December 2008): 122.

McMillian, Rodney. "Pain Should Not Be Ignored: On Facing One's Bogeyman." *Afterall* 18 (Summer 2008): 36–44.

Merjian, Ara H. "Critics' Pick: William Pope.L at the Carpenter Center for Visual Arts, Harvard University." Artforum.com. https://www.artforum.com/picks/william-pope-l-22205.

Mizota, Sharon. "William Pope.L Returns to LA with Twin Gallery Shows Focused on Race." *Los Angeles Times*, November 13, 2015.

Mooney, Amy. "Black Is, Black Ain't: A Historic Prelude." *Nka: Journal of Contemporary African Art* 24 (Summer 2009): 6–15.

Muchnic, Suzanne. "William Pope.L at Museum of Contemporary Art." *Art News*, June 9, 2015. http://www.artnews.com/2015/06/09/william-pope-l-at-museum-of-contemporary-art/.

Myers, Terry R. "William Pope.L: *Trinket*." *Brooklyn Rail*, May 6, 2015.

Myles, Eileen. "What I Saw." *Art XX* 2 (September 2009): 22–23.

Nathan, Emily. "Prospect.2 New Orleans: Beating Heart Biennial." *Artnet Magazine,* November 2, 2011. http://www.artnet.com/magazineus/features/nathan/prospect-2-biennial-new-orleans-11-2-11.asp.

Nelson, Steven. "William Pope.L: The Friendliest Black Artist in America." *African Arts* (Summer 2003): 92–93.

O'Grady, Megan. "Troubled Waters." *T: The New York Times Style Magazine*, March 2, 2018: 90.

Owens, Clifford. "Notes on Critical Black U.S. Performance Art and Artists." Fylkingen's Net Journal, October 23, 2003. http://www.hz-journal.org/n3/owens.html.

Peabody, Rebecca. "The Reassurance Project: William Pope.L in the Archive." *Getty Research Journal* 4 (November 2012): 195–200.

Pogrebin, Robert. "Warhol Foundation Finances Work Rebuffed by N.E.A." *New York Times*, December 21, 2000.

——. "Arts Agency Delays Decision on Two Grants." *New York Times*, December 1, 2001.

Pollack, Barbara. "Superman Enters the Culture Wars." *Village Voice* 47, no. 2 (January 15, 2002): 47.

——. "The Art of Public Disturbance." *Art in America* 91, no. 5 (May 2003): 120–23, 158.

——. “William Pope.L: October Projects.” *Time Out New York* 681 (October 16–22, 2008): 87.

Robinson, Dash. “Consumer Demand: William Pope.L.” *Cambridge Tab* (Needham, Mass.), January 14, 2000.

Rogers, Mike. “William Pope.L.” *ArtUS* 21 (2008): 22.

Rush, Michael. “Art/Architecture: Performance Hops Back into the Scene.” *New York Times*, July 2, 2000.

Russeth, Andrew. “Pope.L Is Raising Funds to Bottle, Sell Flint Water.” *Art News*, August 8, 2017. http://www.artnews.com/2017/08/08/pope-l-is-raising-funds-to-bottle-sell-flint-water/.

Russo, Francine. “Sightlines: Performance Anxieties.” *Village Voice* 44, no. 50 (December 21, 1999): 129.

Shaked, Nizan. “Under the Banner of Contradiction.” *X-tra* 18, no. 1 (Fall 2015): 4–19.

Sharp, Sarah Rose. “Pope.L’s Conceptual Bottled Water Project Calls Attention to the Crisis in Flint.” *Hyperallergic*, October 17, 2017. https://hyperallergic.com/402175/in-flint-pope-ls-conceptual-bottled-water-project-calls-attention-to-a-crisis/.

Siegel, Katy. “Reconstruction,” *Art Journal* 70, no. 3 (Fall 2011): 5.

Sims, Lowery Stokes. “William Pope.L.” *High Performance* 60 (Winter 1992): 46–47.

Smee, Sebastian. “All over the Map.” *Boston Sunday Globe*, January 29, 2010.

Smith, Roberta. “Art in Review: William Pope.L.” *New York Times*, January 30, 2004.

——. “The Expansive Provocateur Pope.L, in Smaller, Potent Doses.” *New York Times*, June 29, 2017.

Stillman, Nick. “William Pope.L: *The Great White Way*, Fulton Street to Reade Street, Manhattan.” *Brooklyn Rail*, June 1, 2003.

——. “eRacism.” *Brooklyn Rail*, February 1, 2004.

Storey, Natalie. “On Your Knees!” *Santa Fe New Mexican*, March 12, 2006.

Taft, Catherine. “William Pope.L.” *Modern Painters* 19, no. 6 (July/August 2007): 83.

——. “C[illegible] Picks: William Pope.L.[illegible]rum.com, November 13, 2007. https://www.artforum.com/picks/william-pope-l-18897.

Terada, Rei. “Saturated Crime: Pope.L’s *Reenactor*.” *Blind Field: A Journal of Cultural Inquiry*, November 7, 2018. https://blindfieldjournal.com/2018/11/07/saturated-crime-pope-ls-reenactor/.

Thompson, Nato. “Hole-ly Moley: The Work of William Pope.L.” *Afterall* 18 (Summer 2009): 28–35.

Thrush, Glenn. “Art: *How Much Is That Nigger in the Window*.” *Downtown Express* (New York) 5, no. 12 (July 25, 1991).

Tousignant, Isa. “Crawl for Your Life.” *The Hour* (Montreal), November 4, 2004.

Trainor, James. “Walking the Walk: The Artist as Flaneur.” *Border Crossings* 88 (November 2003): 82–92.

——. “Ain’t No Such Thing as Superman.” *Frieze* 83 (May 2004): 60–63.

Urist, Jacoba. “How Do You Conserve Art Made of Bologna, or Bubble Gum, or Soap?” *The Atlantic*, June 9, 2017. https://www.theatlantic.com/science/archive/2017/06/how-do-you-conserve-art-made-of-bologna-or-bubble-gum-or-soap/529713/.

Valdez, Sarah. “William Pope.L at Mitchell-Innes and Nash.” *Art on Paper* 13, no. 2 (November/December 2008): 84–85.

Valentine, Victoria L. “Loaded with Symbolism, a Fountain Sculpture by Pope.L Is among New Acquisitions at Carnegie Museum of Art.” *Culture Type*, July 29, 2018. https://www.culturetype.com/2018/07/29/loaded-with-symbolism-a-fountain-sculpture-by-pope-l-is-among-new-acquisitions-at-carnegie-museum-of-art/.

Vanderbilt, Tom. “Preview: *The Last Newspaper*, the New Museum.” *Artforum* 49, no. 2 (September 2010): 162.

Van Ryzin, Jeanne. “Pope.L Takes His Provocative Art to the Streets.” *Austin* (TX) *American-Statesman*, September 11, 2003.

Vogel, Wendy. “Post-Truth Detroit.” Frieze.com, November 8, 2017. https://frieze.com/article/post-truth-detroit.

Volk, Gregory. “Rolo Castillo and William Pope.L at The Project.” *Flash Art* (March/April 1999): 113–14.

——. “Topsy Turvical: William Pope.L in Kansas City.” Grand Arts, August 2008. https://www.grandarts.com/past_projects/2008/2008_09.html.

Wargo, Abby. “Differing, Drawn: Scholar Examines Pope.L’s ‘Skin Set’ Drawings.” *The Elm* (Chestertown, Md.), April 26, 2018. http://elm.washcoll.edu/index.php/2018/04/differing-drawn-scholar-examines-pope-ls-skin-set-drawings/.

Wilson, Michael. “Art Review: William Pope.L., ‘landscape + object + animal.’” *Time Out New York* 765 (June 3–9, 2010): 48.

Wood, Joe. “Color Blinded.” *Village Voice* 35, no. 45 (November 6, 1990): 116.

——. “Cameos: *The Aunt Jenny Chronicles/Journey to Incontinence*.” *Village Voice* 36, no. 42, October 15, 1991: 130.

WORKS IN THE EXHIBITION

member: Pope.L, 1978–2001

All works in the exhibition © Pope.L. Unless otherwise noted, all works in the collection of The Museum of Modern Art, New York, acquired in part through the generosity of Jill and Peter Kraus, Anne and Joel S. Ehrenkranz, The Contemporary Arts Council of the Museum of Modern Art, The Jill and Peter Kraus Media and Performance Art Acquisition Fund, and Jill and Peter Kraus in honor of Michael Lynne.

Works are separated into seven categories and listed in chronological order.

Video

Egg Eating Contest, basement version, 1990
Video: color, sound; 8:04 minutes

The Aunt Jenny Chronicles, 1991
Video: color, sound; 3:04 minutes

Black Domestic a.k.a. Cow Commercial, 1994
Video: color, sound; 2:49 minutes

Member a.k.a. Schlong Journey, 1996
Video: color, sound; 3:39 minutes

Sweet Desire a.k.a. Burial Piece, 1996
Video: color; 4:19 minutes

Sweet Desire a.k.a. Burial Piece, window version, 1996
Video: color, sound; 2:17 minutes

ATM Piece, 1997
Video: color, sound; 1:54 minutes

Eating the Wall Street Journal, Version 3, 2000
Video: color, sound; 2:54 minutes

Eracism, Version 8b, 2000
Video: color, sound; 10:23 minutes

The Great White Way: 22 miles, 9 years, 1 street, 2001
Video: color, sound; 6:34 minutes

Photographs

Times Square Crawl a.k.a. Meditation Square Piece, 1978
Times Square, New York
Five inkjet prints
Each: 10 × 15" (25.4 × 38.1 cm)
Edition 1 of 3, 1 AP

Thunderbird Immolation a.k.a. Meditation Square Piece, 1978
West Broadway, New York
Five inkjet prints
Two works: 6 × 9" (15.2 × 22.9 cm)
Two works: 15 × 10" (38.1 × 25.4 cm)
One work: 10 × 15" (25.4 × 38.1 cm)
Edition 1 of 3, 1 AP

Egg Eating Contest, 1990
BACA Downtown, Brooklyn, N.Y.
Five inkjet prints
Each: 10 × 15" (25.4 × 38.1 cm)
Edition 1 of 3, 1 AP

The Aunt Jenny Chronicles, 1991
PS122, New York
Five inkjet prints
Three works: 15 × 10" (38.1 × 25.4 cm)
Two works: 10 × 15" (25.4 × 38.1 cm)
Edition 1 of 3, 1 AP

How Much Is That Nigger in the Window a.k.a. Tompkins Square Crawl, 1991
Tompkins Square Park, New York
Five inkjet prints
Four works: 10 × 15" (25.4 × 38.1 cm)
One work: 15 × 10" (38.1 × 25.4 cm)
Edition 1 of 3, 1 AP

Eracism, Version 2, 1993
Drew University, Madison, N.J.
Inkjet print
10 × 15" (25.4 × 38.1 cm)
Edition 1 of 3, 1 AP

Eracism, Version 7, 1996
Ko Performance Festival, Amherst, Mass.
Two inkjet prints
One work: 15 × 10" (38.1 × 25.4 cm)
One work: 10 × 15" (25.4 × 38.1 cm)
Edition 1 of 3, 1 AP

Member a.k.a. Schlong Journey, 1996
125th Street, Harlem, New York
Five inkjet prints
Three works: 10 × 15" (25.4 × 38.1 cm)
Two works: 15 × 10" (38.1 × 25.4 cm)
Edition 1 of 3, 1 AP

Sweet Desire a.k.a. Burial Piece, 1996
Skowhegan School of Painting and Sculpture, Maine
Five inkjet prints
Three works: 10 × 15" (25.4 × 38.1 cm)
Two works: 15 × 10" (38.1 × 25.4 cm)
Edition 1 of 3, 1 AP

ATM Piece, 1997
Chase Manhattan Bank, Forty-Second Street, New York
Five inkjet prints
Four works: 10 × 15" (25.4 × 38.1 cm)
One work: 15 × 10" (38.1 × 25.4 cm)
Edition 1 of 3, 1 AP

Eracism, Version 7b, 1997
Mobius Experimental Theater Space, Boston
Two inkjet prints
Each: 10 × 15" (25.4 × 38.1 cm)
Edition 1 of 3, 1 AP

Eating the Wall Street Journal, Version 2, 2000
Mobius Experimental Theater Space, Boston
Inkjet print
9 × 6" (22.9 × 15.2 cm)
Edition 1 of 3, 1 AP

Eating the Wall Street Journal, Version 3, 2000
Sculpture Center, New York
Four inkjet prints
Two works: 10 × 15" (25.4 × 38.1 cm)
One work: 6 × 9" (15.2 × 22.9 cm)
One work: 15 × 10" (38.1 × 25.4 cm)
Edition 1 of 3, 1 AP

The Great White Way: 22 miles, 9 years, 1 street, 2002
Broadway, New York
Three inkjet prints
Each: 10 × 15" (25.4 × 38.1 cm)
Edition 1 of 3, 1 AP

Training Crawl (for The Great White Way: 22 miles, 5 years, 1 street), 2001
Lewiston, Maine
Two inkjet prints
Each: 10 × 15" (25.4 × 38.1 cm)
Edition 1 of 3, 1 AP

Installations and Sculptures

Snow Crawl, 1991–2001/2019
Video: color, sound; 7:42 minutes; and structure made of wood, mirrors, and cardboard with cathode-ray-tube television and DVD player
Dimensions variable

Eating the Wall Street Journal, 2000
Wood-and-metal structure, toilet, newspaper, pillow, fishing pole, Heinz Ketchup bottles, and milk cartons
Dimensions variable

The Black Factory Archive, 2004–
Video (*SUM Film*, 2004–6: color, sound; 7:56:49 [looped]), donated objects, twice-sold goods, ephemera, digital image files, and wallpaper
Dimensions variable
The Museum of Modern Art, New York. Fund for the Twenty-First Century and Deborah Wye Endowment Fund

Package Received But Never Opened #21, 2015
Maisie's Savory Snack Mix, The Popcorn Factory Caramel Popcorn, Emilie Roux Pretzel Snacks, Walkers Belgian Chocolate Cookies, Ghirardelli Dark Chocolate Blueberry Squares, ceramic bowl, plastic, and silk ribbon
18 × 9 × 8" (45.7 × 22.9 × 20.3 cm)
Courtesy Mitchell-Innes & Nash, New York

Package Received But Never Opened #107, 2015
White tissue paper with graphite and coffee stain over unknown contents
9 × 5¾ × ¾" (22.9 × 14.6 × 1.9 cm)
Courtesy Mitchell-Innes & Nash, New York

Package Received But Never Opened #75, 2017
Brown paper with postal markings over unknown contents
18 × 14 × 12" (45.7 × 35.6 × 30.5 cm)
Courtesy Mitchell-Innes & Nash, New York

Ephemera, Objects, and Props

Bra
From *Egg Eating Contest*, basement version, 1990
Cotton and polyester
12 × 16" (30.5 × 40.6 cm)

Jumpsuit
From *Egg Eating Contest*, basement version, 1990
Polyester
63½ × 18" (161.3 × 45.7 cm)

Drawing
From *Egg Eating Contest*, basement version, 1990
Synthetic polymer paint, ink, and tape on paper
33½ × 26" (85.1 × 66 cm)

Drawing
From *Egg Eating Contest*, basement version, 1990
Synthetic polymer paint, ink, and tape on paper
65½ × 42" (166.4 × 106.7 cm)

Street fragment
From *How Much Is That Nigger in the Window a.k.a. Tompkins Square Crawl*, 1991
Asphalt
11 × 9 × 11½" (27.9 × 22.9 × 29.2 cm)

Timberland boots
From *How Much Is That Nigger in the Window a.k.a. Tompkins Square Crawl*, 1991
Leather
Shoe Size: 11½M

Dress shirt
From *The Aunt Jenny Chronicles*, 1991
Cotton
33 × 19" (83.8 × 48.3 cm)

Two music stands
From *The Aunt Jenny Chronicles*, 1991
Plastic and metal
Dimensions variable

Sleeveless shirt with drawing
From *The Aunt Jenny Chronicles*, 1991
Cotton with marker
28 × 19" (71.1 × 48.3 cm)

Belt
From *Black Domestic a.k.a. Cow Commercial*, 1994
Leather
39 × 1" (99.1 × 2.5 cm)

Cow figurine
From *Black Domestic a.k.a. Cow Commercial*, 1994
Plastic and leather
17¼ × 27¾ × 6" (43.8 × 70.5 × 15.2 cm)

Schlong sleeve
From *Member a.k.a. Schlong Journey*, 1996
Two PVC tubes, cardboard, paint, and marker with plastic wheeled base and stuffed bunny
Dimensions variable

Suit, shirt, and necktie
From *Member a.k.a. Schlong Journey*, 1996
Cotton, polyester, and leather
Jacket: 33½ × 18½" (85.1 × 47 cm)
Shirt: 30 × 30½" (76.2 × 77.5 cm)
Pants: 40" (101.6 cm) long
Necktie: 51 × 2½" (129.5 × 6.4 cm)

Timberland boots
From *ATM Piece*, 1997
Leather
Shoe Size: 13M

Africa cloth
From *Eracism*, Version 8b, 2000
Sewn cloth with Velcro
53¾ × 34½" (136.4 × 87.6 cm)

Dress
From *Eracism*, Version 8b, 2000
Cotton, polyester, and tulle
50 × 48 × 36" (127 × 121.9 × 91.4 cm)

Jockstrap
From *Eracism*, Version 8b, 2000
Lycra, plastic, and drawing
Dimensions variable

Bench
From *Eracism*, Version 8b, 2000
Painted wood
38½ × 40 × 10" (97.8 × 101.6 × 25.4 cm)

Table
From *Eracism*, Version 8b, 2000
Painted wood
30 × 48 × 36" (76.2 × 121.9 × 91.4 cm)

Two eyeglass straps
From *Eracism*, Version 8b, 2000
Terrycloth
11" (27.9 cm) long

Headband
From *Eracism*, Version 8b, 2000
Terrycloth
8¾" (22.2 cm) long

Three bottles in suitcase
From *Eracism*, Version 8b, 2000
Glass, plastic, and metal
11½ × 16½ × 4¾" (29.2 × 41. 9 × 12.1 cm)

US cloth
From *Eracism*, Version 8b, 2000
Sewn cloth with Velcro
30 × 23½" (76.2 × 59.7 cm)

Skateboard
From *The Great White Way: 22 miles, 9 years, 1 street*, 2001–09
Painted wood and metal, bungee cords
29 × 8 × 3½" (73.7 × 20.3 × 8.9 cm)

Superman costume
From *The Great White Way: 22 miles, 9 years, 1 street*, 2001–09
Polyester
60 × 24" (152.4 × 61 cm)

Hat
From *The Great White Way: 22 miles, 9 years, 1 street*, 2001–09
Wool
9 × 8¼" (22.9 × 21 cm)

Drawings

Failure Drawing #140: Worm Segment World, 2004
Ink and marker on printed paper (verso)
8½ × 11" (21.6 × 27.9 cm)
Courtesy Mitchell-Innes & Nash, New York

Failure Drawing #34: Chateau Hotel Bats and Piles, 2004–06
Ink, ballpoint pen, marker, and synthetic polymer paint on hotel stationery
5½ × 4¼" (14 × 10.8 cm)
Courtesy Mitchell-Innes & Nash, New York

Failure Drawing #1139: Worm Segments on Green, 2004–06
Ballpoint pen, synthetic polymer paint, stains, and hair on printed paper
4⅜ × 7" (11.1 × 17.8 cm)
Courtesy Mitchell-Innes & Nash, New York

Failure Drawing #355: Steaming Phali, 2006
Ballpoint pen, synthetic polymer paint, and watercolor on printed card
3¾ × 9¹³⁄₁₆" (9.5 × 24.9 cm)
Courtesy Mitchell-Innes & Nash, New York

Books

William Pope.L's "How Much Is That Nigger in the Window": Rap Street Journal, 1992
Artist's book
8½ × 11 × ¾" (21.6 × 27.9 cm × 1.1 cm)
The Museum of Modern Art Library, New York

Live Events

Eating the Wall Street Journal, flag version, 2019
Performance
Courtesy Mitchell-Innes & Nash, New York

Dressing Up for Civil Rights, MoMA version, 2019
Performance

CONTRIBUTORS

Naomi Beckwith is Manilow Senior Curator at the Museum of Contemporary Art Chicago, where her exhibition and book projects focus on the impact of identity and multidisciplinary practices for shaping contemporary art. Prior to working at the MCA Chicago, she held positions at the Institute of Contemporary Art in Philadelphia and the Studio Museum in Harlem, New York.

Mark H. C. Bessire is Judy and Leonard Lauder Director of the Portland Museum of Art in Portland, Maine. At the Institute of Contemporary Art at Maine College of Art in Portland, he curated the first retrospective of Pope.L's work, *William Pope.L: Eracism* (2002), and edited the accompanying publication, *William Pope.L: The Friendliest Black Artist in America©*. Previously, he was a Helena Rubinstein Fellow at the Whitney Independent Study Program and a Fulbright Fellow in Tanzania.

Cynthia Carr is a New York–based writer. Using the byline C. Carr, she reported on experimental art for the *Village Voice* from 1984 to 2003. Her books include *Our Town: A Heartland Lynching, a Haunted Town, and the Hidden History of White America* (1991), the edited collection *On Edge: Performance at the End of the Twentieth Century* (2008), and *Fire in the Belly: The Life and Times of David Wojnarowicz* (2012).

Valerie Cassel Oliver is Sydney and Frances Lewis Family Curator of Modern and Contemporary Art at the Virginia Museum of Fine Arts, Richmond. She formerly served as senior curator at the Contemporary Arts Museum Houston from 2000 to 2017. Her past exhibitions include *Double Consciousness: Black Conceptual Art since 1970* (2005) and *Radical Presence: Black Performance in Contemporary Art* (2012), which toured through 2015. Recently, with Naomi Beckwith, she organized the survey *Howardena Pindell: What Remains to Be Seen* (2018).

Stuart Comer is the Lonti Ebers Chief Curator, Department of Media and Performance, The Museum of Modern Art.

Adrienne Edwards is Engell Speyer Family Curator and Curator of Performance at the Whitney Museum of American Art, New York.

Malik Gaines is Associate Professor of Performance Studies at New York University's Tisch School of the Arts and the author of *Black Performance on the Outskirts of the Left: A History of the Impossible* (2017). Since 2000, Gaines has performed and exhibited with collaborators as the group My Barbarian.

Adrian Heathfield is a writer, curator, and professor of performance studies. His books include *Out of Now* (2009), a monograph on the Taiwanese-American artist Tehching Hsieh, as well as the edited collections *Shattered Anatomies* (1997), *Small Acts* (2000), *Live: Art and Performance* (2004), and *Perform, Repeat, Record* (2012). He is currently a Professor of Performance and Visual Culture at the University of Roehampton, London.

EJ Hill lives and works in Los Angeles. His practice incorporates painting, writing, installation, and performance in ways that seek to elevate bodies and amplify voices that have long been rendered invisible by oppressive social structures. Hill has exhibited or performed at the Studio Museum in Harlem, New York (2016); Future Generation Art Prize at the 57th Venice Biennale (2017); Underground Museum, Los Angeles (2017); Hammer Museum, Los Angeles (2018); and Aspen Art Museum (2018), among other venues.

Danielle A. Jackson is a Curatorial Assistant in the Department of Media and Performance, The Museum of Modern Art.

Thomas J. Lax is Curator in the Department of Media and Performance, The Museum of Modern Art.

André Lepecki is Professor of Performance Studies at New York University. He works and researches at the intersection of critical dance studies, curatorial practice, performance theory, contemporary dance, and visual-arts performance. He is the author of *Exhausting Dance: Performance and the Politics of Movement* (2006) and *Singularities: Dance in the Age of Performance* (2016).

Yvonne Rainer is a dancer, choreographer, and filmmaker. One of the founders of Judson Dance Theater, Rainer transitioned from dance to filmmaking in the 1970s and returned to dance in 2000. Recent publications include her memoir *Feelings Are Facts: A Life* (2006), *Poems* (2011), and the edited collection *Moving and Being Moved* (2017).

Kaegan Sparks is the 2018–19 Museum Research Consortium Fellow in the Department of Media and Performance, The Museum of Modern Art.

Martine Syms is an artist who uses video and performance to examine representations of blackness. Her artwork has been exhibited and screened at The Museum of Modern Art; Hammer Museum, Los Angeles; ICA London; New Museum, New York; Art Institute of Chicago; and the Studio Museum in Harlem, New York, among other institutions. She is on faculty at the School of Art at the California Institute of the Arts, Valencia, and runs Dominica Publishing, an imprint dedicated to exploring blackness in visual culture.

Martha Wilson is a pioneering feminist artist and art-space director who over the past four decades has created innovative photographic and video works that explore her female subjectivity. In 1976, she founded Franklin Furnace, an artist-run space that champions the exploration and preservation of artist books, temporary installations, and performance art, as well as online works.

ACKNOWLEDGMENTS

Pope.L recently mused that "a good collaboration requires two things: space when you need it, and boundaries when you don't." I am deeply indebted to the many dedicated and inspiring colleagues and contributors who have come together to create space for Pope.L at The Museum of Modern Art, including this publication and the exhibition it accompanies, *member: Pope.L, 1978–2001*, which brings the Museum's ambitious acquisition of thirteen performances by Pope.L to its galleries for the first time.

The exhibition is part of the opening season celebrating the Museum's extensive renovation and expansion on its ninetieth anniversary. The show was organized during a period of profound reconsideration and transformation that has repeatedly reminded me what an extraordinary group of people make The Museum of Modern Art what it is. To the many minds and hands at MoMA and beyond that forged and enabled this project, my gratitude knows no bounds. It is a pleasure and privilege to work with such committed colleagues and to be part of an institution that puts artists at its center and supports them on this scale.

This project's commitment to cross-disciplinary thinking benefited from the input of every department at the Museum, led by Glenn D. Lowry, The David Rockefeller Director, who provided steadfast support and guidance at every turn. Former Associate Director and Laurenz Foundation Curator, Kathy Halbreich, now Executive Director at the Robert Rauschenberg Foundation, provided constant insight, inspiration, and support. The encouragement and ingenuity offered by Ramona Bannayan, Senior Deputy Director, Exhibitions and Collections, played an essential role in bringing the exhibition to fruition, and Peter Reed, Senior Deputy Director, Curatorial Affairs, provided helpful assistance at key junctures. Leah Dickerman, Director, Editorial and Content Strategy, offered scholarly exchange and meaningful advice regarding the public reception of Pope.L's work.

Danielle A. Jackson, Curatorial Assistant in the Department of Media and Performance, has been an exceptional partner and the life force of this project. Her diligence in choreographing all manner of practical matters was matched only by her infectious intellectual joy and the care she invested in every detail. Her passion for books and bookmaking has shaped the publication you now hold. Kaegan Sparks, the 2018–19 Museum Research Consortium Fellow, expertly researched Pope.L and compiled the chronology in this book in collaboration with the artist and his studio.

Throughout the development of this exhibition, my inspirational colleagues in the Department of Media and Performance were faithful and attentive interlocutors. Erica Papernik-Shimizu, Associate Curator, and Athena Holbrook, Collection Specialist, were committed custodians of the complex acquisition process. Thomas Lax, Curator, who joined me for the first visit to Pope.L's studio five years ago, offered a steady beat of invaluable insights. Ana Janevski, Curator; Martha Joseph, Assistant Curator; Giampaolo Bianconi, Curatorial Assistant; and Chelsea Airey, Assistant to The Lonti Ebers Chief Curator of Media and Performance, all offered crucial support and vision. The early involvement of Stephanie Weber, formerly Assistant Curator in the Department and now Curator, Contemporary Art at Lenbachhaus in Munich, was integral to bringing this body of work to the Museum.

There would, of course, be no book without its exceptional authors. I offer greatest thanks to Naomi Beckwith, Mark H. C. Bessire, Cynthia Carr, Adrienne Edwards, Malik Gaines, Adrian Heathfield, EJ Hill, Danielle A. Jackson, Thomas J. Lax, André Lepecki, Valerie Cassel Oliver, Yvonne Rainer, Martine Syms, and Martha Wilson. Each brought expertise as a scholar, critic, artist, filmmaker, curator, or poet to cast into language a body of work that can at first appear ineffable. My gratitude extends to the photographers and archives for their visionary images of Pope.L's work and performance-related ephemera, including Luc Demers; Fales Library and Special Collections, New York University; Brian Forrest; Paul Fortin; Franklin Furnace Archive, New York; Lydia Grey; Ellen Labenski; Ellen LaForge; Larry List; The Museum of Contemporary Art, Los Angeles; The Museum of Modern Art Library, New York; *P-Form*; James Pruznick; Sarah Schwartz; Ken Thompson; and Chantal Zakari.

I am ever grateful for Joseph Logan and Katy Nelson's thoughtful and lucid design of the catalogue, which perfectly articulates the work on its pages. Editor Domenick Ammirati treated every word and component of the book with care, and I thank him for his diligence and rigor. I am grateful to Soyoung Yoon for her thoughtful and critical insights.

This publication was delivered with unwavering dedication and commitment by MoMA's Department of Publications. I thank Christopher Hudson, Publisher; Hannah Kim, Business and Marketing Director; Don McMahon, Editorial Director; Marc Sapir, Production Director, and Matthew Pimm, Production Manager; Sophie Golub, Department Manager; Naomi Falk, Rights Coordinator; and Anora Sandhu, Intern, whose keen eyes and sharp mind spared us many an infelicity.

I am also indebted to my outstanding colleagues in MoMA's Departments of Development, Institutional Giving, and Affiliate Programs, including Todd Bishop, Senior Deputy Director, External Affairs; Sylvia Renner, Assistant Director, International Funding; Maggie Lyko, Director, Special Events and Affiliate Programs; Jessica Smith, Assistant Director, Institutional Giving and Global Partnerships; Anna Luisa Vallifuoco, Manager, Institutional Giving and Global Partnerships; Erica Bibby, Development Officer; Meredith Dean, Development Associate; Nora Webb, Assistant Director of Institutional Giving; Leah Asha Allen, Program Coordinator, The Friends of Education; and Courtney Schaefer, Associate Director, Membership and Affiliate Programs.

Pope.L's *The Black Factory Archive* is an important hinge in the exhibition. I am deeply thankful to the Departments of Drawings and Prints and Collection Management and Exhibition Registration for their generous interdepartmental loan and their guidance on this key work: Christophe Cherix, The Robert Lehman Foundation Chief Curator of Drawings and Prints; Esther Adler, Associate Curator; Emily Cushman, Collection Specialist; Margot Yale, Cataloguer; Sewon Kang, Senior Cataloguer; Anna Blaha, Curatorial Assistant; Ana Torok, Curatorial Assistant; Jeff White, Preparator; and Sydney Briggs, Associate Registrar, Collections.

In addition, the exhibition benefited greatly from the intellect and interest of all of the Museum's Chief Curators, including Rajendra Roy, The Celeste Bartos Chief Curator of Film; Martino Stierli, The Philip Johnson

Chief Curator of Architecture and Design; Ann Temkin, The Marie-Josée and Henry Kravis Chief Curator of Painting and Sculpture; and Peter Eleey, Chief Curator of MoMA PS1. Colleagues in the Department of Archives, Library, and Research Collections made their collections available for both display and research. I thank Jennifer Tobias, Librarian, Reader Services, and Nathaniel Otting, Library Assistant.

The very nature of Pope.L's work and this exhibition are rooted in fugitive gestures and materials. I am indebted to my devoted colleagues in the Department of Conservation for rising to the philosophical and practical challenges of guiding material of this nature into the Collection and preparing it for the public to see. My great appreciation goes to Kate Lewis, The Agnes Gund Chief Conservator; Chris McGlinchey, The Sally and Michael Gordon Senior Conservation Scientist; Lee Ann Daffner, The Andrew W. Mellon Foundation Conservator of Photographs; Peter C[illegible], Associate Media Conservator; Ellen Moody, The David Booth Associate Sculpture Conservator; Annie Wilker, Associate Paper Conservator; Amy Brost, Assistant Media Conservator; Caroline Gil, The Andrew W. Mellon Media Conservation Fellow; and Joy Bloser, The David Booth Fellow in Sculpture Conservation. I also thank Tae Smith and Christina Ewald, our textile conservators for the exhibition, for their inventive approaches to costume display.

My colleagues on MoMA's Creative Team and in the Department of Communications helped craft meaningful entry points for the public and press, led by Rob Baker, Director of Marketing and Creative Strategy, and Amanda Hicks, Director of Communications and Public Affairs, with Rebecca Stokes, Director, Marketing Campaigns and Audience Development; Wendy Olson, Marketing Manager; Stephanie Katsias, Building Project Publicity Coordinator; and Maureen Masters, Film, Media, Performance Publicist. On the Creative Team, I would also like to thank Shannon Darrough, Director, Digital Media; Chiara Bernasconi, Assistant Director, Digital Media; Sean Yetter, Video Producer; Natasha Giliberti, Video Producer; Prudence Peiffer, Managing Editor; and Jason Persse, Editorial Manager.

The Graphics team—Rob Giampietro, Director of Design; Damien Saatdjian, Art Director; Kevin Ballon, Senior Graphic Designer; Claire Corey, Production Manager; and Melanie Conrad, Design Operations Manager—brought incredible enthusiasm and care to the graphic identity and installation of the exhibition.

In addition, our colleagues in Imaging and Visual Resources, including Robert Kastler, Director; Jennifer Sellar, Digital Asset Manager; Kurt Heumiller, Studio Production Manager; and Roberto Rivera, Production Assistant, skillfully provided images for the wallpaper elements in the exhibition.

The exhibition benefited from our editors and collaborators in Education, who considered *member*'s public reception. Thanks to Wendy Woon, The Edward John Noble Foundation Deputy Director; Pablo Helguera, Director, Adult and Academic Programs; Jess van Nostrand, Assistant Director of Exhibition Programs and Gallery Initiatives; Leticia Gutierrez, Associate Educator; Rachell Morillo, Assistant Educator; Alethea Rockwell, Assistant Educator, Studio and Artist programs; Jenna Madison, Assistant Director; Kelly Cannon, Associate Educator, Interpretation, Research, and Digital Learning; and Hannah Fagin, Coordinator, Adult and Academic Programs. Particular thanks go to Sara Bodinson, Director, Interpretation, Research & Digital Learning, the embodiment of the project's collaborative spirit, who generously helped in crafting interpretation for this exhibition. The Publications department's Jaclyn Neudorf, Assistant Editor, and Maria Marchenkova, Senior Assistant Editor, were also essential partners in preparing interpretive texts.

The Department of Visitor Engagement, led by Sonya Shrier, Director, and William Umana, Assistant Director, ensured that each visitor was welcomed. In any exhibition that includes live performative actions, the staff in the Department of Security and Operations are our frontline heroes who guarantee the safety of all. We are grateful to Tuniji Adeniji, Director of Facilities and Safety; Daniel Platt, Director of Security; and Tyrone Wyllie, Associate Director of Security.

MoMA's Exhibition Planning and Administration team is a crucial factor in the Museum's ability to deliver exhibitions of such ambition and complexity. I am always proud and delighted to work alongside Erik Patton, Director; Lizzie Gorfaine, Assistant Director and Producer, Performance and Live Programs, who dauntlessly makes our live performance dreams possible; Cate Griffin, former Exhibition Manager; Elizabeth Henderson, Exhibition Manager; Kate Scherer, Manager, Performance and Live Programs; Ginny Benson, Assistant Performance Coordinator; and Beatrice Johnson, Assistant Performance Coordinator.

The show's stunning exhibition design was crafted by Mack Cole-Edelsack, Senior Design Manager. The audiovisual work so central to the show was beautifully installed by Aaron Louis, Director of Audio Visual, and his skilled team: Aaron Harrow, AV Design Manager; Mike Gibbons, AV Exhibitions Foreperson; and Jeffrey Bergstrom, Travis Kray, and Zachary Prewitt, AV Technicians.

Sarah Primm, Assistant Registrar, Collections, coordinated many details of the exhibition with her characteristic grace and good humor. Peter Perez, Foreman, Frame Shop, expertly and elegantly framed the works in the exhibition. Of course, there would be no show without the Art Handling and Preparation team; I am enormously grateful to Sarah Wood, Assistant Manager; Tom Krueger, Assistant Manager; and art handlers Eric Araujo, Bradley Biancardi, Francesca Caruso, Dietrich Kleffel, Mark Murchison, Max Runko, Arkadiy Ryabin, and Peter Teraberry.

As with any acquisition, and particularly one of such scope and intricacy, we benefited greatly from the support of our General Counsel team: Patty Lipshutz, General Counsel and Secretary to the Board; Nancy Adelson, Deputy General Counsel, who was spectacularly committed to this project; and Alexis Sandler, Associate General Counsel.

The network of support for *member* expanded well beyond the Museum's walls and includes a number of people who have been integral to the development of the project. From Pope.L's studio I would like to thank Noelle Africh, Fabienne Elie, Jasper Goodrich, Anaïs Daly, and Dave Lloyd. From Pope.L's gallery, Mitchell-Innes & Nash, New York, I would like to extend particular thanks to Lucy Mitchell-Innes and Courtney Willis Blair, alongside David Nash, Josephine Nash, Isabelle Hogenkamp, Sheldon Mukamal, Peter Tecu, Bridget Finn, and Ebony L. Haynes.

Powerhouse Arts, New York, was essential to realizing the performances of *Eating the Wall Street Journal*, flag version. We are incredibly grateful for the vision and creative problem solving provided by Luther Davis, Art Domantay, Jeremy Gender, Gina Pham, John Michael Swartz, and Kiah Vidyarthi.

This exhibition is one part of *Pope.L: Instigation, Aspiration, Perspiration*, a trio of complementary presentations of Pope.L's work organized by MoMA, Public Art Fund, and the Whitney Museum of American Art. This unique collaboration between institutions across New York City has been an exciting opportunity to work with colleagues and fellow travelers who share our passion for Pope.L's unique and urgent project. From the Whitney, I thank Adam D. Weinberg, Alice Pratt Brown Director, and Christopher Y. Lew, Nancy and Fred Poses Curator, and their colleagues Haley Kattner Allen, Graphic Design Project Manager; Reid Farrington, Audio Visual Manager; Joel Fear, Graphic Designer; Jackie Foster, Senior Digital Content Manager; Hilary Greenbaum, Director of Graphic Design; Maura Heffner, Assistant Director, Exhibitions Management; Zoe Jackson, Director of Marketing; Robert Lomblad, Art Handler; Lindsey O'Connor, Exhibitions Manager; Lindsay Pollock, Chief Communications and Content Officer; David Selimoski, Engineering Manager; Aliza Sena, Digital Producer; Stephen Soba, Director of Communications; Mark Steigelman, Director, Exhibition Design Production; and Ambika Trasi, Curatorial Assistant. We are likewise grateful to the entire Public Art Fund team, with special thanks to Nicholas Baume, Director and Chief Curator; Walsh Hansen, Project Manager; Kellie Honeycutt, Deputy Director; Sara Jones, Graphic Designer; Katerina Stathopoulou, Assistant Curator; and Allegra Thoresen, Associate Director of Communications.

Above all, I would like to thank Pope.L, an artist whose work swiftly betrays the deep intelligence behind its irreverence. He has been as dedicated a collaborator as he has a trickster, diligently scavenging his studio and archive for missing clues and guiding us through the material and immaterial traces of his career, while throwing enough intellectual curve balls to ensure we never took the work or its complexity for granted. Taking on not one but three New York institutions simultaneously is no easy task. I am humbled by his generous dedication to our joint effort.

Stuart Comer
The Lonti Ebers Chief Curator of Media and Performance
The Museum of Modern Art

PHOTOGRAPH CREDITS

Courtesy The Museum of Modern Art, New York, Department of Imaging and Visual Resources, photo by John Wronn: Endpapers, 74 (bottom), 75 (top).

Courtesy Franklin Furnace Archive, Inc., New York: 24, 110.

Photo by Ellen LaForge: 38, 42–44, 48–49.

Photographer unknown: 50, 54, 76, 81.

Photo by Adam Reich, courtesy the artist and Mitchell-Innes & Nash, New York: 55, 61.

Photo by Brian Forrest, courtesy The Museum of Contemporary Art, Los Angeles: 56.

Courtesy The Museum of Modern Art, New York: 60, 86–87.

Photo by James Pruznick: 20, 62, 66.

Photo by Marty Heitner, courtesy Franklin Furnace Archive, Inc., New York: 67.

Photo by Lydia Grey: 68, 72–73, 74 (top), 88, 92–93, 100, 104, 106, 111 (bottom), 117.

Photo by Massachusetts Museum of Contemporary Art/Art Evans: 75 (bottom).

© *P-Form* / Randolph Street Gallery Archives, photo by Paul Fortin, cover design by Chantal Zakari, courtesy The Museum of Modern Art Library, New York: 80.

Photo by Paul Fortin: 82, 94, 98–99.

Courtesy Fales Library and Special Collections, New York University: 105.

Photo by Johnna Arnold, courtesy Yerba Buena Center for the Arts, San Francisco: 111 (top).

Photo by Luc Demers: 112, 116.

Hyundai Card

The exhibition is presented as part of The Hyundai Card Performance Series.

Major support is provided by The Jill and Peter Kraus Endowed Fund for Contemporary Exhibitions and The Jon Stryker Endowment.

Additional support is provided by The Friends of Education of The Museum of Modern Art, Marilyn and Larry Fields, Nancy and David Frej, Barbara Karp Shuster, and Ann and Mel Schaffer.

Leadership contributions to the Annual Exhibition Fund, in support of the Museum's collection and collection exhibitions, are generously provided by the Kate W. Cassidy Foundation, Sue and Edgar Wachenheim III, Mimi and Peter Haas Fund, Jerry I. Speyer and Katherine G. Farley, Eva and Glenn Dubin, The Sandra and Tony Tamer Exhibition Fund, Alice and Tom Tisch, The David Rockefeller Council, Anne Dias, Kathy and Richard S. Fuld, Jr., Kenneth C. Griffin, Marie-Josée and Henry R. Kravis, Jo Carole and Ronald S. Lauder, Anna Marie and Robert F. Shapiro, The Keith Haring Foundation, and The Contemporary Arts Council of The Museum of Modern Art.

Major contributions to the Annual Exhibition Fund are provided by the Estate of Ralph L. Riehle, Emily Rauh Pulitzer, Brett and Daniel Sundheim, Karen and Gary Winnick, The Marella and Giovanni Agnelli Fund for Exhibitions, Clarissa Alcock and Edgar Bronfman, Jr., Agnes Gund, and Oya and Bülent Eczacıbaşı.

Published in conjunction with the exhibition *member: Pope.L, 1978–2001*, organized by Stuart Comer, the Lonti Ebers Chief Curator of Media and Performance, with Danielle A. Jackson, Curatorial Assistant, Department of Media and Performance, at The Museum of Modern Art, New York, October 21, 2019–February 1, 2020.

member: Pope.L, 1978–2001 is part of *Pope.L: Instigation, Aspiration, Perspiration*, a trio of complementary exhibitions organized by The Museum of Modern Art, the Whitney Museum of American Art, and Public Art Fund.

Produced by the Department of Publications, The Museum of Modern Art, New York

Christopher Hudson, Publisher
Hannah Kim, Business and Marketing Director
Don McMahon, Editorial Director
Marc Sapir, Production Director

Edited by Domenick Ammirati
Designed by Katy Nelson, Joseph Logan Design, New York

Production by Marc Sapir and Matthew Pimm
Printed and bound by Ofset Yapimevi, Istanbul

This book is typeset in GT America and Practice. The paper is 120 gsm Munken Polar Rough.

Published by The Museum of Modern Art
11 West 53 Street
New York, NY 10019-5497
www.moma.org

Library of Congress Control Number: 2019943708
ISBN: 978-1-63345-086-8

Distributed in the United States and Canada by
ARTBOOK | D.A.P.
75 Broad Street
Suite 630
New York, NY 10004
www.artbook.com

Distributed outside the United States and Canada by
Thames & Hudson Ltd
181A High Holborn
London WC1V 7QX
www.thamesandhudson.com

Printed and bound in Turkey

Handwritten titles by Pope.L, 2019

Front endpaper: Pages from *William Pope.L's "How Much Is That Nigger in the Window": Rap Street Journal*, 1992. Pictured: *Eating the Wall Street Journal*, early street version, New York, 1991
Front endpaper, pages 1–9: Pages from *William Pope.L's "How Much Is That Nigger in the Window": Rap Street Journal*, 1992. The Museum of Modern Art Library, New York. Redactions by Pope.L, 2019
Rear endpaper: Pages from *William Pope.L's "How Much Is That Nigger in the Window": Rap Street Journal*, 1992. Pictured: *Selling Mayonnaise for 100 Dollars a Dollop*, East Seventh Street and Cooper Square, New York, 1991

Page 74, top: *The Black Factory* performance tour, 2004. Pictured: Julie Hammond and Justin Lauder conducting an experiment in front of *The Black Factory* truck, location unknown
Page 74, bottom: Donated objects from *The Black Factory Archive*, 2003–. Various dimensions. The Museum of Modern Art, New York. Fund for the Twenty-First Century and Deborah Wye Endowment Fund
Page 75, top: Twice-sold objects from *The Black Factory Archive*, 2003–. Various dimensions. The Museum of Modern Art, New York. Fund for the Twenty-First Century and Deborah Wye Endowment Fund
Page 75, bottom: *The Black Factory* truck. Installation view: *The Interventionists: Art in the Social Sphere*, Mass MoCA, North Adams, Mass., May 29, 2004–March 1, 2005

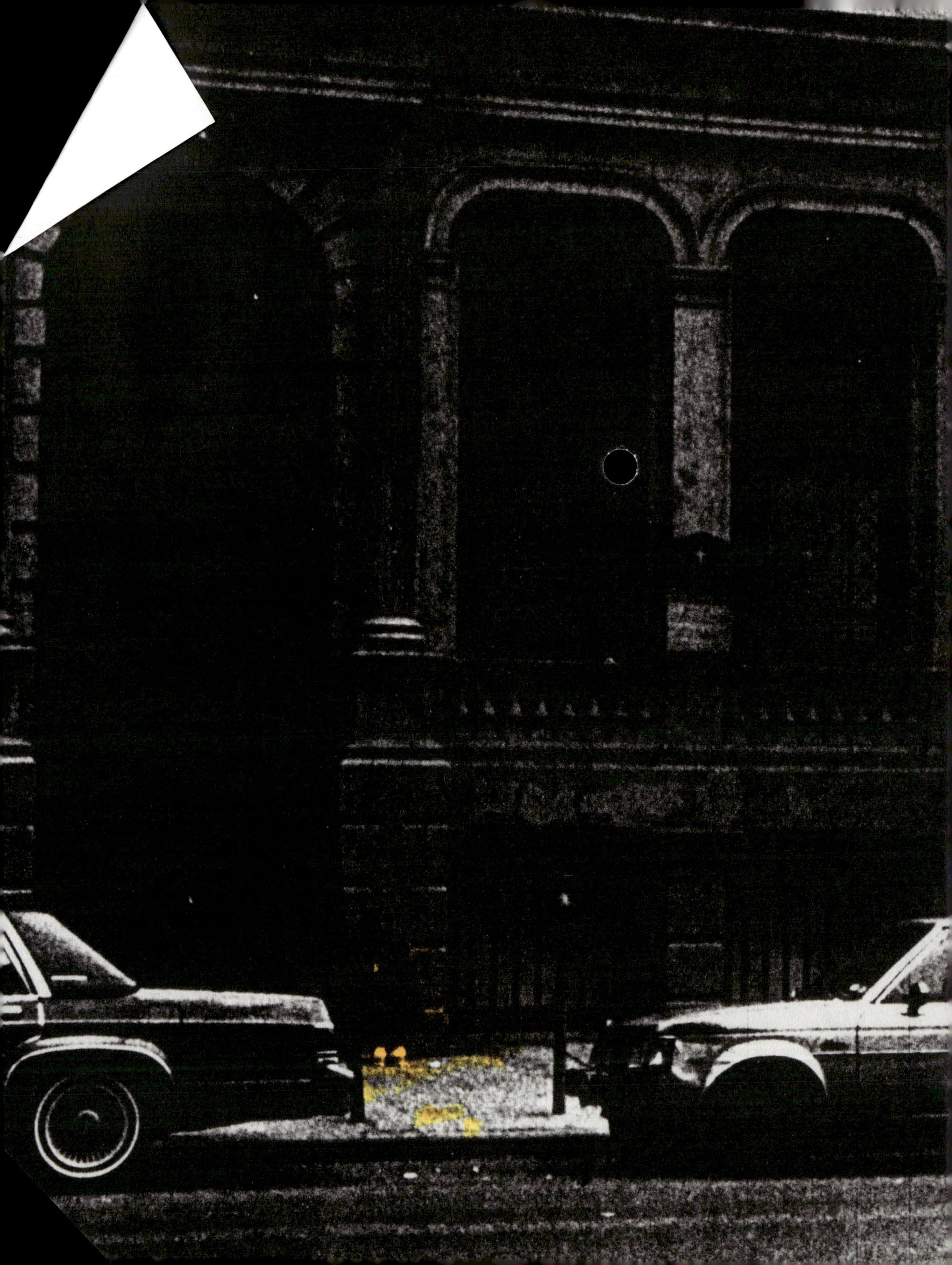